SUCCESS

BREAKTHROUGHS

Published by CelebrityPress®, Orlando, FL.

CelebrityPress® is a registered trademark.

Printed in the United States of America.

ISBN: 978-0-9991714-8-6
LCCN: 2018939862

This publication is designed to provide accurate and authoritative information with regard to the subject matter covered. It is sold with the understanding that the publisher is not engaged in rendering legal, accounting, or other professional advice. If legal advice or other expert assistance is required, the services of a competent professional should be sought. The opinions expressed by the authors in this book are not endorsed by CelebrityPress® and are the sole responsibility of the author rendering the opinion.

Most CelebrityPress® titles are available at special quantity discounts for bulk purchases for sales promotions, premiums, fundraising, and educational use. Special versions or book excerpts can also be created to fit specific needs.

For more information, please write:

CelebrityPress®
520 N. Orlando Ave, #2
Winter Park, FL 32789
or call 1.877.261.4930

Visit us online at: www.CelebrityPressPublishing.com

SUCCESS
BREAKTHROUGHS

CelebrityPress®
Winter Park, Florida

CONTENTS

CHAPTER 1

EVERYTHING YOU WANT IS JUST OUTSIDE YOUR COMFORT ZONE

BY JACK CANFIELD

What could you achieve if you created a major, life-changing goal, and then focused all your effort and actions on accomplishing it? Have you ever wondered what your life would look like if you achieved such a success breakthrough? Would you get a promotion, start a new career or double your income? Would you travel the world, retire early, start a charity or something else?

The good news is that *everything* you want is possible. In fact, much of what you can envision for your life has *already* been accomplished by other people whom you can follow and emulate.

So why doesn't everyone achieve at the level of their dreams? Unfortunately, most people get stuck in their own comfort zone. They know that achieving a breakthrough goal requires learning new skills, having difficult conversations, and working in new ways. It requires them to become a more expanded and evolved person. Often times, they believe it's simply easier to maintain the status quo.

Another reason people may be "stuck" is that the right opportunity, person or situation simply hasn't become available yet. The perfect scenario or circumstances may not yet be ready for you.

That's exactly what happened for me and my *Chicken Soup for the Soul*® coauthor, Mark Victor Hansen.

In the early 1990's, we had very busy speaking careers and seminar companies. As we delivered our talks—and the inspiring stories they contained—audience members would approach us afterward asking if those stories were in a book somewhere.

"My daughter would love that story about the puppy," I'd hear. "That story about the three pennies gave me goose bumps," people would say. Mark and I knew these were stories that people wanted—heartwarming, uplifting, true stories—at a time when people were overwhelmed, hurting, tired and worn. As more and more people asked me about the stories, I hit upon the idea of compiling them into a book that would help heal the soul.

Unfortunately, anthologies of "feel-good" stories simply weren't selling, we were told. After being rejected by 144 publishers, our literary agent gave the book back to us and wished us the best in pursuing another path.

Were we disappointed? Yes. But we were also committed to bringing *Chicken Soup for the Soul*® to market. We persevered. In fact, we decided to start pre-selling it ourselves at our speaking engagements and workshops. We thought that if we compiled enough pre-orders—at least 20,000 books, for example—we would look like a much better risk to a publisher. We asked our audiences to fill out a form with their name, contact information and the number of books they pledged to buy once *Chicken Soup for the Soul*® was published.

In the end, we decided to attend BookExpo America—the largest publishing tradeshow in North America—to talk with publishers in person. If we didn't find a publisher, we told ourselves, we'd self-publish the book just to get these life changing stories into people's hands.

On the last day of the trade show, we gave a copy of the manuscript to Peter Vegso, the cofounder of HCI Books in Florida, and showed him some of the completed forms representing nearly 20,000 pre-sold books. He agreed to read the manuscript on the flight home and wept at the poignancy, emotion and hopefulness of the people and lessons in the stories. It was the first book that had caused that reaction for him, and he immediately sent us a contract.

Getting a publishing deal for *Chicken Soup for the Soul*® and turning it into a bestseller was a major success breakthrough for Mark and me. It literally changed our lives forever. It took us from being known in a few narrow fields to being recognized internationally. It created greater demand for our audio programs, speeches, and seminars. The additional income it produced allowed us to improve our lifestyle, secure our retirement, hire more staff, take on more projects, and have a larger impact on the world.

So how can YOU create a similar success breakthrough in your own life? There's a multi-step formula I recommend, and it starts with *deciding what you want.*

BREAKTHROUGH STEP 1: DECIDE WHAT YOU WANT

One of the main reasons why most people don't get what they want is they haven't decided what that "want" is. They haven't defined their goals—exactly—in clear and compelling detail. After all, how else can your mind know where to begin looking, seeing and hearing if you don't give it specific and detailed goals to achieve?

Clarify Your Vision and Your Values

In just a moment, I'll give you a powerful technique to help you decide what you want in vivid, colorful and compelling detail. But before using this technique to define the compelling life you want for yourself, you first must know what your priorities are. Priorities are "wants" that are personally important to you—not those you believe should be important or those you believe the world expects you to value—but what's truly important to you from the deepest place in your heart.

Once you know your "wants," you must also determine your core values. What kinds of activities and priorities are in alignment with your integrity? Which are outside your acceptable limits?

Think about it. You might "want" all the riches and material wealth that could come from selling illegal drugs, but you might find it very difficult to convince your mind and body of your enthusiasm, especially if breaking the law and contributing to broken lives went against your basic values. In fact, engaging in an activity you don't agree with often causes low self-esteem, depression, despondency, even anger. So be sure that what you want matches your values and your life purpose.

Don't Live Someone Else's Dream

Be certain, too, that what you "want" isn't someone else's version of what you should want.

I once met an anesthesiologist who made $350,000 a year, but whose real dream was to work on cars. He had wanted to be a mechanic, but he knew his parents, both of whom were doctors, wouldn't approve. My solution for him?

"Give yourself permission to buy a bunch of cars and then work on them on the weekends," I said.

What the anesthesiologist wanted in his heart didn't match his picture of what he and his family thought he should be. Unfortunately, the sad reality for most people is they simply aren't honest with themselves. If they were, they would realize their "want to's" are almost always bigger than their "shoulds."

Make an "I Wants" List

One of the easiest ways to begin determining what you truly want is to ask a friend to help you make an "I Wants" list. Have the friend continually ask you, "What do you want?" for 10-15 minutes, while pausing to write down each answer and then again asking you, "What do you want?" You'll find at first that your "wants" aren't all that profound. In fact, most people usually hear themselves saying, *I want a sports car. I want a big house on the ocean.* But by the end of the 15-minute exercise, the real you begins to speak: *I want people to love me. I want to fully express myself. I want to make a difference. I want to feel powerful*—wants that are deeper expressions of your core values.

Is "Making a Living" Stopping You?

Of course, what often stops people from expressing their true desire is that they don't think they can make a living doing what they love to do.

"What I love to do is hang out and talk with people," you might say.

Well, Oprah Winfrey makes a living hanging out and talking with people. And my friend Diane Brause, who is an international tour director, makes a living hanging out and talking with people in some of the most exciting places in the world.

Another woman once told me that her favorite thing to do was to watch soap operas.

"How can I make a living watching soap operas?" she asked.

Fortunately, she discovered lots of other people loved watching soap operas, too, but often missed their favorite shows because they also had to go to work. Being very astute, she created a little magazine called *Soap Opera Digest*. Every week, she watched all the soap operas, cataloged the plots and wrote up little summaries, so that if a viewer missed their soap operas that week, they would know who got divorced from whom, who finally married the doctor, and so on. Now this woman makes a fortune watching and publishing information about soap operas.

See how it's possible to make a great living doing what you want to do? You simply have to be willing to risk it.

Visualize What You Want

In addition to the "I Wants" list above, you can also decide what you want (and write it down) through visualizing it. Have a friend read the following exercise to you (or audio-record it yourself on your smartphone or on your computer in a slow, soothing voice, and then listen to it with your eyes closed). If you record it, be sure to pause for a minute in between each category so you'll have time to write down your answers.

Begin by listening to some relaxing music and sitting quietly in a comfortable environment. Close your eyes. Then, begin visualizing your ideal life exactly as if you are living it.

1. First, visualize your ideal financial situation. How much money do you have in your savings, how much do you make in income? What is your net worth? How is your cash flow?

Next, what does your home look like? Where is it? What color are the walls? Are there paintings hanging in the rooms? What do they look like? Walk through your perfect house visually putting in all of the details.

At this point, don't worry about how you'll get that house. Don't sabotage yourself by saying, "I can't live in Hawaii because I don't make enough money." Once you give your subconscious mind the picture, your mind will solve the "not enough money" challenge. Simply be honest with yourself about what you truly want.

Next, visualize driving your ideal car and any other possessions you want to own and enjoy.

Open your eyes and write down what you see, in as great a detail as possible. Or give your friend the exact details to jot down.

2. Next, visualize your ideal career. What are you doing in your career? Where are you working? With whom are you working? What kind of clients do you have? What is your compensation like? Is it your own business? Do you have partners? Staff?

3. Then, focus on your free time, your recreation time. What are you doing with your family and friends in the free time you've created for yourself? What hobbies are you pursuing? What kinds of vacations are you taking? How many times a year?

4. Next, visualize your body and your physical health. Are you strong, flexible, pain-free? Are you exercising regularly? Where and with whom? Are you playing sports? Running a 10K marathon?

Now focus on your ideal emotional and spiritual life. Are you free and open, relaxed, in an ecstatic state of joy all day long? Are you meditating, spending time in nature, and going on retreats? What does that aspect of your life look like?

5. Then move on to visualizing your relationships with your family and friends. What is your relationship with your primary partner like? What about the rest of your family? Who are your friends? What is the quality of your relationships with your friends? What do

those friendships feel like? Are they loving, supportive, inspiring, empowering? How much time do you spend with your friends?

6. What about your personal growth and development? Do you see yourself going back to school, taking workshops and trainings, working with a coach, reading more books, taking online classes, seeking therapy for a past hurt, or growing spiritually?

7. Move on to the community you live in, the community you've chosen. When it's ideal, what does it look like? What kinds of community activities are you participating in? What about your charitable work? What are you doing to help others and to make a difference? How often do you participate in these activities? Who are you helping?

Remember to take time to write down all the details of what you are imagining in your vision of your ideal life—either as you go along or all at once at the end.

BREAKTHROUGH STEP 2: SET GOALS

Once you've made your "I Wants" list and visualized your perfect life in the seven areas above, it's time to refine them by making them measurable and targeted.

It's time to set some goals for creating your success breakthrough.

Experts on the science of success know that the brain is a goal-seeking organism. Whatever goal you give to your subconscious mind, it will work night and day to achieve. To make sure a goal unleashes the power of your subconscious mind, it must be specific and measurable. In other words, a stated goal must include two criteria: how much (some measurable quantity such as pages, pounds, dollars or points) and by when (a specific time and date). Your goal must be stated in a way that you—or anyone else—would be able to measure it. For instance, if you say you want to lose 30 pounds by June 30th, you can step on the scale today, then again on June 30th and know for certain that you've achieved your goal—or not.

Where there is no deadline or basis for measurement, that goal is simply a good idea, a wish or a vague intention. And one of the best ways to guard against getting stuck at the level of simply having good ideas is to be very clear about a goal of something you want to be, do or have and write it down in clear and compelling detail—always adding how much and by when. If there is a certain house you want to own, write down its specifics in vivid colorful detail—its location, size, style, landscaping, furniture, artwork, and floor plan. Then provide a date by which you want to own it.

Create a Breakthrough Goal

Goal-setting is such an important step to becoming more successful, but unfortunately, most of the goals we set focus on small improvements to our life in the immediate future. Get the house painted. Finish my sales report. Clean the garage. Lose 20 pounds.

But what if instead you were to focus on a single goal that would amplify everything you do—from your career to your relationships to your income to your lifestyle?

Wouldn't that be a goal worth pursuing with passion? Wouldn't that be something to consistently focus some time on each and every day until you achieved it?

Think about it.

If you were an independent sales professional and knew you could get a better territory, a substantial bonus commission and maybe even a promotion once you landed a certain number of customers, wouldn't you work day and night to achieve that goal?

And if you were the coach of a football team, whose typical strategy was to gain four yards on every play, what if your players instead worked toward completing a breakthrough 60-yard pass?

If you were a stay-at-home mom whose entire lifestyle and family finances would change by earning an extra $1,000 a month, wouldn't you pursue every possible opportunity until you achieved that goal?

That's what I mean by a breakthrough goal. Something that significantly changes your life, brings you new opportunities, gets you in front of the right people and expands every activity, relationship or group you're involved in.

I call this kind of goal a Breakthrough Goal—a goal that will quantum leap your life and your results, and that will require you to grow to achieve it…and that can be achieved within one year from today.

Some breakthrough goals that my students and past clients have set are: write and publish a bestselling book, double my income, double the number of the people in my multi-level marketing company downline, get twenty new coaching clients, get my realtor's license, get my MBA degree, learn Spanish, get my product sold on Amazon.com, have my own internet radio show, start a podcast, and hire an assistant.

BREAKTHROUGH STEP 3: TAKE ACTION

When Mark Victor Hansen and I published the first *Chicken Soup for the Soul*® book, we were so eager and committed to making it a bestseller. But candidly, we were overwhelmed by the many tasks and methods for promoting the book. We didn't know where to start, plus we both had our speaking and seminar businesses to run.

We sought the advice of Ron Scolastico, a wonderful teacher and guide, who told us, "If you would go every day to a very large tree and take 5 swings at it with a very sharp ax, eventually, no matter how large the tree, it would have to come down."

How very simple and how very true! Out of that we developed what is called *The Rule of 5*. This simply means that every day, you commit to doing 5 specific things that move you closer to completing your goal.

What might you accomplish if you were to do a little bit—five things— every day for the next 40 years toward the accomplishment of your goal? If you wrote 5 pages a day, that would add up to a total of 73,000 pages of text—or about 243 books. If you invested $5.00 a day at 6% interest, at the end of 40 years you'd have amassed a small fortune of $305,357.

Do your dreams for your life seem overwhelming, too?

A lot of people tell me, for example, that their dream is to own a house in Hawaii. While I'm excited for them, I also have to ask them to get clear about all of the steps they'll have to take to get there.

You have to find out where the best locations are, decide which island, find out how much homes cost there, determine how much money you'll need to save, research where you can get financing, furniture, any renovations or repairs needed…and on and on.

Once you break down your big goal into "bite-sized" pieces, you can begin accomplishing the small tasks that you've determined will lead to achieving your breakthrough goal.

Preparing to Move Forward Isn't the Same as Taking Action Itself

Preparation, research, planning, getting it perfect—these are all areas where people get bogged down in the "take action" process. Don't let that be your outcome. Practice *The Rule of 5* and ensure that you consistently move forward a little bit each day.

BREAKTHROUGH STEP 4: CELEBRATE YOUR SUCCESSES

Finally, once you do accomplish these steps—and especially when you accomplish your breakthrough goal—be sure to celebrate.

That's right, have some fun!

Not only does celebrating help you acknowledge each success to your subconscious mind (which loves winning), as humans, we simply don't feel complete until we've been acknowledged and recognized. That recognition is particularly important. For instance, if you spend weeks producing a report and your boss doesn't acknowledge it, you feel incomplete. If you send someone a gift and they don't acknowledge it, there's this little incomplete taking up attention units inside of you. Our mind's natural cycle needs to move to completion.

Of course, even more important than completing, the simple, enjoyable act of rewarding our successes causes our subconscious mind to say, "Hey, succeeding is cool. Every time we produce a success we get to go do something fun. Jack will buy us something we want or take us someplace neat. Let's have more of these successes, so Jack will take us out to play."

Rewarding yourself for your "wins" powerfully reinforces your subconscious mind's desire to want to work harder. It's just basic human nature.

Whatever you choose to do, be sure it's fun, safe and nurturing. Don't go out and get drunk, overeat or buy yourself something you can't really afford yet.

CONCLUSION

As you start down your path to future success breakthroughs, my final advice to you is this: you have control over just three things in your life ... the thoughts you think, the images you visualize and the actions you take. How you make the most of them determines the outcomes you experience in life.

If you don't like what you are producing and experiencing, choose now to change your responses. Change your negative thoughts to positive ones. Change what you daydream about—only visualize what you want to happen, not what you don't want to happen. If you don't like the way people treat you, stand up and say something about it or spend your time with different people. Remember, nothing will change for the better until you change your thoughts, what you imagine, and your behavior (which includes what you do and the words you speak).

If you keep doing what you've always done, you'll keep getting what you've always gotten. In fact, if what you are currently doing was capable of producing the "more" that you are seeking in life, the "more" would have already shown up. If you want something different, you're going to have to do something different![1]

The day you begin to do that is the day your life will begin to change for the better.

---

1. For more principles and techniques to create the ideal life you want, read *The Success Principles: How to Get from Where You Are to Where You Want to Be* by Jack Canfield and Janet Switzer. (New York: William Morrow, 2015)

About Jack

Known as America's #1 Success Coach, Jack Canfield is the CEO of the Canfield Training Group in Santa Barbara, CA, which trains and coaches entrepreneurs, corporate leaders, managers, sales professionals and the general public in how to accelerate the achievement of their personal, professional and financial goals.

Jack Canfield is best known as the coauthor of the #1 New York Times bestselling *Chicken Soup for the Soul®* book series, which has sold more than 500 million books in 47 languages, including 11 New York Times #1 bestsellers. As the CEO of Chicken Soup for the Soul Enterprises he helped grow the *Chicken Soup for the Soul®* brand into a virtual empire of books, children's books, audios, videos, CDs, classroom materials, a syndicated column and a television show, as well as a vigorous program of licensed products that includes everything from clothing and board games to nutraceuticals and a successful line of *Chicken Soup for the Pet Lover's Soul®* cat and dog foods.

His other books include *The Success Principles™: How to Get from Where You Are to Where You Want to Be* (recently revised as the 10th Anniversary Edition), *The Success Principles for Teens, The Aladdin Factor, Dare to Win, Heart at Work, The Power of Focus: How to Hit Your Personal, Financial and Business Goals with Absolute Certainty, You've Got to Read This Book, Tapping into Ultimate Success, Jack Canfield's Key to Living the Law of Attraction*, his recent novel, *The Golden Motorcycle Gang: A Story of Transformation and The 30-Day Sobriety Solution.*

Jack is a dynamic speaker and was recently inducted into the National Speakers Association's Speakers Hall of Fame. He has appeared on more than 1000 radio and television shows including Oprah, Montel, Larry King Live, the Today Show, Fox and Friends, and 2 hour-long PBS Specials devoted exclusively to his work. Jack is also a featured teacher in 12 movies including *The Secret, The Meta-Secret, The Truth, The Keeper of the Keys, Tapping into the Source*, and *The Tapping Solution*. Jack was also honored recently with a documentary that was produced about his life and teachings, *The Soul of Success: The Jack Canfield Story.*

Jack has personally helped hundreds of thousands of people on six different continents become multi-millionaires, business leaders, best-selling authors, leading sales professionals, successful entrepreneurs, and world-class athletes while at the same time creating balanced, fulfilling and healthy lives.

His corporate clients have included Virgin Records, SONY Pictures, Daimler-Chrysler, Federal Express, GE, Johnson & Johnson, Merrill Lynch, Campbell's Soup, Re/Max, The Million Dollar Forum, The Million Dollar Roundtable, The Young Entrepreneurs

Organization, The Young Presidents Organization, the Executive Committee, and the World Business Council.

He is the founder of the Transformational Leadership Council and a member of Evolutionary Leaders, two groups devoted to helping create a world that works for everyone.

Jack is a graduate of Harvard, earned his M.Ed. from the University of Massachusetts and has received three honorary doctorates in psychology and public service. He is married, has three children, two step-children and a grandson.

For more information, visit:

- www.JackCanfield.com
- www.CanfieldTraintheTrainer

CHAPTER 2

OPTIMAL SUCCESS

BY TOLA GBADEBO

The Oxford English dictionary defines 'Success' as the attainment of fame, wealth and social status. This narrow definition of success overlooks other important measures of success. For instance, Mother Theresa, the charitable doyenne, is regarded by many as being successful in her lifetime despite not having fame, wealth and social status. Success is subjective and should be an inner fulfilment of an individual's dreams rather than be about conformity with societal standards. Since success is categorically individual, it is crucial to understand and accept what space one occupies in the world. What is your personal definition of success? What will ultimately give you fulfilment?

A good foundation for defining personal success is the identification of an individual's 'raison d'être/purpose, vision, actions, habits and core values'. Core values define a person, just as a company's core values ultimately define the company's culture and brand. Core values are our internal navigation system. Studies have shown that individuals experience a greater sense of fulfilment when they live by their values because there is soul harmony. What habit must you start or stop doing to achieve your definition of success?

Your beliefs become your thoughts. Your thoughts become your words. Your words become your actions. Your actions become your habits. Your habits become your values. Your values become your destiny.
~ Mahatma Gandhi

Identifying your purpose and core values enables you to establish what is most important to you in life and to define success on your terms. Otherwise, no matter how successful a person is perceived to be by others, there will always be an inner void. Many will perceive a CEO as highly successful, yet I have worked with CEOs who lacked fulfilment and considered life as hollow because life was not value driven.

Research has shown that having purpose and meaning in life increases overall well-being and life satisfaction, improves physical health and ultimately longevity.

In Okinawa, Japan, where there is a high proportion of centenarians; many residents put their longevity down to having 'Ikigai'. Ikigai is a concept meaning 'reason for being'. Ikigai encourages people of Okinawa to strive to find a purpose and mission in everyday life.

Unlike the Western idea of success, success to the people of Okinawa is about finding one's happy combination of life satisfaction. It is a scientifically-backed concept that life satisfaction and fulfilment tend to stem from a balanced wheel of life. That balanced wheel is my personal definition of Optimal Success.

Success is liking yourself, liking what you do, and liking how you do it.
~ Maya Angelou

To attain optimal success, it is fundamental to focus on the right measures of success. Using myself as an example, as a fresh Law graduate, I set out to make a difference in the world but later became trapped on the hamster wheel of life. I exhausted myself striving for perfection but was often out of balance. When we don't honour our values, our mental, emotional and physical state suffers. The loss of a loved one led me to a paradigm shift. I redefined what success meant to me. I want to live authentically; a life that is value-based and purpose-driven. I did not want my eulogy to be unevenly tilted towards my professional, marital or parental accomplishment. I have always had a deep desire for the wheel of my life to be well balanced. I embarked on a self-discovery journey, which helped me to realize, that I lacked a clear vision of the masterpiece that I was creating. I required the creative energy of a vision that will help transform that caterpillar into a butterfly.

A vision is the springboard that will enable you to make the right choices, take pertinent actions and propel you into the desired future. Vision is essentially the same for individuals and companies.

Research has shown that vision and purpose-driven organizations ultimately achieve success. For example, Amazon.com Inc.'s vision is "To be Earth's most customer-centric company". The Harris Poll survey ranked Amazon.com as having the best reputation among the most visible 100 companies in the United States for two consecutive years. Indeed, the company's vision has translated into success.

Establishing your purpose and vision does not need to be a 'pie in the sky' dream. The exercise can be achieved through self-examination and the use of the '5 W's' which are useful in problem solving and information gathering.

- *Who* am I?
- *What* do I stand for and would like my legacy to be?
- *Where* am I headed?
- *When* do I experience most joy or satisfaction?
- *Why* do I do what I do?

Discovering your purpose is the easy part. The hard part is working on yourself daily to the point where you become that purpose. Goals are "how" you achieve your vision, the steps you must take to achieve the vision. Goals trickle into daily disciplines and actions.

Success is 1% inspiration, 99% perspiration.
~ Thomas Edison

Admittedly, it is all quite philosophical. Many people will rather live a life of chaotic indulgence. As Seneca, the Roman Philosopher, once said, 'Life without a design is erratic.' Without being conscious and purposeful about life, you will naturally decline. *Without a vision/dream, a people perish.* [Proverbs 29 v 18].

Even with a perfect blueprint, life is unpredictable. Unexpected problems emerge. These 'life issues' are the biggest hurdles to success and the reason why we need breakthroughs for success.

What are the unseen blocks delaying your *Success Breakthroughs*?

Could it be limiting beliefs programmed into your subconscious through education, culturization and life experiences? To achieve *Success Breakthroughs*, you must recognize there will be obstacles and prime your brain to overcome those obstacles; just like a chess expert concentrates on the pieces that can make or break the game. We cannot control the circumstances of life, but we can control our reactions.

There are hardly any success stories without initial setbacks. If you really look closely, most overnight successes took a long time. Often, life is considered as a linear narrative, when, it is usually a scattered graph of random dots. Challenges are sometimes the key to our growth – just as the oyster spins the pearl out of its discomfort.

The part of the success many focus on is the tip of the Iceberg that is visible to all, ignoring the mass that lies beneath; years of hard work, sacrifice, failure, disappointment, dedication and persistence. Some have said grit is the single-most important trait to become successful. No one has it together every day. The pains, defeat and challenges are all part of the success story. Success rarely happens by accident. Success at any level and in any field comes from building skills and expertise. Once you have defined what success means to you, create a supportive environment for your goals and dreams.

Success is a science; if you have the conditions, you get the result.
~ Oscar Wilde

Success leaves clues. Successful people take common deliberate steps to make sure they reach their goals. Here are some tips for *Success Breakthroughs*, which highly successful people apply.

- **Write the Vision and Goal.** The palest ink is better than the best memory. Use paper or electronic tools to record your vision and goals. Many have attested that a vision board helped to bring their dreams to life. Michael Phelps, the greatest swimmer and Olympian of all time has said one of his key secrets to winning is the use of mental imagery. Before each race, he visualises every detail of the race.

  Not everyone will be good with the mental exercise of visualization or the self-discipline required for goal setting and tracking, but technology offers some empowerment tools – e.g. Freemind or Coggle, these are tools that can help you structure and prioritize your ideas.

For goal setting and tracking, Strides and TrackMyGoals are apps that will support accountability, by measuring your progress in accomplishing what you set out to achieve.

- **Self-Awareness:** Self-Awareness has been identified as a predictor for success. Self-Awareness is having a clear understanding of one's personality, beliefs, motivations, talents, strengths and weaknesses. These insights help us to identify valuable traits we possess, as well as weaknesses to conquer.

Daily journaling or online personality tests are ideal for raising self-awareness. The University of Cambridge Psychometrics Center has a free, psychometric test titled, 'My Personality 100-item'. The DISC personality assessment is also a popular tool used by organisations for assessing self-awareness.

- **Daily Affirmations:** There is a direct correlation between the words we speak and the quality of our lives. Affirmations have been proven to reprogram the mind for success. Affirmations help to remove limiting beliefs and replace them with empowering ones. Several celebrities have mentioned affirmations as integral to their success breakthroughs. Denzel Washington, a multiple award-winning actor has confirmed that affirmations helped him overcome problems that held him back and contributed to his success.

There are tools that can automate the process for daily affirmations, helping to replace negative thoughts with positive counter thoughts. Think Up is an affirmation app that allows you to record affirmations in your own voice, and schedule these for notification at your preferred time.

- **Growth Mindset:** A common thread that runs through the lives of many successful people is their commitment to reading. Jack Canfield, America's No. 1 success coach considers continuous learning as the minimum requirement for success in any field. Warren Buffett and Bill Gates confirm that reading is key to their successes. Read to bridge your knowledge gap. If you are struggling to cultivate a reading habit, you may require the assistance of a book discovery site. Goodreads and Riffle are free book discovery sites that let you create a wish list, keep track of your reading lists and include a recommendation service.

- **Accountability and Supportive Relationships:** When questioned about their success trajectories, many successful people give credit to coaches or mentors who helped them fulfil their potential. A support system from a mentor or coach can greatly improve the likelihood of success. Similarly, organizations with strong coaching cultures have been identified to report above-average revenue, compared to their peers.

  Even if you do not have a direct Coach or Mentor, you can sustain motivation by subscribing to YouTube channels of proven coaches and joining interactive group sessions on social media.

- **Associations:** One of the most overlooked factors for achieving success is the association one keeps. Jim Rohn, a foremost Business Philosopher famously said that we are the average of the five people we spend the most time with. People are our biggest influences because beliefs, values and habits are contagious. Observe the five people you spend the most time with and ask yourself if the ambitions and efforts of these five individuals propel you towards or deter you from your vision of success. Be the weakest link in your chain.

Surround yourself with the dreamers and the doers, the believers and thinkers, but most all, surround yourself with those who see greatness within you, even when you don't see it yourself.
~ Steve Jobs

What success will be achieved in the next five years is directly linked to the actions taken today. The articulation of a vision, the implementation plan, the knowledge that is acquired and the associations that are nurtured. Visualisation, Verbalisation/Affirmation, Thoughts, Beliefs and Actions must be aligned for *Success Breakthroughs* to occur, otherwise there will be cognitive dissonance. To attain *Optimal Success*, a lot of time and intense effort is required, and the loftiest of visions can transform into a successful and fulfilling reality.

Whatever your personal definition of success is, aim to be a person of value rather than just a person of success. Be relentless in the pursuit of what sets your soul on fire. Remember to live life on your terms, be uniquely you and be the best of whoever you are.

About Tola

Tola Gbadebo is a Consultant, Speaker and Success coach. Tola is an expert at empowering people and organizations at strengthening commitments to their Vision. Tola provides valuable and strategic insights in delivering best in class service to her clients. She excels in advising clients on Regulatory risk management, Governance and project execution.

Tola's career spans 20 years with clientele across the business map. She has worked for leading global banks and has had experience of multi-disciplinary projects in Africa, Europe, Australia and the United States. Some of the clients she has worked with include: ExxonMobil, Barclays Bank, Credit Suisse Goldman Sachs, Bank of America, Morgan Stanley and many others. Her experience working for several industry leaders has equipped her to distinguish between good and bad practice in leadership, management and change projects.

Tola has been an invited speaker at expert panels, seminars and conferences. She has been part of Lord Mayor of the City of London's business delegation to Asia and Africa, to promote trade and investment. She is acknowledged as an influencer and a communicator.

Tola holds a Master's degree in Financial Regulation, Corporate Governance and Economic Law from IALS, University of London; and is a certified Life Coach with the University of Cambridge.

Tola is a sought-after author and speaker, most recently co-authoring *Success Breakthroughs*. She is naturally skilled at stirring the innate gifts of others and helping them discover their destiny. Tola aims to transform lives and empower leaders across all walks of life; inspiring people to live their dream life, and encouraging them to be the best they can be. Tola works with business leaders, high-potential managers and top talent individuals, helping them to improve their leadership, decision making, influence, and overall fulfillment. Tola's vision is to make a difference in people's lives through expert advice, personal empowerment, and compassion.

As an executive coach, Tola works with major business leaders, high-potential managers and top talent individuals, helping them to improve their leadership, decision making, influence, and overall fulfillment. Tola has dedicated her life to continual personal and professional development.

To access Success empowerment tools, you can connect with Tola at:
- www.optimalsuccess.org

or
- Email: Tola@optimalsuccess.org

CHAPTER 3

ENERGIZING YOUR INNER P.O.W.E.R.

BY JUNE RYAN, RADM, USCG (Ret.)

I know it sounds crazy to some individuals reading a book about Success Breakthroughs, but I achieved many historical firsts in my field without ever setting those specific goals. I was a trailblazer, breaking through many gender barriers that I didn't know existed when I joined. One of the most recognizable achievements was becoming the first woman, in the over 220-year history of the United States Coast Guard, to rise from the rank of Seaman Recruit (E-1) – a small boat deckhand, to Rear Admiral (O-8). I achieved these successes through the persistent and dogged employment of my inner "P.O.W.E.R."

As a young high school student, I enjoyed being a night owl like my mother, watching television late into the evening, and frequently into the early morning hours. During one of these late nights, I saw a 30-second television commercial that changed my life.

The advertisement detailed generations of individuals, all from the same few families, that served as lifesavers off the Outer Banks of North Carolina. Black and white vintage photos, and short clips of more modern-day news and documentary film footage highlighted the rescue oarsmen. Dressed in white sailor uniforms, they patrolled the beach on foot and horseback. They ascended tall watchtowers connected to the one-story white rescue stations, scanning the horizon for ships in peril or for newly washed-up debris on the beaches, evidence of a ship in danger.

When a wreck was spotted, the station came alive in a well-orchestrated beehive of activity. The heroes ran into the boathouse, emerging moments later with equipment, and their heavy wooden-planked rescue boat that they quickly transported to the ocean's surf-line. One by one the crew pushed the surfboat into the breaking waves, each oarsman climbing aboard as the lifeboat violently rose and fell over successive crashing waves like a bucking bronco as they set out to sea.

With the unmistakable sound of modern day music, the commercial cut to footage of recent rescues with helicopters and small boats battling the elements and arriving back at the stations with survivors. "Since 1790", the narrator declared, "members from these families have served in the Lifesaving Service, a predecessor to the United States Coast Guard, and they continue to serve today." The 30-second commercial ended with the tagline: "Start your own family tradition. Be a lifesaver. Join the United States Coast Guard."

As soon as the commercial ended, I bolted to the short, dark brown wooden bookshelf at the top of the stairs that held our family's World Book encyclopedia. I looked up "United States Coast Guard" and read the meager few pages on the organization's 200-year history. That one-30 second commercial, and a few pages in a World Book encyclopedia sent this Iowa-born patriot on a 35-year odyssey, as a member of the United States Coast Guard.

I didn't join the Coast Guard to make history; in fact, I hadn't planned to join the Coast Guard on a full-time basis at all. I enlisted in the Coast Guard Reserves. The one-weekend-a-month commitment with added training opportunities in the summer, allowed me to continue my college career, and provided me with a small income, until I could find a "real job."

My success was not one of goal setting, reevaluation, and more goal setting. In fact, it was quite the opposite. I learned early on in my military career, if you share your promotion goals with your peers, you are often teased as a "Lifer" or "rate-grabber" (someone who others see as promoting too quickly, without truly learning the craft), or other equally derogatory term that was sure to leave you out-in the-cold. As a woman in the military, being set apart was already a steady way of life, and I didn't need to create a larger chasm between me and my peers by announcing some half-baked, obscure career ambition. After all, many of the individuals I served with had never met a Coast Guard officer, and those that had met officers, generally walked away with a strong disdain for them.

Despite the lack of encouragement from my peers at the time, I began to reach out and quietly ask officers, "How do you apply to Officer Candidate School?" "Do you think I have the 'right stuff' to make it?" Although I had many doubts, fueled by a deeply entrenched lack of self-esteem, I was encouraged to apply.

Those small steps led to thirty-five years in a Coast Guard uniform that took me from Bettendorf, Iowa to destinations around the globe, including Ireland, England, Spain, Germany, Hungary, and Russia. I had the honor of meeting several Presidents, world leaders, and international celebrities. I participated in formal Head of State arrival ceremonies with the President and world leaders, later observing meetings on a wide variety of topics from formal nuclear arms treaties negotiations to informal dialogue on the news, weather and sporting events. I served my country aboard three Coast Guard cutters, two as the Commanding Officer ("the Captain") and in numerous shore-side assignments, including three additional commands, carrying out the Coast Guard's 11- statutory missions from search and rescue, to law enforcement, to counter-terrorism, and military defense.

My historical firsts started just 18 months after graduating Officer Candidate School, landing a job as the first female Commanding Officer of the Coast Guard Cutter CAPE MORGAN. Then a tour at the Maritime Law Enforcement School where I became the first woman to qualify as a Defensive Tactics Instructor. My second command was on the Coast Guard Cutter NEAH BAY, again a first for a woman aboard that cutter as well. At the national level, I was honored to serve as the Military Aide to the President of the United States, only the third woman in United States history to "carry the football," and the first woman to serve as Military Advisor to the Secretary of Homeland Security. The final assignment of my Coast Guard career was yet another first, as the first woman to serve as Commander of the Ninth Coast Guard District, leading the six thousand plus men and women of the Great Lakes region. My Change of Command and retirement ceremony was my final "first." It marked the first time in Coast Guard history that one female Admiral was relieved by another female Admiral as a Coast Guard District Commander.

With each year that passed, and each successful tour completed, my confidence grew, and the awards and accolades mounted. The medals that filled my chest, at my retirement ceremony, read like a novel that chronicled my three decades of service, Command Ashore and Afloat insignias, service badges for the White House and Department of Homeland Security, along with numerous personal awards. Yet, not one of them did I purposefully set out to accomplish.

I am living proof that a shy, awkward teenage girl from Iowa could join the Coast Guard, and not only thrive, but could make military history during three decades of service, without ever having those initial goals in mind.

You can *breakthrough* to success through the persistent and steadfast use of your inner P.O.W.E.R.

What is inner P.O.W.E.R?

P: Be Positive. No matter your circumstance, assume a positive, "can-do" attitude. The world is a mirror. When we radiate positivity, the world responds back with positivity. I learned this very early in my career. Although among the most junior individuals assigned, I often found myself designated to serve as the unit's representative during visits from families or high-ranking VIPs. I would provide the unit brief, and lead the tours. Later, when I asked my supervisors why I was selected over more senior (and presumably more qualified) individuals, they always replied, "your positive attitude." As my career progressed, I began to notice I was hand-selected to serve on special study groups or investigations. What I didn't realize at the time was my steadfast commitment to doing high-quality work regardless of the task, coupled with my positive outlook became an attraction. The more positive I was, the more high-visibility, trustworthy and positive assignments I was given. If you want to breakthrough to Success, maintain a positive attitude.

O: The "O" stands for "Oh! What the heck, go for it anyway." I was first introduced to this phrase listening to the *Self-Esteem and Peak Performance* cassette tapes narrated by Jack Canfield, published by CareerTrack. Jack described how, when many of us were small children, we first learned to jump off the diving board, by experiencing the fear and doing it anyway. Like that high dive, we must also feel our uncertainties, but take action anyway. Were there times I got burned? Yes, like when I volunteered for a "special assignment" that turned out to be cleaning the heads (the bathrooms) that were crusted with dried urine. But I committed myself to excellence; I finished the task with far more cleanliness than they had seen from preciously assigned individuals and was justly rewarded and never assigned that type of task in the future.

When I was junior, and offered positions of increased responsibility like the command of a ship, or as Military Aide to the President, there were some thoughts of self-doubt that crept into my head, "are you really ready for that job?" However, armed with "Oh what the heck…", I powered though the doubt. I rested, confidently knowing that my prior assignments had laid the foundation for my future. Each success served to build my experience base, build my expertise, and build my self-confidence. Maintain an "Oh!-What-the-heck-go-for-it-anyway" approach to your career, and you too will go farther than you ever thought possible.

W: The "W" in P.O.W.E.R stands for "We". We are strongest when we are in the service of others. Each time we contribute to the success of others, we share in that success. Just like physical fitness and exercise builds muscle, success builds future successes. Therefore, the more we assist others in achieving their goals, the more our confidence builds, and the more successful we become as a result. Surround yourself with successful people. Use the momentum, and strength gained from each other, and watch your success skyrocket.

E: Ralph Waldo Emerson once said, "Nothing great was achieved without enthusiasm." The "E" stands for Enthusiasm, the tireless pursuit of your endeavors with the tenacity to stay with it, no matter what. Many team coaches and Olympic athletes will tell you, those athletes who achieve greatness were not always the strongest, the fastest or most talented athletes when they started the sport. They were the athletes who stuck it out, who didn't quit. When some folks ask how I became an Admiral (an O-8 on the military officers' promotion scale)? I tell them I didn't retire as a Lieutenant Commander (an O-4). I stuck it out. You too can achieve greatness in your endeavors, by sustaining tireless enthusiasm.

R: Rest and Re-assess. Taking a pause, and assessing where you are, is one of the most important aspects of any breakthrough to success. Aboard our Coast Guard cutters and small boats around the world, navigators "take a fix," finding the vessel's position. Once the position is known, the navigator will then assess if the vessel is on-track or off-track from the vessel's intended route. If the vessel is on-track, no adjustment is necessary. If the vessel is off-track, the navigator will order a course change to get the vessel back on-track. I used this same approach throughout my career. As each tour of duty approached completion, my husband and I would "take our fix" to determine where we were, and where we wanted to go moving forward. I attribute the success in my career to this process. Travel a distance, take a fix, assess my position, and moving forward: one tour of duty at a time. At the end of each tour, I'd look back and deeply appreciate the distance I traveled, the lessons I learned, and incredible experiences I gained along the way.

Today, I continue the journey. In the fall of 2017, after 35-years of dedicated service, mentoring and coaching many along the way, I altered course…slightly. I chose to retire from the Coast Guard and pursue my passion of helping others achieve their success. As a Jack Canfield Certified Trainer®, I am blessed to be able to work with company executives, college and high school students, church and veteran groups, and individuals as they travel on their journey. I am proof-positive that you can achieve success breakthroughs by consistently and diligently energizing your inner P.O.W.E.R.

About June Ryan

Rear Admiral (Ret.) June Ryan is a motivational speaker, seminar leader, and corporate trainer. She energizes and empowers her audiences through her effective use of humor and inspirational stories. She is a Success Trainer and Coach drawing upon her 35 years of military service and formal certification in the *Success Principles - Getting from Where You Are to Where You Want To Be®*, by Jack Canfield, co-Author of *Chicken Soup for the Soul®*.

During her career, June was a trailblazer, achieving many historical firsts for women – including the first enlisted woman in the Coast Guard to rise to the rank of Rear Admiral, the first woman to serve as the Military Advisor to the Secretary of Homeland Security, and the third woman in our nation's history to serve as the Military Aide to the President of the United States.

During her 35 years as a distinguished military leader, June served in a wide variety of leadership roles including five separate command positions; two aboard Coast Guard cutters (ships), three regional units ashore. She also served as the Chief of Staff of Coast Guard Pacific Area, an area that encompasses 6 of the 7 continents, 71 countries, and more than 74 million miles of ocean from U. S. Western States to Asia and from the Arctic to Antarctica. Prior to her retirement in October 2017, June served as the Commander, Ninth Coast Guard District (Great Lakes Region), leading the 6,000 men and women of the Coast Guard across an area of responsibility that spanned 8 states and a 1,500-mile international maritime border. She again made history as the first woman to hold that assignment. Even her final Change of Command was historic. It marked the first time in U.S. history that a female Coast Guard Admiral was relieved as District Commander by another female Coast Guard Admiral.

June holds a Bachelor of Science degree in Biology from Bowling Green State University, and a Master of Arts degree in Adult Education from the University of South Florida. She is a graduate of the National Preparedness Leadership Initiative (NPLI) from the Harvard School of Public Health/Harvard Kennedy School of Government. Her personal military awards include the Coast Guard Distinguished Service Award, two Defense Superior Service Medals, three Legion of Merits, and six Coast Guard Meritorious Service Medals among others. She has earned the Presidential Service Badge, the Secretary of Homeland Security Service Badge, as well as the Advanced Boat Force Operations and Coast Guard Cutterman pin.

June is an active community leader, board member, and community volunteer. In her spare time, June enjoys spending time with her family. Her husband of 30+ years is a research analyst for a financial firm, and a retired Coast Guard Chief Warrant Officer.

They both volunteer in the community and at their church, serving on various parish leadership councils. On the weekends, they can be found along the many regatta race courses cheering-on their daughter's high school crew team, traveling, and working on many home improvement projects.

Visit June at:

- Website: JuneRyan.com
- Facebook: https://www.facebook.com/juneellenryan/
- E-mail: JuneEllenRyan@gmail.com

CHAPTER 4

RESILIENCE AND THE HUMAN SPIRIT

BY NINA M. KELLY, Ph.D.

Direct your eye right inward, and you'll find
A thousand regions in your mind
Yet undiscovered. Travel them, and be
Expert in home-cosmography.
~ Henry David Thoreau

The search for bliss—often confused with success—beckons to each of us. Yet at almost every period of life, joy appears muddled with the trials and tribulations that befall mankind. The question of whether one's life has been a success may present itself at any time, but especially at moments when tragedy arrives uninvited at one's doorstep or when the seeker is reassessing ideals set in place earlier in life. Each life chapter makes a distinctive imprint that later influences one's answer to the question, "Has my life been purposeful and successful according to my standards?" The measure of success is as unique to the individual as is their story. We all desire a happy ending and also want to believe that as long as our story chronicles a meaningful and purposeful life, it can be characterized as a success.

In his book *I and Thou*, Martin Buber reminds us that for man/woman the world is not simple and is ever unfolding. He suggests that one must enter into a personal relationship with oneself to examine whether the phantoms of exaggerated fears have been allowed to take ownership of one's life. I would encourage reflection as a means of measuring whether

45

your life has met your personal standards. Periods of solitary, meditative thought, of personal reflective contemplation, call forth inklings that answer the revelatory question, "Have I fulfilled my destiny?"

I once knew a man who was homeless and had endured many years of horrific and tragic circumstances. Yet, when I met him, he carried a white bucket as an emblem of his dream to be independent. He had obtained consent from a parking lot owner to begin his own car-washing service. Carrying his water bucket and his determination, he tenaciously remade his life by washing automobiles that belonged to businesspeople that parked in the city's central district. He did this with enthusiasm, bent on changing his status and restructuring his situation. Mr. Scott eventually moved from the homeless shelter. He acquired a small apartment, a used car, and a television to watch sports. I remember asking him, what he would like his legacy to be? At first, he did not quite understand the question. After I explained further, he replied, "I wish to leave whatever possessions I may have to help another. Others have helped me. I also wish to acknowledge my belief in God, and if I can give those gifts to anyone, then I have done something with my life."

This pure, strong voice touched me, and I knew then that Mr. Scott was an authentic success. He had become a man of compassion at the same time as finding personal independence. I have never forgotten Mr. Scott and the light that reflected from his eyes. He was his true self, and that honesty was priceless beyond measure. He never seemed angry at his position in life. He never displayed aggression. Rather, always believed in a better dream. Meeting individuals like Mr. Scott has concretized my belief in the resilience of the human spirit in the face of tragedy, the unwavering spirit of humankind in the search for something better. His belief in himself coupled with his strong spiritual conviction was enough. It was galvanizing. I am honored that he chose me as one of his friends. Mr. Scott is no longer around, but his memory lives on. No one could ever deny that his was a true and outstanding breakthrough to success.

Viktor E. Frankl acknowledges in his book, *Man's Search for Meaning*, that the human condition demands a time of personal reflection when one faces the limits of one's existence. His writings grew from a moment of human tragedy and suffering, when many were forced to confront the limits of their lives. He described the intensely painful and horrific environment prisoners in the concentration camps endured during years when their freedom—if not their lives—was taken from them without just cause. Not to diminish such unimaginable suffering, even those lucky enough to have been spared terrible outward trials will find that the human mind often puts its own terrible barriers in place. I am suggesting that to break through in life is to identify the prisons that limit us, steal our joy, and impede our freedom to soar. Self-awareness, and with it the capacity to disengage from those internal prisons, is the first step toward a successful life. The question we each must answer is, "Am I willing to set out on the long journey of life and allow resilience to be my companion in the arduous task of self-discovery while gaining freedom from the prison that holds my spirit captive?" Prisons, whether physical or personal, confront us with limits against which we may measure the success of our lives.

What matters, according to Dr. Frankl, is not the meaning of life in general, but the specific meaning of a person's life at a given moment. Each life is a road to self-discovery. Each time one must choose among paths or weather a crisis, the resilience that lies deep within the human spirit springs forth, comforting and shaping the individual. When one does not succumb to the weariness of the trials but rather reflects upon the story of one's own life and continues to explore, then there is the opening for awareness.

Maya Angelou calls this, "The quality of the human spirit that continues to rise despite the slings and arrows of outrageous fortune." She counsels, "Rise out of the physical pain and the psychological cruelties. Rise from being victims of rape and abuse and abandonment to the determination to be no victim of any kind. Rise and be prepared to move on and ever on." This determination not to accept the forces that weigh upon us but rather to find the place of "higher ground" and move forward toward a more positive, active outlook and future is a talent anyone may cultivate. It benefits its possessor and inspires others. Maya Angelou's breakthrough came through her creative gift with words. I believe that simple words and the stories they enable us to tell are the most powerful tools bestowed. When paired with a positive attitude and a directed purpose, the spirit that seeks higher ground can overcome almost any obstacle. Angelou's life and writing are proof that one can choose to live in the place of higher ground.

It has been my experience that the more we call forth and witness the resilience within ourselves, the greater the treasures we find spread before us. These treasures lure us into the journey of critical exploration and thus create the transformative process that allows our unique success to blossom in our path.

The ancient Greeks counseled, "Know thyself," and Shakespeare advised, "To thy own self be true." In theory this sounds wonderful and easy. However, the authentic road to self-awareness more often than not presents unforeseen difficulties. Thankfully, the human spirit is far more resilient than any of us fear.

The ability to understand one's own story is the thread that holds the individual together, and the creative act of telling oneself one's story brings forth much that might otherwise be hidden from the conscious mind. I am implying that the path toward personal discovery, and with it a sense of one's destiny and the meaning of success, is self-examination. One undertakes this examination by implementing the most blessed tool of all, the art of positive imagination and creative thinking. We might even name it "magical" thinking, because of the vibrancy and vitality it brings to the imagination. This positive thinking invites the authentic self to show up and leads one to explore truths that are often hidden in the far reaches of one's psyche.

Anyone who has spent time with them knows that the minds of small children are filled with imagination and playfulness. They see their world through the eyes of playfulness. Wouldn't it be something if we could return, from time and time, to the child's mind? The playfulness that comes naturally to the young child, and can be called upon in an instant, is one of the most powerful gifts we possess. People confuse the joy of playfulness with not using one's intellect. Yet one can play intelligently. Why not accomplish goals and bring forth success with playful joy and imagination? It is my position that the natural state of playfulness invites the imagination to soar. It opens the door for laughter and joy, and hence creativity abounds. This state of play is not lack of discipline. Behind it lurks the desire to move forward toward higher ground that is essential to making an authentic breakthrough. A complete person comprises numerous dynamic facets that work together to guide them to a sense of accomplishment.

Miguel de Cervantes wrote the inspiring story of Don Quixote while imprisoned, in Spain, during the late 1500s. The novel shows how belief in the impossible brings forth a hero. And perhaps because it does it with playful humor and imagination, the novel remains alive and vibrant today. The character Don Quixote represents the dreamer in all of us, who seeks an outcome that's different from that life offers. "I know who I am," Don Quixote states. And we discover that that means no situation will deter his belief in the goodness of life. Cervantes does not hide the shadow side of humanity that remains a necessary part of life, but through Don Quixote he shows that reality need not be what it appears. Don Quixote's resilient determination to remain true to his belief, his purpose, his desire to do good and to serve, to "right the wrongs" and not give up on humanity, regardless of its flaws, is as real as the flawed world he rides out to encounter.

Today more than ever the voice of communities around the globe speak out to this very theme. Darkness cannot be ignored. Light cries to have its place in the world and help maintain the balance of justice.

Life will always consist of contraries. In *The Marriage of Heaven and Hell,* the poet William Blake explains that "without contraries" there is "no progression." "Attraction and Repulsion, Reason and Energy, Love and Hate," he writes, "are necessary to Human existence." From the play of these forces, human progress emerges.

I would encourage each person not to be afraid to explore what is true for him or her. Look within and identify your gifts and talents. Soulfully review your traits. Then accept yourself and thrust forward. Love yourself. Learn to be more playful. Engage in laughter, as it truly is the heart's best medicine. Give of yourself and be open to receiving the knowledge and wisdom that life and others offer to you. Find the time to open new vistas. Have a child's mind filled with imagination. Engage in more positive thinking and embrace affirmations that enrich your life. Above all, discover your relationship with the Divine, the creator of the cosmos, and soon you will see with fresh new eyes, hear with newly-opened ears, and your heart will readily explore the wonders of this world. Forgive those who have harmed you and make peace with all you may have harmed.

Every new breath yields the opportunity of success … in the end called wisdom.

About Nina

Nina M. Kelly is an Amazon best seller as one of the co-authors with Jack Canfield in *Success Mastery.* She is a mythologist with an emphasis in depth psychology, storytelling, author, humanitarian, and cultural and arts activist. She also is an Archetypal Pattern Analyst and Dream Pattern Analyst. Nina's sense of adventure has always been sparked through learning more about people and their cultures. Believing that if you understand a person's culture, stories, myths, and rituals, then you more readily open your world to greater compassion.

Her passion for the art of healing through stories brought her to the place of writing Grace Has A Silent Voice, where she honors the silent heroes and the resilience of the human spirit. Working with death and dying patients, she acquired a tremendous respect for the proper honoring of story. In her book, she acknowledged the silent heroes that walk into our lives for a moment, then quickly disappear. This inevitably leaves an imprint that continues to remind us that there is beauty in humanity.

Nina's doctorate is from Pacifica Graduate Institute in Mythological Studies and Emphasis on Depth Psychology, and her dissertation research was completed through Louisiana State University Medical Center in New Orleans, Louisiana. Her dissertation was entitled: *Myth Making and Modern Medicine, A Case of Kidney Transplantation.* Her research work included reducing the rejection episodes post-transplant, implementing the power of stories and images. She published T*he Lost Heritage* in Psychology at the Threshold.

Nina is also an Archetypal Pattern Analyst and Dream Pattern Analyst where she completed her studies from Assisi International Institute and published, *Weaving Story Into The Web.*

As an executive film producer for the short film, *Dandelion,* the film won the judges award and has been shown at several film festivals. She has also served as president of the New Orleans Opera Association, president of Southern Repertory Theatre, Chair for Loyola University School of Music Visiting Committee, president and CEO of the Children's Bureau, publishing the history of the Children's Bureau, *Saving Wednesday's Child,* authored by Mark Cave, and authoring the introduction and acknowledgements. Throughout her tenure, she has served on numerous non-profits boards.

Nina continues to challenge us through the inspiration and motivation of storytelling. She continues to believe that the art form of storytelling and story sharing originate from the heart of everyone searching for expression – thus healing both listener and teller.

You may contact Nina at:

- Nina@ninastime.com
- www.ninamkelly

Dear Joan —

Thanks for everything

This chapter was tough
to write but necessary

And it's where the
origins of AMIT eden
come from.

1/19

CHAPTER 5

SUCCESS THROUGH FAILURE
FIVE STEPS TO USE FAILURE TO ACHIEVE SUCCESS AND MEANING

BY DR. PAUL ANDERSON

When you are a doctor and a patient dies, it is never pleasant, but it is something you adjust to as part of the job. When it is a child who dies however you never really adjust. Two decades ago I was working with a family and their child. The child was a twelve year old boy named Billy who had a brain tumor. In traditional cancer care we did not have a great deal of success with these types of cancer so I was working with Billy and the family on integrative cancer therapies to see if we could help either his quality of life or extend his life. The therapies I was including in Billy's care were "state of the art" at the time, and I would later be considered an innovator in these therapies. We worked hard with Billy and tried all our best therapies. Sadly, Billy lost his battle with this brain tumor and eventually died despite all the best efforts from both standard and integrative cancer care.

The death of Billy set me on a path to discover what we could do to get better and improve cancer care. While there is no cure for cancer, both the standard and integrative worlds of cancer care evolve over time. What drives this innovation and evolution is the idea that "people who have cancer die, and we have to do better."

Fast forward twenty years. Another family with a child affected by a deadly cancer contacted me. When we met they brought their beautiful four-year-old daughter Lilly. She was diagnosed at eleven weeks of age with this severe form of cancer. She had early treatment and had been in remission until now. She now had fallen out of remission and her only option was the same treatment that got her into remission the first time. The trouble was that her blood counts were bad, and she could not have the potentially life-saving treatment until her blood counts normalized. The real problem was that there were no treatments in standard cancer care that could get her blood counts to normal. The family and our team were in a conundrum and needed to find a way to get her blood counts normal so she could qualify for the other therapy.

Lilly was a joy to work with and know. Her tiny blonde presence was the source of limitless joy, personality and life. She lifted everyone around her and became an uplifting fixture at our clinic.

In the two decades since Billy's death, I had been involved in a great deal of innovative clinical cancer practice. That led to work in a federally-funded cancer research project where I had the opportunity to not only try innovative cancer therapies, but also to track those therapies and see if they actually work. When I met Lilly I had been working in this program for a few years and had brought many of the innovations of the past decades to our integrative cancer practice.

We went to work and tried a therapy which failed. Then tried another that failed. We tried more innovative therapies and they failed. We tried combining some of the therapies and that strategy failed as well. Lilly's blood counts were getting worse and our therapies were not helping. There was a therapy that made complete sense "on paper" (from a scientific point of view) but we had only tried it with one person. It was helping that one person, but they were an adult and had a different kind of cancer. We were out of ideas and options so I proposed this new therapy to the family.

When I met with the family I proposed this new therapy idea. The family said "so, you have tried this on one person so far?" "Yes" I replied, "and it has been safe and makes a lot of scientific sense." They continued and said "and this is an adult who has a different cancer from Lilly?" I had to agree this seemed very "outside the box" but it was the only option I could see trying next. The look from them was "please tell us you are joking, and that you have a better idea." I was not and I did not.

The family and I decided to proceed. We knew there were no other options and our only goal was to get her blood counts normal so she could have the other therapy. Without getting her blood counts back to normal she would lose any chance for the other therapy and really lose any chance for living very long.

We began the new therapy and she responded very well. It was safe, well-tolerated and her blood counts were back to normal within three weeks. We kept the therapy going and her blood counts stayed normal. Thinking this may be a fluke, we stopped the therapy for a week and her blood counts were abnormal again. We had two trials without the therapy and both times her blood counts were not controlled. After that we never stopped the experimental therapy again, because it worked. All this work and her blood counts being normal allowed her to start the standard therapy. We also did some preparatory integrative treatment to prepare her body for the standard therapy, another innovation of the years prior.

After this, the standard therapy worked and Lilly went into remission. She responded well to the treatment and we were ecstatic. We continued the original experimental therapy to keep her in remission and to keep her blood counts normal. The goal was to keep the latent cancer cells quiet and nonfunctional. Finally the whole plan worked together and she had time that was relatively normal and healthy with her family.

Three years later, she was still in remission and a relatively healthy, happy child. Then, as happens with these severe genetically-based cancers, the cancer figured out a way around all the therapies and started to be active again. This time the cancer came back forcefully. We quickly started to try innovative therapies to get her back into remission. We came close and another standard therapy was tried. That standard therapy did not help and her cancer progressed. Ultimately, as nothing was working, an experimental chemotherapy was tried. During this treatment she died, not from the cancer but due to side effects of the chemotherapy.

I was in her hospital room as she was passing away. Her family was around her and while a difficult time, was also a touching and beautiful time for her transition. Her family asked if I would speak at her memorial service which was an extreme honor. Lilly packed many decades of life and love into her eight years.

If the story ended there, for either Billy or Lilly, it would just be a sad story. The real benefit of their (and all the other patients) stories is what we can learn from them. You may be thinking "I'm not a doctor, what can I gain from these stories?" Anyone can take principles from these experiences which can illustrate pathways to success through any failure. Below are the five primary success attributes I have found when working through seemingly impossible odds and failures.

THE FIVE STEPS TO MOVE THROUGH FAILURES TO SUCCESS

1. PERSISTENCE

Persistence is a universal quality of all successful endeavor. One reason many will fail to move forward in the face of overwhelming odds is the extreme difficulty experienced when trying to be persistent while failing. To relate this to my story, what would have happened if I were to have given in to my desire to quit integrative oncology when Billy died? What if I had not gone on the quest to learn more and innovate, would Lilly have had anything new available to her? It is during our worst failures we are often being taught our most profound lessons. One key to persistence is to remember that a failure is just that, one point in time, and you have the rest of your life to learn from it and move on. Easy to say but hard to do. Persistence can lead you to step two.

2. BE A CURIOUS LEARNER

Curiosity and learning go hand in hand with innovation. Learning and curiosity can be separate, but when combined create a powerful position for you to move through failures and on to the next breakthrough. Curiosity is that force that is creative and motivating while learning is the stabilizing and grounding force that makes sure your curiosity leads to innovation. It is easy to forget that innovation and success after failure is rarely a single event. You are usually knocked down repeatedly in the process of moving through a failure. Without the combination of a curious mind to search for solutions and the ability to learn from (and not repeat) past failures, it is too easy to fall into despair and become stagnant. Curiosity propels you beyond each failure with a knowledge that you do not know everything but the answers are out there. You can literally see that there is more than we know "out there" and that eventually you will find it. "Finding it" requires the next step.

3. INFORMED BOLDNESS

Just as the combination of curiosity and learning take those two processes to the next level, combining boldness with being informed allows the action which can propel you to the next level. Boldness alone is a good quality, but if it is not informed can lead to disaster. Being informed is important but the world is full of people well informed but afraid to act. You need to "do your homework" and be informed, but you also then need to act. Why is this so rare? It is easy to act and it is easy to be informed, but when informed it is more comfortable to sit back and let someone else act. "What if I act and it doesn't work?" your mind will say. This fear is the most common reason people do not move forward. It is uncomfortable to take the leap to informed action but moving past your comfort is required to find success through your failures. When you do take the leap, you come face to face with the next inevitable step.

4. THE TRUTH OF "YOU ARE NEVER"

Once you take the leap past failure using informed action, you come face to face with the truth of the "you are never" reality. You are never done learning, never done trying, never done failing, never in possession of all the facts, your curiosity is never satisfied and so on. Once you can see the power of this step you realize that every day (instead of a day full of answers and success) can be a day of challenge, exhilaration and joy in discovery. It is the greatest generator of hope one can have in this process. *Use the power of "never" and you will truly never be the same.* Once you embrace this step you can enter the most powerful step.

5. PASS IT ON

There is little point in achieving successful breakthroughs if you keep them to yourself. What good is an invention or innovation if nobody else knows about it? My experience is once you find success through your failure and share it, then the journey (including the trials and setbacks) becomes worth it. I passed the therapies learned from Lilly and her remission on to other physicians and scientists for free, and now it is the basis for an entire system for treating cancer used in many places around the world. Successes come at too high of a price not to share them and better the world we live in. Without persistence, being a curious learner, informed boldness, the truth of "never" and passing it on, we cannot move from our inevitable failures to success.

About Dr. A

Dr. Paul Anderson ("Dr. A") is an author, speaker, media host and physician.

He is the CEO of the Anderson Medical Group which includes a
[Photo credit: A. Atkins]   state-of-the-art integrative medical clinic in Seattle, Washington, serving people with cancer and advanced chronic illnesses. In addition to this, he operates a medical education website, a Radio show / Podcast on CTR Radio Network and a patient outreach and medical education services firm.

Dr. A uses his over two decades of work as a physician and four decades total in medicine to bring a unique view of medicine to patients, physicians and the public. His vision is that of returning to the medical ideal of "treating the whole person," while incorporating all that modern science can add. And while medicine is often divided into sections ("western medicine", "Chinese medicine", "traditional medicine", "botanical medicine", etc.) there are in reality only two kinds of medicine: good medicine and bad medicine, and that good medicine takes the best of all forms and integrates them. In this way the patient is afforded the very best that history and science have to offer.

His training as a naturopathic medical doctor was also unique and eclectic, spanning traditional hospital training as well as integrative and natural medical training and practice. He has blended both worlds of medicine in practice and now trains other physicians in advanced medical therapies and true medical integration. In recognition of his clinical work, Dr. A was named as one of the "Top Doctors" in Seattle three times.

For five years, Dr. A was involved in a National Institutes of Health research project innovating and evaluating integrative cancer therapies. He has combined that experience and his other clinical and research work to offer, teach and write about truly cutting-edge integrative cancer therapies. Out of this research work, he was able to author a number of cutting edge clinical guidelines for integrative oncology. He has taken this work to the next level in his own conference series, "Advanced Applications in Medical Practice" – a twice-yearly advanced continuing medical education seminar series.

Dr. A also published a book for cancer patients and their families called *Outside the Box Cancer Therapies* (Hay House Publishing) based on both his and his co-authors clinical experience and the cancer research he had been involved in.

When he is not on the road or working from his Seattle offices, Dr. A enjoys time with his wife Lori and their family. They have five adult children and five grandchildren who provide endless opportunities for fun and interaction. His family has always been his driving force, motivation and joy.

Learn more at:

- www.ConsultDrA.com
- www.advancedmedicaltherapies.com
- www.aampconferences.com
- www.DrAbooks.com

CHAPTER 6

MARRIAGE MASTERY

BY JENNIFER N. PRICE

What do you do when you're looking for the help you need but can't find it? You become it. So, I did.

After a ten-year journey of healing from an unhealthy marriage that ended in a devastating divorce, and after a hefty dose of personal development and deep soul-searching, I dedicated my life to helping married couples worldwide save their marriages and create successful and passionate relationships.

My definition of greatness and success are one and the same: turning pain into purpose. As a result, I took the pain from my experience and turned it into my life's purpose.

You see, hell hath no fury like an unhealthy marriage. I fully understand its destructive effects on self-worth and the emptiness it creates. I understand the deep heartache when you witness your spouse slip on their wedding ring when they return home from a weekend away. I understand the frustration that accompanies years of failed marriage counseling, the death of romance and affection, and the inability to resolve conflicts.

I understand the spiritual pain that occurs in one's soul when trying to honor your vows amidst emotional and verbal abuse because "God hates divorce." I understand trying to be a good Christian and not dishonoring your spouse by discussing your marital woes with family and friends — all in the name of soldiering on.

I understand alcoholism. And I hate it. Evident was our need for a professional diagnosis, education, and solution, but I couldn't find anyone capable of helping us. The professionals said, "There's no hope, there's nothing that can be done, we don't know how to help you." Metaphorically, I was punched in the gut, gasping for air, and slowly suffocating to death.

Thus, I began my quest for understanding, healing, and a real solution (even if it was too late for my marriage). After years of study, I understood what went wrong. I found solutions and wanted to help others. But first I had to learn to love and honor myself again to be good for, and capable of, serving others. I dove into personal development and made a path for healing. A great power was unleashed within me, so I could go out into the world and do work that matters. To me, *Marriage Matters.*

I became a Marriage Interventionist and learned a radically different approach to marriage improvement that works. As you may suspect, there are no shortcuts to authentic change. It takes commitment, effort, and the right knowledge, but you might be surprised at some of the eye-opening remedies and how fun they are.

Allow me to help your relationship, beginning with this chapter. Which leads me to beg the question…

DO PEOPLE EVER BECOME MASTERS OF MARRIAGE?

Don't be fooled. It doesn't mean a relationship without hurt feelings, messiness, or arguments. I'm talking about individuals who have mastered the art of union: those who remain committed to creating a successful partnership; who never cease to foster connection, passion and communication; who triumph through conflict; who possess humility and aren't afraid of making (or owning) mistakes; and those who respect the sanctity of marriage. When struggling, marriage is the least fulfilling entity in life. Despite this, I am convinced that when marriage is mastered, it's the most fulfilling. It is possible for you to master your marriage — anyone can with the proper strategies, tools, and knowledge.

Why Marriage is Important and Worth Fighting For:
Let's first look at why people should get (or stay) married. Inscribed on the human heart is the desire for a permanent and monogamous

commitment to one person. Studies suggest that happily married couples have better health, wealth, sexual intimacy, and live longer than singles. Children in loving families also tend to be healthier in all areas (mind, body, and spirit) than children from divorced parents. A healthy marriage provides security, stability, love, passion, and fulfillment.

In a healthy marriage, selfishness recedes, and you live to love and serve your mate. You experience total acceptance because of complete trust and loyalty. You help improve each other through personal growth. Beautiful freedom exists when you attain security in your relationship: the kind that allows you to be you, no pretenses, and you share your innermost desires, fears, and goals.

How to Achieve a Healthy and Prosperous Marriage:
I won't say it's easy, but with a commitment to success, the right knowledge, and perseverance, anyone can do it. Yes, *anyone*. It begins with one of the cornerstones of a healthy and successful relationship: *SELF*. Self-understanding, self-development, self-worth, self-respect, and self-discipline. You become the type of person you'd want to be married to. Then, you create a compelling future together, fulfill each other's needs, learn successful communication, and create passion.

START WITH SELF

The first cornerstone of marital growth begins with *self*. Personal development involves many intricate entities, but it starts with forgiving and letting go of past pain, knowing and understanding yourself, and committing to a life of growth and gratitude.

You'll never learn and understand your spouse until you know, understand and develop yourself. Yet, most people enter marriage without personal development, and this sets you on the fast-track to divorce because you'll be incapable of fulfilling each other's needs.

Included in self-development is having your own friends, hobbies, and goals, so your identity isn't defined by your spouse or children. The healthiest people live beyond their home and family life by contributing to society. Individuals experience happiness and fulfillment, which goes full circle to create a happier, more fulfilled marriage. This also fosters connection between partners because it provides excellent conversation topics when you regroup after spending time apart. You'll create a lifetime of intimacy and deep connection if you commit to continually discovering new things about each other and yourselves.

We enter marriage with a plethora of specific expectations regarding married life — communication, satisfying each other's needs, holiday traditions, vacations, the running of home life — and this contributes to how we communicate, act, react and feel. It's helpful to examine your expectations and whether they are serving you and your marriage well or causing conflict and dissatisfaction. Tony Robbins teaches us to replace expectations with appreciation; it's the fastest route to happiness and contentment.

CREATE A COMPELLING FUTURE

The second cornerstone to marital success involves creating a compelling future as a united team. This helps keep your eye on the prize and enables you to cope with daily stressors and conflict more easily. Without a compelling future, it's difficult to have hope for improvement, and you're more likely to suffer depression or anxiety. Creating new standards for yourselves as individuals and for your marriage fosters teamwork and connection within relationships.

Decide precisely what you want in every area of your life (deeper spirituality, personality characteristics you want to improve or develop, marriage desires, dream home, career goals, saving and investing targets, and whatever else is important to you). Create a plan of action, list obstacles you foresee and how to eliminate them, and list anyone you'll need help from. Develop short-term and long-term goals for yourselves as individuals and together as a couple, and create target dates for the completion of your goals. Create a vision board with all your goals and hang it in a location where it can be seen daily. Then, commit to making it happen.

COMMITMENT

Many people think marital commitment means staying faithful, but genuine commitment is rooted in transparency, truth, forgiveness, respect, and fulfilling each other's needs. When couples concentrate on these dynamics, the rest follows suit.

When your spouse is your top priority, you'll immediately improve your marriage. You'll reach ultimate depth in love and connection, and that depth of connection breeds trust, then healthier communication, and finally attraction and passion. Ultimately, you'll no longer fear for the health, success, or longevity of your marriage and will have peace.

Commitment allows couples to share everything with each other knowing they will be safe, respected and honored, even when disagreeing. This provides the strength necessary to cope with daily stress and challenges, and hope of a long, happy life together. A healthy connection offers the sense of teamwork and fosters a mature love that expects nothing in return. This level of maturity allows you each to encourage one another and want the best for each other in all areas of life.

Tips to foster a deeper connection:

- Greet each other sincerely every time you reconvene.
- Put your spouse's preferences first, and they will eventually reciprocate.
- Make daily time together, without children or other distractions, for at least 30 minutes.
- Treat your spouse the way you want your children to be treated in their future marriage. They are watching you and learning about love and marriage.
- Pray and/or meditate together daily.
- Exercise caution and have boundaries with opposite-sex friends. Limits need to be in place that you and your spouse agree on.
- All email, banking, and social media accounts should be open to each other; share passwords.
- Choose friends wisely for they influence your marriage.
- Refrain from pornography. Mental commitment is just as significant as physical because mental/emotional often leads to physical.
- Always wear your wedding ring. It's a reminder of your dedication and priorities and tells the world you're taken.
- Always defend each other.

Part of commitment is not judging your spouse. They will feel connected to you when they feel understood.

COMMUNICATION

Communication points clearly to massive differences between men and women, and can make or break a relationship. The nature of the differences is apparent, but the reason for those differences escapes our understanding. Perhaps it's to teach men to be more detailed and patient, and to teach women to be more efficient and to the point. Whatever the reason, men and women must learn practical communication skills to understand one another more successfully.

When breakdowns in marriage occur, contempt materializes in the form of frequent conversational interruptions, dismissal of spouse, and stonewalling (withdrawal from important communication). This provides a dangerous domino effect that yields resentment and lack of vulnerability, intimacy and ultimately, commitment. Thus, the factors that make up effective communication, such as proper self-expression, understanding your partner, body language, and self-control, are all key to nurturing a relationship. Seven percent of communication is verbal, and 93 percent is non-verbal (facial expression, body language, eye movements, and tone of voice), so be mindful of your physicality.

A huge part of communication is learning successful conflict management. Here are a few tips to get you started:

- Listen to understand, not to react or respond.
- Promote and protect the right of your spouse to communicate their opinions, beliefs, perspective, needs, and desires. You both have the right to communicate your position, even if you disagree.
- Always find humor during conflict.
- Give your spouse the benefit of the doubt when it comes to their intentions. Remember they probably have positive intentions, even if it doesn't feel that way in the moment.
- Maintain physical touch when discussing difficult topics: it's soothing, diffuses anger, and promotes understanding and teamwork.
- Arguments should occur in private, not in front of family or friends.
- If you have children, maintain a united team in front of them.
- Remember the magic 5:1 ratio: have at least five positive communications for every negative. Even better in my opinion, is a 10:1 ratio.
- Make lots of eye contact.

- For further understanding, try: "Sweetheart, I'm confused by your statement when you said _____. When can we talk about this more so I can understand?"
- For clarity, try: "Babe, I heard you say _____. Did I hear you correctly?"

PASSION

Creating passion in marriage is the ultimate goal because it involves intense emotions of love, hope, desire, and excitement to share life together. This level of intensity usually represents a thriving relationship.

Lack of passion causes a host of problems: feelings of insignificance, boredom, frequent fighting, discontent, then communication diminishes, connection fades, trust suffers, and it goes downhill from there. Passion naturally occurs at the start of a relationship, but once the honeymoon phase is over, couples must work daily to create it. Affairs don't happen, and marriages don't end because of lack of love; relationships dissolve due to lack of passion.

Practices that create great passion:

- Sincerely say "I love you" frequently.
- Go to bed at the same time together, share pillow talk, and wake at the same time daily.
- Never withhold sex, and never force it. Passionate intimacy develops when mutual submission occurs.
- Create non-sexual intimacy daily: a 10-second heartfelt embrace, a 10-second passionate kiss, shoulder/foot massages, holding hands. The more non-sexual intimacy that occurs, the more passionate sexual intimacy is.
- Develop and achieve goals together.
- Flirt playfully with your spouse.

There's one last element that will blow your passion off the charts: polarity. Polarity is opposites attracting each other. Think positive and negative ends of a magnet. In marriage, polarity is created when masculine and feminine energies collide. If both spouses predominantly dwell in the same energy, they will repel each other (if man is effeminate and woman is feminine *OR* if both man and woman display a masculine disposition). When polarity exists, passion ensues!

Women, maintain beautiful femininity: approach him with softness, be gentle, playful, and seductive. This will drive him wild. What will drive him *crazy* is nagging, critical attacks, and a controlling demeanor (all non-feminine). Allow him to search internally and if he doesn't reveal all feelings, realize this is a biological trait for men. Respect that, be patient, and give him space — he will be grateful. Allow him to be a masculine man. A Warrior. Your Champion.

Men, step up and maintain your masculinity by first examining your identity and integrity. List the masculine traits you want to embody: leadership, courage, humility, honesty, provider, protector. Explain to your wife your desire to grow in masculinity. It may take some adjustment, but she'll love and respect you for it. In time, she'll become more attracted to you. Her deepest desire is for you to become an outstanding leader (firm, yet gentle with her), provide for and protect her, and make her feel loved and cherished.

Above all, live in constant gratitude. If you focus on what's lacking, you'll remain frustrated and unsatisfied. Being grateful every day for what you have is the blueprint for receiving more blessings and abundance. Take time daily to feel gratitude for your spouse and their positive characteristics. Wake to see the sunrise together, hold one another in the moonlight. Celebrate each other always, for a gratuitous heart breeds love.

Dedication
This chapter is dedicated to God, for His abundant grace; to my son, John Michael, for teaching me unconditional love; to my family, for your love and support; and to Tony Robbins, for Unleashing the Power Within me.

About Jennifer

When a couple experiences marital breakdown, they often encounter suffering in every area of life. Jennifer Price, BCC has a passion for helping couples break through their marital conflicts and create beautiful, fulfilled relationships. Jennifer is honored to help couples all over the world transform their marriages and their entire lives through one-on-one coaching, her online programs, and destination marriage retreats.

Jennifer firmly believes the adage "to whom much is given, much is expected," so she volunteers her time and expertise by serving members in her Facebook group, *Marriage Matters*, where she interacts with and gives advice to people worldwide.

Jennifer is a Robbins-Madanes Center Board Certified International Strategic Interventionist. Additional professional designations include:

- Executive Certificate of Advanced Negotiation: University of Notre Dame - Mendoza College of Business
- Certificate of Strategies for Conflict Management: University of Notre Dame
- Certificate of Intercultural Management: University of Notre Dame
- Author, speaker, educator

You can connect with Jennifer at:

- www.jenniferprice.com
- www.facebook.com/groups/MarriageDoesMatter
- www.instagram/MarriageMastery

CHAPTER 7

LISTEN TO YOUR BODY AND SUCCEED IN A HIGH-STRESS WORLD

BY STACEY GRIFFIN, Ph.D.

Joy bubbled up within me and started to spread. I felt vibrant and could feel the joy take root in my body. I started to laugh. I thought, "Oh! There's my joy!" I had been looking for it. I was doing some guided visualization focused within the body, with an intent to learn how to listen to the subtle messages my body was telling me for greater health and well-being. I have since learned just how important this is, but I have not always had a consistent relationship with listening to the messages my body gives me.

Five years ago, when I hit the burnout wall, I wasn't listening. I still have a vivid memory of walking out to my car in the parking lot of my office building, feeling dizzy, wobbly and a bit nauseous. The feeling you get coming off a spinning ride at the fair. It was late and dark. Not many other cars were left. I got in my car and put my head back, closing my eyes and willing the feeling to go away. I had been in this place for a while, but this was the first time I had started to let in the voice that I couldn't live like this. I was trying to hold on to my high performance by working long-hours, but it was slipping. With the constant organizational change, back-to-back meetings, politics, never ending e-mails, long hours, and disconnected relationships, I had become cynical and my sense of humor was gone. I was physically, mentally and spiritually exhausted. I had allowed myself to get this far by pushing myself and ignoring signs that

I wasn't dealing well with the adrenaline and cortisol surges from the high-stress environment. I had lost touch with myself, and was seriously burned out.

With the amount of people reporting to be burned out and struggling with high stress levels, I am not alone in my experience. So many of us live in this high stress, fast paced, look-at-what-I-can-accomplish life style, and as a result, we have become a society fatigued and disconnected. There is so much coming at us, it is hard to process. Curious about my experience and path back to health, I started researching burnout prevention and recovery. I also looked at what the opposite experience of burnout would be, focusing on energetic vitality and joy. In doing this research, I found the importance of integrating body and mind, and it forced me to realize this experience of embodied vitality and joy had been left behind as I prioritized reaching my next accomplishment. So, I turned my goal of going back to a "neutral" or non-burned-out state into one of vitality and joy, even in a high-stress environment.

If you want to thrive and succeed in a high-stress environment while also feeling healthy and balanced, learning to listen and engage your body is a great place to focus. The following practices are just a few of the ones I have found most helpful for myself and my clients.

BODY CENTERED PRACTICES

Engage Your Senses

Research has shown that focusing on your senses is a great way to reduce stress hormones. The good news is this can be done easily. Getting into nature and tuning into your surroundings is one of best ways to do this, but you can also do this in just a minute or two in everyday situations like sitting in a meeting or taking a shower. I use this practice frequently and find that taking a few minutes between meetings to walk in the garden, feel the air on my skin and smell the plants, makes a positive impact on my focus and mood.

As you read this, give the following a try:

- Take a deep breath, letting the air fill your lungs. Exhale slowly and notice the feeling of the air as it moves out of your body.

- Notice any breeze across your skin. Is the air soft, hot, or cold?
- How do your clothes feel against your body?
- What do you smell in the air around you?
- What sounds do you hear?
- What tastes do you notice?

Just observe without judgement. Let your body be immersed in all the senses it perceives. Notice any shifts in your body, mood or stress levels afterward.

Connect with Inner Wisdom

To truly connect with ourselves, to feel on a cellular level what is going on for us, is a lost art. I am not talking about paying attention to our physique by going to the gym and working out. That is great, but often that's the mind telling the body what to do. I am talking about pausing the running narrative in your mind and bringing your attention to within your body. And listen. To recognize and trust the messages.

When you learn to quiet the mind and go within, you can more easily connect with what your body is telling you it needs. Next time you feel out of sorts or your energy lagging, take a moment and sit quietly, bringing your awareness within.

- Ask what it is your body needs right now?
- Do you need to move, walk around, stretch your muscles?
- What senses want to be engaged?
- Do you need to eat, sleep or drink some water?
- What kind of food does your body need?

Pay attention if your mind makes excuses why fulfilling any of those needs isn't possible, or that they aren't valid. Just notice what your body is telling you and ask what would happen if you did? How can you honor those requests?

Honor Your Cycle of Renewal

In our world where constant stimulus, the search for increasing productivity, and a fear of stillness and quiet rule, many of us are forgetting to honor the need for rest and renewal. We forget that rest is an integral part of the growing and achievement process. The pull is strong to live in the glory of busy accomplishments, to do more and do better, to be the one who replied to the most e-mail overnight, who worked the longest hours. We push ourselves, ignoring signs of fatigue, and end up burned out, stuck on auto-pilot, disconnected from our creativity and passions that nurture our energy. What felt good and accomplished begins to fall flat. Our creativity wanes. Giving more effort doesn't equate to the same sense of satisfaction. Like a plant that needs the seasonal downtime to nourish its roots and come back stronger, you also need to honor your own cycle of renewal, whether for a season, a week, a day, or even for just a few minutes.

When was the last time you felt deeply rested? When your body gives you messages that you need rest, what do you do? If you find yourself feeling drained and tired, is your mind saying yes to more when your body wants to say yes to rest? How might you equate success with renewing yourself? How can you allow your roots to store nutrients and energy, so that your next productive cycle can bring forth new blooming brilliance?

Release Embodied Barriers to Success

Emotions live in the body in the form of energy, and if not felt and released, can create tension, constrictions, and physical bracing over time. Unfortunately, suppressing emotions is something we are conditioned to do. Take a look at kids. They get angry, yell, cry, kick their feet, then a few minutes later they are running around laughing. The emotional energy moves through their body and dissipates as it is felt. But as we age, the full expression of emotions becomes socially awkward at best.

When we live in high stress situations, such as feeling criticized in a meeting, anxious after getting a call from the school about your child, or fear over hearing there will be another round of layoffs, we often ignore the emotional energy until it tries to get our attention with symptoms like back pain and headaches. This suppression of energy can also create unconscious barriers to making changes in our life. We can set a goal to accomplish something or make a change, but the held feelings, such as fear, shame, or resentment, become barriers to progress until we address them.

The following exercise can help tap into those held emotions and set them free if you choose to. I invite you to bring to mind an area of your life you want to shift. This could be anything like lose weight, be less anxious, apply for that promotion, become a better parent, or get rid of chronic pain doctors can't diagnose. Anything that you want to shift or change. Be specific.

Next, get in a comfortable position lying down or reclining. Close your eyes and take a breath, letting your belly and rib cage expand, extending your exhale until all the air is out of your lungs. Repeat this two more times, keeping your attention focused on your breath. Slowly scan each part of your body with your mind, moving from the top of your head down to your toes. Relax any areas of tension you find.

Recall what it is you want to shift in your life. Where do you feel the challenge in your body? Focus on that area. What emotion are you feeling? Spend a long moment really feeling it in your body. Next, bring to mind an image that is a symbol of your emotion. It could be an image of anything or just an impression like a color or shape. Let this image become detailed in your mind. What color is it? How big is it? Is it moving? Ask this image what purpose it serves you. Ask it what it needs. Take as long as you need to let the answers come to you. After you listen to these answers, ask yourself if you still need this image to live in you. If you do, then ask how it can give you protection but still allow the flexibility and freedom to make the shift you desire. If you don't want to keep it, thank the image for serving you in this way and give it permission to leave. Watch it leave. Next, replace it with an image you want there, one that will serve you in your new purpose. When the image forms, take time to notice how it feels. If you want, you can spread that feeling throughout your body. When you are complete, open your eyes.

CONNECTING TO JOY AND VITATLITY

We have gotten used to paying attention to our bodies only when something is wrong or hurts. But if you think of these as symptoms your body uses in trying to get your attention, that something new is trying to emerge, you can address your needs before they limit your life, and you can use your body intelligence to help you achieve your goals and successfully thrive in a stressful world.

I have learned that in order to shift a habit or way of living in the world, you must also engage your physical body on that journey too. By tapping into the wisdom of my body and really listening, I recovered from my burnout and embodied joy again. I released the stored burnout emotions keeping it down and I learned how to engage my body to allow vitality to be experienced. I am still on my journey and I invite you to join me.

About Stacey

Stacey Griffin, Ph.D. is an experienced executive coach, consultant and executive with over 25 years of experience. In group and one-on-one sessions, she helps clients embrace new behaviors that bring about powerful changes, allowing them to stretch into their potential. With passion for helping leaders, teams and organizations manage the fullness of complex, chaotic environments, she loves partnering with clients to find the positive, energetic spark that moves them from high stress, declining performance and burnout to overall vitality and effectiveness. Her past clients have reported an increased resourcefulness to solve problems creatively, greater health and resilience to handle ups and downs of life, renewed sense of optimism about the future, better relationships at home and work, and an increased awareness about assumptions, fears, and how they are preventing them from reaching their goals.

Stacey has provided coaching and consulting services to a variety of organizations and industries, from not-for-profit to Fortune 500. Prior to working for her own consultancy, she led the organizational development and talent management teams for over 13 years for a large health system, where her work included executive coaching, change management, culture assessment, employee engagement, and performance and talent management. She has also held leadership positions in property and facilities management and has successfully started and led her own facilities management business.

Stacey is a certified coach from the Hudson Institute of Coaching and the International Coaching Federation, a certified MindBody Bridge Practitioner, has a B.A. in psychology and a M.S. and Ph.D. in organizational psychology, and is trained in a number of leadership and organizational assessments and methodologies. She is a member of various professional groups, including the national Organizational Development Network, International Coach Federation and Association for Talent Development.

Stacey can be reached at:

- Stacey@GriffinCC.com

CHAPTER 8

INFLECTION POINTS: AMERICA, THE BEAUTIFUL

BY SUMIT GANGULI

Great things are not done by impulse, but by
a series of small things brought together.
~ Vincent Van Gogh

They say to be forewarned is to be forearmed. I need to warn you, that my story is not about a major transformational experience. In my story there is no pot of gold with a leprechaun at the end of the rainbow. Between the mundane and the sublime, I have decided to focus on the mundane.

My life experience is about the smaller steps with a few hard knocks and a lot of resilience and cultivated mindfulness, that has led to some Success Breakthroughs. I have become very mindful of every moment, as these could be inflection points that slowly but surely change the trajectory of life.

Inflection point is primarily a differential equation term, the point where a concave curve becomes a convex curve. According to Howard Stevensen of Harvard Business School, *"Inflection points change the way we think about things. They present an opportunity that only occurs periodically. And they possess a kind of latent motivational energy, which, when recognized and harnessed, can unleash potential that one wouldn't seize otherwise."*

I grew up in Kolkata, a city in the eastern part of India. My father was a doctor with the Indian Railways and my mother was a home maker, and we lived in a gated community for railway employees beside the Ganges river. It was good sheltered living; I went to the neighborhood catholic school and played soccer, cricket and field hockey with my friends. And I was a dreamer: I created my own world, acting in school plays, building make-believe computers and rolling an occasional cigarette out of my friend's father's cigarette paper and tobacco. The latter, of course, landed me in a great deal of trouble.

During one of those happenstance moments, I chanced upon a coffee table picture book that my uncle from London had given me. It was an unusually large book with glossy paper and big colorful pictures. As I leafed through it, I was transported into the beautiful English countryside. There were these quaint English brick houses, cottages, villas with paved driveways, manicured gardens, undulating fields and bright red doors with an unassuming bottle of milk at the door step. There were pictures of various seasons, the pristine snow of winter, the riot of colors of fall and the lush green of summer. For years during the lazy summer afternoons of Kolkata, I would thumb through these photographs and distinctly found myself placed within these beautiful pictures. I was all of 5 or 6 then, but I had resolved to live in this fantastic land.

And that dream got fulfilled when I came to America, and after a few years was able to buy land near Princeton, NJ and build a home, not unlike one from the photographs in the coffee table book, with the brick finish, large bay windows, pavers in the driveway, landscaping with specimen trees and an undulating field for my backyard. Although I still have not gotten someone to deliver milk bottles to my door step, I was able to literally construct an image that I had sustained in my mind over two continents and over two score and five years. This has been a very personal Success Breakthrough.

When I was around 10 years old, my father had taken up a new assignment to run a few hospitals, and we had moved from Kolkata in the eastern part of India to a port town in the western part of India, almost 1400 miles away. It was a small town and we would often visit the ships that would dock at the port and be invited to dinners hosted by the ships' captains. During one of these events, I chanced upon a National Geographic magazine. This particular month's issue was about the advent of silicon chips, and how the microprocessors and integrated chips would transform the world. There were blown up pictures of the Intel chips with their spidery connectors, the beautiful picture of the valley in the suburbs of San Francisco, and smiling young men and women ushering in the new era. While relishing my dessert - peach melba - and leafing through the magazine, I was awestruck by the story and the potential of the chips and computers. That evening, I decided that it would be rather cool if I could be associated with computers and software, and that could be my passport to the countries of my dreams. So, a number of unrelated and happenstance moments led to my decision to pursue a degree in electrical engineering and computers.

It was in 1992 that I came to America and had a choice to set up business in the Bay Area or near New York, but the pictures from the coffee table book of the various distinct seasons were still vivid in my mind, and I decided to make New Jersey my home. I incorporated a new company, that was a division of one of the larger Indian conglomerates and started promoting software services in the US.

Today's media in the US has made it fashionable to often criticize and dump on America. TV news derive some perverse pleasure in highlighting some of the worst that America has to offer. But after I landed in America, I jumped right into the ways of America and felt truly welcomed by the people I interacted with. I felt most comfortable with the system that the country functioned on, I could rent an apartment, lease a car, buy furniture and conduct business with some of the largest companies in America within a matter of few months. This is a testament to what this country is about. I was a foreigner, but I fit right in and became an integral part of the society. I have been mentored and guided by senior leaders, personally supported by American friends and have never really felt that I was ever treated differently.

I may have been fortunate, but I have travelled across the country visiting Birmingham, AL, Baton Rouge, LA, Midland, MI, Cedar Rapids, IA, Kansas City, KS, Columbia, SC and many more cities, and at most of the places I have been greeted with warm and courteous behavior. I have had the occasion to work in many parts of the world: Western and Eastern Europe, the Far East and the Middle East, including my birth country of India. But I can unequivocally say that no other country is more open, more welcoming and fairer than America, especially for someone who is willing to put in some good old hard work. I feel protective about this country, and while it may have some imperfections, it is so important that the values and principles of America survive, because this is how the world will look like in the future.

At one company where I worked, we were able to pursue a joint venture with a US-based software company and subsequently got a Fortune 5, 125-year-old conglomerate to invest in our company and open up opportunities to execute large, world-class software projects. But here again, as an observer of my life, I have come to the conclusion that one of the most important ingredients for success or to make a breakthrough in our chosen field is to have an unbridled sense of optimism and a sense of purpose. My favorite quote is from Henry David Thoreau that captures this sentiment: *"I know of no more encouraging fact than the unquestionable ability of man to elevate his life by conscious endeavor."*

But it has not always been a walk in the park for me. As the mild-mannered philosopher Mike Tyson once said, *"Everybody has a plan until they get punched in the mouth."* In early 2001, I had joined a computer services company that was backed by a foreign bank, as the Group CEO. We had plans to do multiple acquisitions, then eventually do a management buyout and focus the merged companies on the high-tech field of embedded systems. This would be the fruition of my ambition and dreams. It was in the morning; I had just parked my car and was walking into my office when my assistant rushed in and took me to watch the events unfolding on TV. Rumors were swirling that America was under attack... there were multiple flights in the air ready to attack America, and then we saw the second plane hit the World Trade Center. It seemed everything was happening in slow motion and then, for the next many months of 2001 and 2002, everything went by excruciatingly – in slow motion. The bank had invested in forty-one companies, and all their investments had gone under water. The software business had dried up, clients were refusing engagements and we had to retrench people in droves. The company was teetering, and I had to leave the company and take up another assignment that was a step down from the role of a Group CEO.

We often identify ourselves through work, status and other social trappings, and this incident caused significant upheaval in my life and I was gripped with self-doubt. The initial reaction was to regress and wallow in self-pity and all this uncertainty was further exacerbated by a personal crisis. I was always a hands-on father and was very involved with my son, Sohan. Tending to him, taking him to activities and sports, focusing on his studies and guiding him through his adolescent period was my therapy. My son's evolution as a caring and sensitive young man, overcoming the travails of being a teenager and attending college to become an engineer, could very well be the pinnacle of my personal success. I am a rationalist and a man of reason, but I still have not been able to decode this almost overwhelming sense of affection and protective feeling that one feels for one's scion.

I think it was Churchill who had said that one of the best ways to resolve a crisis is to drive through it, and that is what I did. I did not have the luxury to step back; my first-generation immigrant insecurities kicked in, and I invested everything in my work and in my son. Both gave me immense pleasure, and both defined me as a person.

Finally, as I have soldiered on, I have learned to pace out the days and not seek short-term professional gratifications. I think the greatest gift that America provides its denizens is this indefatigable and almost audacious chutzpah to believe that they can really achieve their dreams, and this is not just a platitude. I am amazed and almost envious of Elon Musk and Jeff Bezos' large bold pursuits. I keenly follow Satya Nadella of Microsoft's efforts to reconcile seemingly contradictory themes of being a world-beating technologist, a successful corporate leader and a humanist. I seek out stories of Jim McKelvey, who was working at IBM's Scientific Center, while simultaneously teaching as a glass blowing instructor. Jim channeled his frustration of not being able to sell his glass-blowing sculptures because of issues with credit cards, towards partnering with Jack Dorsey and inventing the revolutionary payment device, Square.

I try to block out all the contradictions of Travis Kalanick, founder of Uber, and marvel at his idea to create a technology platform for one of the most basic and commonly available utilities like taxis, and then having the temerity to promote this against all odds around the world. I am humbled by the virtuosity of Israel as a country where despite being in the throes of unrest and war, it has become the most prolific innovation destination producing the most eclectic inventions from cherry tomatoes, drip irrigation, pill cams, Pentium chips, IT security software, and many more.

The above leaders and ideas are my mile markers to define my success and I have tried to do that at GAVS Technologies, the company that I now lead. At GAVS, we are harnessing the powers of artificial intelligence, predictive analytics, cloud technologies, and robotics, and have promoted the ground-breaking concept of the Zero Incident Framework, as well as many other products that vastly improve the reliability of the computer infrastructure within large enterprises. We are now competing with the largest computer software companies and are being written about by industry watchers. We are humbled that some of the largest companies in the USA, Asia and Europe are working with us.

Kahlil Gibran in the Prophet had said, *"When you work you are a flute through whose heart the whispering of the hours turns to music. Which of you would be a reed, dumb and silent, when all else sings together in unison?"*

For me and my colleagues, we want GAVS to be able to create truly sweet music. We are obsessed with creating a culture that promotes innovation and instills a sense of belief in our team members, that we are creating a company with a purpose. A company that is going to continue to create disruptive technologies, a company that will engender digital transformation for our enterprise clients.

GAVS has been sponsoring half-marathons in Chennai to raise funds for prosthetic limbs for the specially-abled. I would never trade the exhilaration that I felt when we presented prosthetic limbs to some of the participants, heard their personal stories, and then ran with them for a short while after the half marathon. We are also sponsoring and maintaining one of the impoverished villages in the interior of India and are supporting the villagers to make them self-sustained through a project named Venu Madhuri.

We believe that we need to move from STEM (Science, Technology, Engineering and Math) to STEAM, incorporating Art into the science and technology curriculum so that we can create multidimensional programmers and technologists. To that end, we have promoted art exhibitions by handicapped artists. As I mature in age, some of these projects are becoming dearer to me, as they provide me with a sense of purpose and are my Success Breakthroughs.

So as a journeyman, I have learned to be intellectually humble, always waiting for those inspirational inflection points. For me, Success Breakthroughs do not come through impulse, we need to nurture it with incurable optimism, sustain it with dedicated resolution and then let it blossom in all its splendor. We also need to cultivate our inner stoic and count our blessings. I have tried to develop a sense of gratitude for everything that we have received and for everyone who has played a role in our lives.

And in the spirit of gratitude, I cannot end without an ode to my adopted and welcoming country, America.

> *America, America may God thy gold refine*
> *Till all success be nobleness*
> *And every gain divined.*
> ~ Sung by Ray Charles

About Sumit Ganguli

Sumit Ganguli is an entrepreneur in residence at Basil Partners, a Private Equity firm focusing on IT services companies. He is the CEO and Member of the Board at GAVS Technologies (www.gavstech.com) and at a few other IT Services companies. At GAVS Technologies he is focused on promoting new technologies in the Digital Transformation space - GAVEL and Zero Incident Framework are based on Predictive Analytics and Artificial Intelligence, and support companies' computer infrastructure.

In the past, Sumit has been a member of the leadership team of a NASDAQ listed company overseeing M&A, Global Sales and Strategic Consulting. He has been the Group CEO of a publicly-listed international software company and has pursued multiple M&A initiatives. He has been a founding employee of a leading IT company in the US and had pursued a joint venture with a Fortune 5 company.

He has a degree in Electrical Engineering and a post graduate degree in Management from IIM Kolkata. He has an Advanced Professional Certificate from Sterns School of Management, NYU. He has served as an Adjunct Professor at Rutgers State University, New Jersey, teaching International Business at the Executive MBA and part-time MBA program. He speaks at various industry forums including TedX and is a Charter Member of TiE, New Jersey and Philadelphia Chapter. He is presently pursuing the OPM Program at Harvard Business School (2016 - 2018).

Sumit is a strong proponent of organizational culture and intellectual humility and believes in the axiom, "Culture eats strategy for breakfast."

To connect with Sumit Ganguli:

- SumitGanguli@gavstech.com
- Tweeter: @SumitGanguli
- LinkedIn: SumitGanguli

CHAPTER 9

WHAT IF EVERYTHING YOU KNEW ABOUT VIDEO... WAS WRONG?

BY GREG ROLLETT

According to FortuneLords.com, the total number of people who use **YouTube** is now 1,300,000,000. That reads 1.3 billion, with a B.

They also state that 300 hours of video are uploaded to YouTube every minute. *Almost five billion videos are watched on YouTube every single day.* In an average month, eight out of ten 18-49-year-olds watch YouTube. And these stats are just for YouTube. They do not include the number of videos being uploaded and watched on Facebook or Instagram, Snapchat or on private video servers and platforms like Vimeo or Wistia.

Small businesses and entrepreneurs are still behind the eight ball and not creating enough content for the platform, especially when they need to compete with bigger, more established brands. Let's say you are a financial advisor. Someone heads onto Google or YouTube and starts searching for retirement advice. They find your YouTube account which has two videos, both filmed by your secretary on your iPhone, with no lighting or outline and talks about your firm and who you are and what products and services you offer. This is what most business owners and professionals have filmed and put online and on their websites.

Then, right next to your two homemade videos are 1,851 professionally filmed and generally helpful videos put on YouTube by Dave Ramsey.

Instead of just telling people who he is and what products he wants to sell you, he has videos that address the needs and problems of his market. He addresses them in a fun, engaging and entertaining way.

His videos are titled: *The Secret to Not Being Broke, How to Get Out of Debt and The Truth About Financial Infidelity.*

Yours is titled: *How to Work with Jim Smith Financial.*

Which expert is more helpful for someone looking for financial advice? Who builds more trust with their audience? Who has more authority and positioning within the market? The answer is obvious. Yet so many business owners and entrepreneurs will complain that video just doesn't work for them. Or, for that matter, any marketing whatsoever.

But this is what you were taught. This is what you were told to do. You were told to just film a video and put it online. You were told to use that great smartphone that's in your pocket to film your videos. You were told that camera was just as good or better than a point-and-shoot camera from the electronics store.

But it's not. And your content is not good enough to break through the noise. So how do you break through and get a piece of the billion plus views happening online every day?

Some of the BIG Questions you need to ask yourself right now are:

WHAT IF EVERYTHING YOU WERE TOLD ABOUT USING ONLINE VIDEO TO GET NEW CLIENTS...WAS WRONG?

Just because someone is telling you about a brand-new trend or that you have to do something, doesn't mean that you should do it. In the case of online video, you not only shouldn't do it, but it needs to be at the top of your list. You already saw that billions (not millions but billions) of videos are being played on YouTube every single day. Add billions more on Facebook and you can really start to see where consumer behavior and attention is going.

This is how we spend our time today. We spend it watching videos on platforms like YouTube and Facebook and we do it every free minute in our schedule, whether that is waiting in line at the supermarket or in between calls at the office.

Your job as a business owner is to effectively generate the attention of people who need your services. The best and most effective way to do that is through video. But not just any kind of video, as you can see with the Dave Ramsey example above.

When putting videos online, you need to directly reach and speak to your market. And you need to do it in a way that makes you and your business appealing to them, otherwise your video will be seen for mere seconds before a viewer clicks onto the next one. You need the right approach to video marketing or else your videos will merely just be the noise that clutters up our Newsfeeds, instead of helping you to get clients and customers.

WHAT IF YOUR SMARTPHONE IS NOT THE BEST CAMERA TO USE TO CREATE CLIENT-GETTING VIDEOS?

We all have cameras in our pockets and in our hands. This one device has changed everything about how we communicate with each other. Whether it's instant access to social networks, taking photos of our food, texting emoji's to our friends, parents and bosses, or actually calling someone, we have an all-powerful communication system in our pockets.

The data also shows that we are spending a lot of time on that mobile device watching video. The analytics firm Flurry, says that the average person spends five hours on their phone every single day. They also stated that 51% of those five hours are spent watching video or consuming media.

Your phone is the greatest content-consumption device ever created. But just because you and your market are watching video on your smartphone doesn't mean you should be creating video content with it.

Case in point: I'm sure you've seen someone filming a video for Facebook Live or just posting a video to social media that was filmed in selfie mode. For those unaware, selfie mode is when you turn the camera to face you and not out towards the world. This causes many issues in video production. First, most of us are not trained cinematographers and have no concept of lighting, backgrounds or environment. This leads to video with bad lighting, bad sound and McDonald's wrappers in the background. All of this is bad when it comes to producing videos to get clients.

And that's just the start. Add in the concept of angles and where you hold the camera and you can end up with a double chin, an exposed forehead or people seeing way too much of what you have going on in your nostrils. This happens because whatever is closest to the camera appears the biggest. If you hold your phone over your head, pointing down, your forehead will appear larger than it is in reality. If you hold it down and facing up, you get the double chin or the exposed nostrils. Add in poor sound, wind and shaky hand syndrome and you will quickly find out that people do not want to tune in to your videos.

So remember, even though you have a video camera in your pockets, you might want to think twice before you try and use it to get clients.

WHAT IF YOU DON'T NEED TO FLY OUT TO HOLLYWOOD TO GET THE WORLD'S BEST VIDEO TEAM?

Now that you know your smartphone is not the best video studio for you to use to film client-getting videos, you might be thinking that you need to book your flight to Hollywood and go all out on a full-scale video production.

Here's the truth: almost all good video guys today can point the camera at you and make you look decent in an online video or TV show. What the average (or even above average) video guys don't know is the marketing side. They don't know how you will use the video, what platform it's going on, how your prospects and market will interact with it, how to get their attention and film the video so that after your prospects watch it, they will take action and want to work with you.

This is the missing link in so many videos. Even if your video looks great and is produced at a high level, it likely will never convert because it's essentially a brochure in video format. This is not what is going to help you grow your business.

The reason we do episodic online TV shows for our clients is that each episode is crafted as a hook to get the attention of your market. Each episode is meant to tug at their emotions, question their beliefs and make them understand that they need help to solve their problem. And you are the solution. Every episode includes a call-to-action and next steps, in addition to genuinely helping your audience to get informed and educated.

You don't need a Hollywood budget to do this. You need someone that thinks like a marketer.

WHAT IF YOU DIDN'T CRAM EVERYTHING YOU DO INTO ONE 10-MINUTE VIDEO?

I love the ads that used to appear in the Yellow Pages when I was studying marketing in school. The ads would have a photo of an attorney and an 800 number and all around him in bright bubble letters were all of the specialty areas for which that firm could potentially help you. He was not only a bail bondsman, but a bankruptcy attorney, a family law attorney and a personal injury specialist.

This is not how you want to come across in your online TV show. If someone can't quickly identify how you can help them, they will not call you to help them. You need to be the definitive expert in your market, not a jack of all trades.

One of the best marketing lessons that has stayed with me for decades now is that:

"A confused mind won't buy."

When you try to cram everything you do into one video, you leave your audience confused. This audience will never convert into a client, no matter how hard you try. We film episodic online TV for our clients, because every week we can hyper-focus on one topic. We can go deep and showcase our subject matter expertise in 3-6 minutes. At the end of the episode, the viewer is explained a problem, taught the solution and shown that you are the expert that can help deliver a solution.

This is the most important thing to remember if you are trying to use online video to get clients. You're not trying to do too much. You are trying to show the world that you are the most uniquely qualified person on the planet to help deliver a specific result to your market. Remember this over time as you go to shoot a video. Ask yourself, "Why am I shooting this video?" That will ensure that you hit your target every time.

WHAT IF YOU DIDN'T HAVE TO GO VIRAL TO GROW YOUR BANK ACCOUNT?

We all want to go viral. I would be straight up lying to you if I told you I didn't want millions of people to see my videos. And we do have videos with hundreds of thousands of views.

However, the majority of my videos are seen by only a few hundred to a few thousand people. Even though these numbers are not gigantic or newsworthy, they have provided me the ability and the good fortune to build an incredible business and fuel my life with my family. We vastly overestimate the number of people we actually need to reach in order to make a great living. This isn't to say that we don't want to reach more people. It's not about quantity, it's about quality. Not everyone in your community needs your help. You need to show your videos and TV shows to the people that are most likely to hire you and buy your services.

The good news is that through platforms like Facebook and YouTube you can advertise your video to the exact people that match your perfect prospect profile. Many times you can pay these companies mere pennies to show your episode to that perfect prospect. This is an incredible way to make an impact without having to pay for the people who cannot or do not have the means to utilize your unique gifts and talents.

No matter what the next guru or expert is peddling to you about video and getting millions of viral views, be proud that your video actually made a difference in the lives of the people who see it, and that your business keeps getting bigger every time you put out a new episode.

HOW MANY VIDEO MARKETING MISTAKES ARE YOU MAKING IN YOUR BUSINESS?

For starters, if you are not filming regular, consistent video content, in the form of an online TV show for Facebook and YouTube, you are making the biggest mistake of all. This is not something to plan for in the future or when you get to it. This is the here and now. I don't want you and your great business to go the way of Blockbuster video and virtually disappear overnight because you didn't adapt and change.

The opportunity is staring at you, but it's up to you to use the ideas posed by my big questions in this chapter. Do it correctly and you will get the short term benefit of new clients and business and the long-term effects of brand building that can only be done by constantly and consistently pushing out new episodes of your online TV show. I cannot wait to see what you do with online video to grow your business.

About Greg

Greg Rollett is an Emmy® Award-Winning Producer, Best-Selling Author and Marketing Expert who works with experts, authors and entrepreneurs all over the world. He utilizes the power of new media, direct response and personality-driven marketing to attract more clients and to create more freedom in the businesses and lives of his clients.

After creating a successful string of his own educational products and businesses, Greg began helping others in the production and marketing of their own products and services.

Greg has written for *Mashable, Fast Company, Inc.com, the Huffington Post, AOL, AMEX's Open Forum* and others, and continues to share his message helping experts and entrepreneurs grow their business through marketing. He has co-authored best-selling books with Jack Canfield, Dan Kennedy, Brian Tracy, Tom Hopkins, James Malinchak, Robert Allen, Ryan Lee and many other leading experts from around the world.

Greg's client list includes Michael Gerber, Brian Tracy, Tom Hopkins, Sally Hogshead, Coca-Cola, Miller Lite and Warner Brothers, along with thousands of entrepreneurs and small-business owners across the world. Greg's work has been featured on FOX News, ABC, NBC, CBS, CNN, *USA Today, Inc. Magazine, Fast Company, The Wall Street Journal, The Daily Buzz* and more.

To contact Greg, please visit:

- http://ambitious.com
- greg@ambitious.com

CHAPTER 10

THE BIRTH OF MY ENTREPRENEURSHIP

BY DIDI WONG

"What do you want to be when you grow up?"

Every child gets asked this question. At the age of seven, my answer was, "I want to be a gymnast." At age twelve, I replied, "I want to be a dancer." When I asked myself at age seventeen, when I was about to end my British boarding school years and take the SATs so I could go to America for college, my answer was, "I want to be a chorus girl on Broadway." Even at the age of twenty-two, after graduating from Boston University with a degree in Communications and French, I was still asking myself that question; and the answer was, "I want to be a pop star!" My dream of performing onstage was the connecting link to all my answers. I never once thought of being a business owner, and the word "entrepreneur" wasn't even in my vocabulary.

But during my twenties in New York City, all the makings of being a great entrepreneur were being developed as I pursued my career as a performer, running from audition to audition, promoting myself as a brand, and networking at parties to create a great support team of friends, agents, casting directors and producers. I was taking lots of singing lessons, dancing and acting classes to better my skills; and waking up every day, motivated to do whatever it took to achieve my goal.

After five years of trying to make it as a triple threat on Broadway, on the small and big screen, and after having met Michael, the love of my life, my maternal instincts kicked in. I found myself at age thirty without having made much money doing what I thought I'd wanted to do, and my motivation for working in the entertainment industry was rapidly fading. I faced the facts: there weren't that many breakthrough roles for Asian women and if I wanted to make the sort of money that I knew I was capable of, I'd better be smart and practical and forget about my name in lights on Broadway.

My husband and I moved to Los Angeles so he could take his acting career to the next level. At first, I was feeling somewhat lost. I spent a good deal of quality time alone. I didn't know anyone in LA and turned inward. I discovered yoga and found that it made me so happy, I practiced it four times a week. I stopped auditioning, having realized that I didn't really like being an actress because I didn't like pretending to be someone else. I was more comfortable and happy being me.

Yoga took me back to Hong Kong, where my family lives, to immerse in a four-day intensive conference. I was doing physical poses up to five hours a day. Just before I fell asleep, after completing the fourth day, my body was exhausted; but my mind was in a euphoric state. I felt a sense of total peace and harmony, as if I was floating on cloud nine and nothing bad could penetrate that elation. The whole conference had an immense impact on me. I woke up after that last day at 4:30 AM and intuited a "calling". It came out of a dream where I saw a white tank top with the pose *downward facing dog* on it. Underneath the pose, "Akdo Muka Savasana", was written in Sanskrit; and I even saw the back of the tank top with the English words "Downward Facing Dog" on it. The vision of this tank top was so clear and vivid, I was riveted. I knew at that moment of awakening that I must give up my desire to be an actress, singer or dancer once and for all, for a much bigger mission.

I immediately called Michael, who was in Los Angeles, and told him of my revelation. He was happy for me. I asked my parents and sisters what they thought of my idea, and all of them fully supported me. I had no background in business, I had no idea how to start a company; and I didn't know anything about finances, marketing or manufacturing; but nothing was going to stop me. In fact, I didn't even think about not knowing this or that, all I thought was, "I am going to do this!" "How hard can it be?" "It's just common sense, right?"

I began my new journey as soon as I landed back in Los Angeles. I went to Barnes and Noble and bought four books on how to start your own business. I researched yoga, because I knew from my dream that I wanted to create a yoga-inspired apparel brand, specifically to educate my customers on yoga poses. I even took the time to get certified as a yoga teacher. I attended every workshop and seminar I could find on how to become a business owner. I learned the different ways I could get a loan. After all I spent on educating myself, I had less than $1,000 in my bank account. I decided to give myself ten months to prepare and come back to the same Asia Yoga Conference to launch my product line. I did everything as if I was accelerating at one hundred mph to give myself an MBA in entrepreneurship.

At this point, I realized that as a complete beginner with no business background, it'd be very hard for me to get a loan from a bank. I had great credit but no income and no assets. It became clear that the only solution was to ask friends and family to borrow. I first went to my father. He was a very sensible and successful businessman in his own right. Wisely, he didn't want to just give me the money and hope for the best. Instead, he asked if I was truly serious about opening up a business; and if so, then I must have a business plan.

A business plan? What is that? I went back to the drawing board. I found out that a business plan is a very detailed notebook, consisting of pages of information about your business, your mission, your product description, your ideas, your team, your timeline, what you project to spend your money on; and how much profit you predict in one year, three years, and five years out? This was the document I had to produce in order to prove to my father that I was serious.

I spent 80+ hours creating my business plan with intense focus and dedication. It included intricate graphs and sensible calculations. My father was satisfied with my plan. *Phew!* He granted me $100,000 to open up *Chakras by didi*. What a lucky girl I was to have such generous parents who believed in me! I used $35,000 of that to buy an economical Prius, which I still have to this day, and began my business with $65,000.

Throughout my first year, I worked diligently to accomplish my goal of launching within the year. I asked lots of questions, I educated myself and I put thoughts into action. I didn't have a design degree nor any skills with illustration or design software, but I knew visually what I wanted with my first collection. The creative process was easy for me, but the legal, accounting and the manufacturing fields were more challenging. I was a one-woman-show, but I was so ambitious that whatever challenges came my way, I simply tackled them one at a time. I'd ask anyone who had proven experience in business, question after question. Nothing was going to get in my way.

Fast-forward one year. I launched *Chakras by didi* at the Asia Yoga Conference and made a profit of $9500 after expenses in three days. Not bad for a complete amateur business owner and a brand-new fashion line with only twelve tank tops to sell! I had an impressive profit margin of 760%. My tank tops were made of quality fabric with trendy designs that made yoga clothes sexy, stylish and comfortable. I had a spectacular marketing campaign with models of all ethnicities and sizes. I landed five wholesale orders in my first three days of business, expanding my line to Thailand, Indonesia, Philippines, Japan and Australia. These buyers continued to support me and became long-term accounts.

In the nine years that *Chakras by didi* was in business, I created designs for women, men, toddlers and infants. My company became an international best-selling yoga apparel with the brand expanding into seventeen countries. Every year I returned to the Asia Yoga Conference, and my customers were overjoyed. Some told me they came just to buy my clothes. The last year there, I wrote orders for $63,000 over just four days.

No success comes without failures. There were many rejections along the way, and there were a couple assistants who turned out to be bad eggs. Wholesale and retail business has its drawbacks with maintaining the right inventory as the number one biggest hassle. But each time I "fell", I got back up again and kept on going.

In 2012, *Chakras by didi* received an invitation to be showcased at the Daytime Emmy Awards. It was the only apparel brand selected for the gifting suite out of thousands of other apparel brands they were considering. My company also participated in the Grammy's gifting suite, plus the ESPY's and the Hollywood Show gifting suites. After attending so many gifting suites, I saw how they worked as a business structure and could gauge how much money the organizer would make, by calculating how much I paid as a vendor, counting how many vendors and attendees there are, the cost of tickets to attend, what kinds of celebrities they bring, and finally by estimating how much they'd pay these celebrities to attend. I saw the whole process and my mind started ticking.

I am such an entrepreneur at heart that I find it exciting to determine the ways in which other people make money. It was clear to me that the organizers were doing very well when they could charge for tickets to the event so fans could meet their idols; and also charge for celebrity pictures, autographs and memorabilia, and make money off of the vendors who're there to gift their products to the celebrities. I was adding it all up and realized this was a viable business to be had!

I then thought back to my extensive experience in special events with the New York City Ballet and Pier 59 Studios, planning huge events for Keanu Reeves, and fashion shows for Tommy Hilfiger and Ralph Lauren. I could start up a gifting suite business and take the idea to a whole new level. I wanted to create high-end gifting suites and feature them at Five Star Hotels, with food and beverages included so people would be coming not just to a gifting suite, but a party. I discussed it with my Director of Social Media and friend, Stephanie Jags. She paired this idea with exchanging the celebrities for social media influencers! *What a brilliant idea!*

At that moment, we co-founded Social Spotlight Events, a special events company that brings brands and influencers together to highlight a cause. Building the Social Spotlight Events business was a fun and adventurous ride but, just like building any business, it didn't come without its challenges. It required massive pitching, a good deal of rejection, and phone call after phone call that didn't lead to anything, and a lot of time spent attending parties and events. We were constantly networking and making new acquaintances that required follow-through and diligence. But through it all, we made some amazing contacts. Social Spotlight Events is now the go-to company for charity fundraisers. We were so honored to partner with Girl Up, a United Nations Foundation, where we had big name celebrities such as Jamie and Corinne Foxx as our hosts. In a short time we'd made a mark in the elite gifting suite and charity fundraising event industry. I am very proud of what we've accomplished, especially in our relationship capital.

While becoming an angel investor and a serial entrepreneur, I was introduced to a man whom I call "My Ultimate Mentor", David Meltzer. He is a Forbes and Entrepreneur's Top Keynote Speaker. David has one of the top five podcasts on iTunes *The Playbook*. He is the Executive Producer, Co-Creator and Chief Judge on *Entrepreneur Elevator Pitch*, the #1 digital business show. He's a two-time best-selling author and co-author with Cynthia Kersey and Jack Canfield in his newest book, *Be Unstoppable*. David invited me to be a judge on *Entrepreneur Elevator Pitch* where we reached twenty million views in the last episode. Thanks to David, I am also filming a feature documentary, *Impact*, chronicling my life as a motivational speaker. Through this experience, I founded my sixth company, The Yes Academy. Finding the right mentor is *crucial* to an entrepreneur's success. In fact, I would say this is the most important part of being an entrepreneur.

THANK YOU DAVE!

The Yes Academy is an educational program for students, teaching them how to conceive your perfect 60-second elevator pitch, how to find self-worth and self-confidence, and all the practical steps you must take to become a successful entrepreneur.

The seven steps to successful entrepreneurship are:

1) Find your ultimate mentor.
2) Work on your self-confidence and self-presentation.
3) Be real and authentic.
4) Be a person of your word.
5) Accept failures as a part of your journey to success.
6) Network effectively.
7) Surround yourself with people who lift you up.

Each one of these are essential to your success. Each one takes time to assimilate and put into practice. Each one I have spent my whole life exercising. As a result, I can honestly say that I have found my whole self. I have tackled my mental, emotional, physical and spiritual self with honesty and integrity. I am living my best life. And I am proud to be a successful entrepreneur.

About Didi

Born in Hong Kong, raised in England, and now residing in Los Angeles, Didi Wong is an international serial entrepreneur and angel investor with expertise in the industries of entrepreneur education, event planning, public speaking, mentoring, interior design and real estate.

Didi is the Founder and CEO of multiple businesses including **The Yes Academy**, "the Entrepreneur School", a results and success-driven educational program for entrepreneurs and mothers, focusing on branding yourself, mastering your 60-second elevator pitch, social media and marketing mindset, and how to get investors and everyday people to say "yes". **Social Spotlight Events** is a special events company focusing on fundraising and gifting suites where Didi leverages her relationship capital for philanthropic endeavors by introducing mega social media influencers and celebrities to top billion-dollar brands like Lexus and Nestle, and charitable organizations in initiating multimillion-dollar deals. Didi and her husband Michael own an interior design company, **J2D2 Designs**, that does full multimillion-dollar renovations with the design focus on their signature transitional style and Feng Shui. They are also seasoned real estate investors.

As an international award-winning speaker, Didi is the recipient of the highest level award of "Women of the Decade for Entrepreneurship and Venture Capital" from the Women Economic Forum with over 75,000 members in over 150 countries. She has also been a speaker at the Global Entrepreneurship Initiative at the United Nations, New York City.

Didi is a judge on the #1 digital record-breaking business show *Entrepreneur Elevator Pitch* where the last episode in Season One had 23 million views. She is also currently filming the feature movie documentary *Impact,* about her life as a public speaker, due to launch in early 2019.

She has been featured as a Master Practitioner of life coaching expert with POPSUGAR, NBC News, FOXNews.com, Yahoo!Style, Telemundo, Bustle, Brit & Co. and more. She is a co-author of the book, *Success Breakthroughs,* with the legendary Jack Canfield.

Her *super powers* lie in the fact that she manages her four children under the age of seven (including a set of identical twins), and all five of her businesses, always with a smile on her face. Didi says, "Raising four kind, respectful and all-rounded humans is truly more challenging than managing a multimillion-dollar company!"

You can connect with Didi at:

- didi@didiwong.com
- INSTAGRAM: @didiwongofficial
- FACEBOOK: @didiwongofficial

CHAPTER 11

DIAMONDS IN THE ROUGH

BY YOLANDA PAYNE

Who you are is truly tested during times of conflict and crisis. Pain doesn't discriminate or have any boundaries. If you've struggled with finding value in rough times, you're not alone. My philosophy is: search deep enough and you can find diamonds in any situation. Yes, even in the mist of hurt, loss and crisis.

I believe you can always find the good in any situation or learn a lesson if you look hard enough. However it's a bit challenging when you're the one experiencing loss or pain. Dealing with hurting people is nothing new. With over twenty plus years of experience as a leader and chaplain experiencing the continual crisis of others was somewhat normal for me. I considered myself somewhat a master at finding what I called diamonds in critical life situations. My diamonds were valuable lessons I learned through supporting those that were experiencing rough times, loss, etc.

Oftentimes, I experienced that the strongest trials or failures produce the strongest people. Little did I know my quest to find my ultimate diamond began on August 26, 2012.

One day after returning from Sunday services, my life changed forever. My husband found my twenty-three-year-old son dead in his apartment. Truth be told this was one of the worst days of my life. What do you do when life breaks? How do you react when reality becomes a nightmare? What do you do when you've helped hundreds process their pain and loss only to awake one day and realize you are on the other end of hurt?

Parental grief in my opinion is a pain that penetrates the soul. The spiritual place where mother and child connect is a miracle in itself. This is the only way I can explain my grief; it felt like a part of my soul disconnected and I was left with a void.

Life after my son's transition felt empty. Yes, I was still helping those hurting and experiencing rough times but no longer looking for diamonds. I lost hope and no one seemed to recognize I was stuck. I would encourage others often, only to come home and cry myself to sleep . Everything I thought I knew appeared to no longer have meaning. My husband busied himself with work and our daughter processed her pain silently. Of course, I continued to support those dealing with life issues on a daily basis while struggling to make sense of my own chaos.

After a long day, I would read the book of Jeremiah – the eighteenth chapter. The passage where he was told to go to the Potter's house to watch how the potter works with the clay. There were days I felt like the clay and my life was the wheel. I felt stuck, yet I knew I had to rise above my pain. I devoted my life to being a supportive voice of hope to hundreds even thousands over the years, yet I found myself struggling to find my support. When you're a leader, people tend to look at your strength as a part of you. However experiencing death and loss as a part of life is different to grasp when you're the one weakened by the blow. I found myself processing grief on multiple levels. I experienced the shift of hearing the voice of two children calling me mom become one. I began to grieve the change. It was exhausting. I continually prayed asking for guidance and healing.

I remember standing to speak and often forgetting passages of scriptures that were definitely a part of my daily life. Without warning, my thoughts would become foggy. I would be driving and forget my destination. Daily I would pray asking God to help heal my broken heart. The heart is a powerful yet fragile vessel. I understand why we are told in scripture to guard it. I've experienced a broken heart before, but not on this level. When the heart is broken, it feels like no one can mend it. I believe a broken heart affects the soul. Well it affected mine. The essence of a person's worth is embedded in his soul.

A couple of years before my son's death I received a diamond ring as a birthday gift from him and his sister. About a year before he died, I misplaced it. I searched everywhere and couldn't find it. I remember being devastated. One day while cleaning, I found the ring behind my bed. I guess I had left it on my night stand and somehow lost it. It was so dusty I almost didn't recognize it. Of course, I became emotional and couldn't bear to look at it, so I placed it in my jewelry box for safe keeping. It wasn't until months later while going through boxes that I realized I journal a lot. I would record my thoughts , dreams, fears, etc.

I didn't realize it had been years since I wrote my true feelings. Often dating and recording the time helped me use it to reflect and monitor my life progress. I found a journal that was timed and dated the morning of the day of my son's death. It was simply titled "DIAMONDS". I was beginning a new journal the morning of his departure. How profound. I had been praying for guidance. Sometimes your breakthrough shows up where you least expect it. Something shifted. Was I still hurting? Yes! Was I still grieving? Yes, but my will to get breakthrough became real. Slowly my perspective changed and I was on the hunt once again for diamonds. This time my quest was to find the DIAMOND in me. Accepting the loss of my son was the most challenging. Transforming my pain to empower my life became my ultimate quest. Exploring ways to re-connect with my purpose was challenging. Clearly I was not the same person after the loss of my son. The way I supported those in crisis changed. I found myself focusing more on the meaning of life. Looking for diamonds in rough places became a quest on my journey to empowerment.

Life took on a different meaning. Of course, I had years of experience helping others with loss. However, it looks and feels different when you experience it first-hand. My perception of the millennium generation shifted after the loss of my son. My perception changed. I begin to look at diamonds differently. I thought about the image a diamond projects. The diamond my children gave me was given as a symbol of love.

I've often heard it is hard for the naked eye to detect a real diamond. Not surprised. It was just as hard to detect one as a metaphor to life lessons. I believe everything that happen to us in life can be used as a teacher. Except a seed falls to the ground, only then can it live was my daily quote as I searched for meaning. During challenging moments, I had to learn how to center and focus on the task at hand. In the midst of my distress, looking for meaning was the last thing I wanted to do – however, it was necessary.

The shadow of emotions after any type of loss in my opinion is dimensional, whether it's the loss of a loved one, career, relationship, job, etc. However, I learned that the shadows of emotions were necessary in order to find my light. In my quest for meaning, I searched the definition of a shadow on Wikipedia.org. Its meaning was: "A shadow is a dark area where light from a source is blocked by an opaque object." There it was, my diamond lurking in the shadows of my pain. That's when I realized that the valley of death or loss of any kind has a potential light attached to it. If there is a shadow, there is definitely a light that's blocking your breakthrough. Often, I had to silence my inner critic when I tried to go on with life after loss. There was days I would almost feel normal and I would feel guilty for going on without my son. These were the times I would have to locate my voice and shout peace into my future.

It didn't feel like I would ever get through the pain. It felt like the shadow would never lift. Finding a new perspective was challenging and transforming; searching for new ways to relate to my pain was empowering. I started to share my story of grief with all who would listen. I spoke of my beautiful boy as often as I could while helping other look for their diamonds in the rough places of life. I don't know when it happened, but one day I realized the shadows were gone. I could see and feel the light of joy once again. Looking back, I now understand the phrase 'diamonds in the rough'.

Searching and finding true meaning in the face of loss and adversity is a valuable life lesson. I believe every person on earth has a purpose to fulfill while living in this world. Living intentionally became a way of life after my son's death. Each of us is given twenty-four hours a day and a teacher to help us in the journey in life. I'm conscious about minding my twenty-four. This teacher I believe is "life" and daily we are given lessons, tests and trials as we journey on life assignments. My faith helped me process my pain. I believe that God set in motion spiritual laws that govern life and time here on earth. Finding my new normal connected me stronger with my life's purpose. I constantly reminded my self during my search that all things would work together for my good according to my purpose.

Grief of any kind in my opinion is very spiritual. My experience left me with a feeling of loneliness yet it caused me to search for something deeper and greater than myself – life forced me to go inward for answers.

There is something spiritual that occurs when the soul is wounded or broken, something shifts dimensionally. I experienced change on all levels – the spiritual, soul and physical plane. Experiencing others searching for meaning, as I wrote earlier, was the norm for a leader. However, my own search for diamonds transformed my life forever.

Based on my experience, I learned what I call my **Diamond Lessons**:

❖ Remember – After my son's transition, I utilized his Facebook page to share stories, photos , anniversaries and memories. This helped me cope with loss in the days, months and years after.

❖ Allow to Release – I learned to allow myself to feel the pain for it was reality. I didn't project being happy if I was sad. This helped me to move my emotions in truth, as I processed my pain.

❖ Focus – I implemented my faith to help me better focus on daily goals. Praying, Meditation and daily scriptures were used as my support.

❖ Journal – I created a Book of Diamonds. Daily, I wrote my feelings, my memories and experiences. At the end of each day, no matter how challenging, I would write a lesson I learned or hoped to learn on my journey.

❖ Be Patient – I learned not to be so hard on myself. It takes time to process loss on any level. Dealing with my loss in seconds, minutes, hours and days helped me to process it one day at a time, in increments. I had to realize my situation was different, and no two people process loss the same.

❖ Live – Give yourself permission daily to breathe, laugh and live. Surround yourself with people who encourage you.

❖ Re-Invent – Search and discover the purpose of your pain. When you find it, use it as fuel to add value and empower others.

❖ Empower – Find someone that's hurting or experiencing loss and help them find their 'diamonds in the rough'. Share your experience to help others succeed to empower.

Understanding and overcoming your life transitions on any level is beyond successful. Finding your diamond in the mist of it is more than breakthrough success, it's life empowering.

About Yolanda

Yolanda Payne is a spiritual entrepreneur, visionary and thought leader. She is also an independent Certified Leadership Speaker, Trainer and Coach with The John Maxwell Team, as well as a published author of the book, *Prophetic Destiny Defined*.

Her career is centered on empowering individuals to reach their maximum potential. She is seasoned with revelatory insight and experience that inspire, motivate and transform destinies. Yolanda is an international autonomous Chaplain, a law enforcement, spiritual care and bereavement Chaplain with over twenty plus years combined experience in transformational leadership. She has acquired a unique ability to connect and empower those experiencing life crises. She holds degrees and certifications in the areas of Divinity and Spiritual Education.

Yolanda is the founder of the "Yo'Payne Empowerment Group", Paradigm Empowerment Coaching and the Remnant 7000 Project. Her goal is to prophetically equip and empower 7000 prophetic coaches and leaders to be a spiritual resource for the millennium generation. Her desire is to be an agent of change and a global voice of hope and empowerment to those in crisis.

You can connect with Yolanda at:

- www.yolandapayne.com
- www.johnmaxwellgroup.com/YolandaPayne
- www. Facebook.com/yopaynecoach/

CHAPTER 12

ALIGN YOUR DREAMS, GOALS, AND VALUES FOR LASTING SUCCESS

BY J.W. DICKS, ESQ.

In the many training sessions I have hosted over the years, I have noticed a great number of people have a difficult time with goal setting. They understand intellectually the value of setting goals, but they can't see how it applies to their own lives.

Maybe this sounds self-evident, but I'll say it anyway: Before you can set a goal, you have to understand what a goal is. Simply put, _a goal is a dream fixed to a certain time_. The dream is something you desire. The time element affixes it to your personal world and your reality. The dream is no longer simply floating in space; now it has a real "time meaning" attached to it, and it must be dealt with.

Second, the goal must relate to a personal value. Goals are the answer to the question, _"What is important to you in life?"_ Values are the answer to why you want to accomplish those goals. If you don't relate your goal to your values, that goal will remain as lost – floating in space – as it was before you attached it to the reality of time.

This is one reason why you can't simply adopt someone else's goals for your life. The chances that you'll share that person's deepest values are incredibly small. Therefore, a goal that makes sense to another person isn't likely to make much sense to you.

111

It is also why it is foolish for parents to push their children onto a particular career path, or – worse – into accomplishing something that they had not been able to achieve for themselves. Why? Because the goal that is being set for the child is based on the *parents'* dream rather than the child's. Yes, you can help someone nurture his or her own dreams, but you can't dream for someone else. The most rewarding thing a parent can do for a child is help that child discover their own dreams and learn how to fulfill them.

SHAPE YOUR DREAMS

In order to reach a goal you set for yourself, you must first learn to *define it specifically.* If you are unsure of your objective, it will be easy for you to become distracted. For example, if you start only with the general desire to "make more money," you may achieve that goal – but chances are you won't *keep* the money. You'll soon discover that there is no end to the amount you can spend if you don't relate it to certain standards. The 2,500 square-foot house will become the 5,000 square-foot house. The "first new car" will evolve into the "first luxury car," which will evolve into the "top of the line new car traded in every two years."

Because you have no specific goal, you will be trapped on the 'up escalator'. You will spend more and more, because you think that the very acquisition of things will make you happy. Yes, you will find yourself in new, more luxurious surroundings – but instead of worrying about how you are going to make your $700 per-month house payment, you'll be worrying about how you will make the $4,000 per-month house payment.

You achieved your vague goal – *more money* – but somehow things got worse. The topic of worry (lack of money) has stayed the same, but now the practical burden you bear has become far heavier. You had a certain number of options to find replacement cash flow for the $700 per-month payment on your smaller home. But now that your payments are $4,000 per-month, the options available to you for producing that much money are far fewer.

To stay off the up escalator – to avoid the "more money" treadmill – you need to decide what you do want, and in very precise terms. You need to *shape your dreams* by attaching them to time frames and specifics. At the same time, <u>you need to make sure that the goals you set are aligned with your values</u>.

Why? Because your values are the focal point of your internal happiness. If you set and achieve a goal that is in conflict with your values, not only will you be unhappy about having obtained that goal, but the result will have a negative influence on your desire to set and achieve *other* goals. Psychologically, you will begin to regard goal setting as an unhappy experience, even though that wasn't the problem in the first place. The *real* problem was that you didn't align the goals with your values.

I have some very good friends who worked for years to build a large company out of an idea they came up with together. They longed for the day when they could buy a huge house on the water in a very exclusive area of our town. Because of their diligence and hard work, the company prospered, and they achieved their goal of purchasing their dream home. Unfortunately, the achievement of that goal didn't make them happy. Why not? Because that purchase separated them from their friends and their church, both of which – as it turned out – were things that they valued far more than that new house on the water.

And just to make things worse, they began to feel guilty about their newfound wealth. They worried that people might think they were showing off – even though that had never been their intent – and that people might become less friendly toward them. And in fact, their friends did begin to associate with them less frequently – in part because of their own feelings of jealousy and insecurity, and in part because their old friends now seemed different in their fancy new house. They seemed guarded and defensive rather than open and friendly.

While this couple came to understand the causes of what had happened, it didn't make them feel any better. The mistake they made was not in buying a big house on the water. (There's nothing inherently wrong with that goal.) The mistake they made was that they had defined and achieved a goal that didn't match their values. How do you keep your goals and valued aligned?

I have summarized the process in a series of seven steps:
1. Create a list of goals and values.
2. Prioritize your goals.

3. Establish a plan to achieve your goals.
4. Take action on your goals.
5. Create success habits.
6. Rebalance your key objectives.
7. Enjoy, actualize, and repeat the process.

GOAL-SETTING STRATEGY NO. 1:
CREATE A LIST OF GOALS AND VALUES

Values are what you believe about yourself. Goals, on the other hand, are targets that should capture those values and – once achieved – reinforce those values. In the case of my friends who became isolated, their goal was a hollow one, because it took them away from their fundamental values of friends and church. The goal was clearly at odds with their values. Without an alignment between values and goals, there will be no satisfaction. In fact, the only possible outcome is dissatisfaction.

Discovering your own values is one of the most important things you can do. And yet, very few people have ever even considered their values. Here is a short helpful exercise. Sit down in a quiet room and write down five personal values that you consider important. Don't think too hard about it – just start writing what comes into your mind. They will come to you. If you put down more than five, that's fine (you won't be graded).

If you need help getting started, that's OK, too. Just glance at this list of values shared by many people. Remember that while lists of values may overlap (in other words, you may use the same words as someone else), the order of the words and the weight you place upon them make the lists very different.

A close relationship with your mate
A good relationship with your family
A meaning of life
A relationship with God
Being highly regarded
Control of your destiny
Fame
Friendships
Giving to others
Good health

Happiness
Influence
Living to old age
Peace of mind
Possessions
Power
Purpose to work
Respect
Retirement
Security
Sense of accomplishment
Travel
Wealth

YOUR VALUE LIST:

1._____

2._____

3._____

4._____

5._____

Now that you have made your list, rank your values from more important to less important (even though every value on this list is important).

Look at the result. Did you get it right? Are you happy with this summary of your values? If so, congratulations, because coming up with this list may be the most important thing you will ever do. Why? *Because it is truly your road map to happiness.*

Here's why. Let's assume that your number one value is a close relationship with God, and your number two value is a close relationship with your family. And let's also assume that at the present time, you are pursuing a career that pays well and earns you lots of kudos and recognition but requires you to spend a great deal of time away from your family.

Well, if that job doesn't somehow help you to develop a closer relationship with God, you are likely to be one miserable human being – and chances are, you won't even know why. Most likely, you are working hard, banking a lot of money, and feeling mostly empty inside. Your values are your essence. If you hope to achieve a happy life, you have to live a life and aspire to a future that captures and expresses those values.

Assume for a moment that a certain individual (let's call her Jane) has the following values:

1. A close relationship with God
2. A close relationship with family
3. Peace of mind
4. Security
5. Good health

Conspicuously absent from Jane's list is anything about "making lots of money." True, you could make the case that goals 3 through 5 presuppose financial security. But the point is, "making money" didn't make Jane's list.

Can you see the importance of this discovery? If Jane spends all of her time trying to become a millionaire, she is almost certain to be a very unhappy millionaire (if, indeed, she ever gets there). For Jane to be successful in her own eyes, her goals must be aligned with her values. To sharpen the point, let's consider the following question: Which of the following goals, if achieved, would make Jane happier?

1. Making $1 million
2. Setting up a faith-based charitable foundation with an endowment of $1 million

See the difference? Putting $1 million in the bank would probably make Jane feel OK, up to a point. But wouldn't endowing a faith-based charitable foundation do a lot more to make Jane feel satisfied with her life?

Let's take this illustration a step further. What if you changed the second goal to read: "Setting up a faith-based charitable foundation with an endowment of $1 million, in which all of my family members would work together." Wow! Do you see what that would mean to Jane? The better she understands her values, the more likely it is that she can set the right goals, give herself a life's mission, and live her life with passion.

So, here's our next exercise, which builds directly on the last one, as well as on Jane's example. Take a few minutes to review the values you've written down and ranked. Now write down five goals that, if achieved, would capture and reinforce those values.

LIST GOALS

1._____
2._____
3._____
4._____
5._____

GOAL-SETTING STRATEGY NO. 2:
PRIORITIZE YOUR GOALS

Now that you have established a list of goals, rank them. Renumber them as you did your values list, lining them up in their order of importance to you. And although we don't want to complicate the assignment too much, we encourage you to think about making two such lists: one ranked in order of importance, and the second ranked in order of urgency. Which goal is of the greatest enduring importance to you, and which do you want (or need) to accomplish first?

For example, if one of your goals is to build a $2 million retirement nest egg and another is to put your kids through college five years from now, it doesn't make a great deal of sense to concentrate on your retirement plan when you have a much more urgent need – unless, of course, the retirement plan is of far greater importance to you. If the goals are of equal importance, then urgency takes over, and your priority quickly becomes the tuition bills.

GOAL-SETTING STRATEGY NO. 3:
ESTABLISH A PLAN TO ACHIEVE YOUR GOALS

You have your goal. It is your top priority. Now, what are you going to do about it?

When my children were younger we went on trips by car, I would call the American Automobile Association – "Triple A" – and ask them to do a trip plan. In a couple of weeks, AAA would send back a nice, bound series of maps that told us the best way to get to our destinations. (Now, of course, you can do it all online.) If there was construction along the way, AAA would either suggest detours or carefully mark the construction area and advise us that there was a bumpy road ahead.

Wouldn't it be nice if life were like that? You could set your goal, call up AAA, and get a plan laid out for you. Unfortunately, life isn't quite that easy. But with the help of the simple concepts you can learn how to do the plan yourself. The key to reaching any financial goal is to have a plan. Surprisingly, it's not so important that you pick the perfect road or the perfect investment system. Instead, the important thing is to pick a specific plan and stick with it until you reach your destination.

How do you create a plan to achieve your goals? The same way that you create a plan for a trip. You write down the moves that you need to make, step by step, to get to your destination. Just as you follow a map from AAA to get to a geographic destination, you follow a specific plan to get to a goal destination.

GOAL-SETTING STRATEGY NO. 4:
TAKE ACTION ON YOUR GOALS

My father always said, "A turtle never gets anywhere unless he sticks his neck out." He was right. Ultimately, we have to take action. Otherwise, all our values, goals, and plans aren't worth the paper we put them on.

But taking action proves difficult for a lot of people, because they are filled with anxieties and insecurities. Did I put down the right goal? Is my plan a good one? These doubts paralyze the worrier, just like a deer caught in headlights.

Nevertheless, you must take action on the plan you create. Think of it as something like scaling a cliff. If you had to climb a cliff for the first time, how would you do it? You'd start out slow and easy. You'd pace yourself, going up foot by vertical foot. You don't have to break any speed record or take any unnecessary risks. Well, it's the same with acting on a goal plan. You don't have to reach your goal overnight. Success is an endurance event – a marathon rather than a sprint. Take off slowly, build to a comfortable pace, and stride to the finish.

How do you get started? It's easy. Take a look at your goals list. Pick the one goal on your list that seems the easiest to accomplish and also has near-term importance. Let's say that you wrote down, "Make $10,000 more this year." That's a good goal. It's near-term, and it's specific. So let's use it to take action. Below your goal, create a plan to achieve the goal by listing the specific action steps you'll take to get there:

Goal:- Make $10,000 more this year
Plan:- Increase salary by $3,000

Action Step 1: *Ask for a raise.*
  • Create a list of reasons I deserve a raise.
  • Make an appointment with my boss.
Action Step 2: *Start a small business.*
  • Research businesses of interest.
  • Pick a business in 60 days.
  • Start the business in 90 days.

If you are like a lot of people who have never properly learned the techniques of goal setting, this method is likely to come as a pleasant surprise. For the first time, not only do you *see* your goal, but you see specific action steps that you can take to achieve it.

While the goal may seem difficult, the action steps to achieve the goal are often much easier. You will discover that taking each step puts you closer and closer to your goal, which in turn makes the goal appear easier and more attainable the closer you get to it.

GOAL-SETTING STRATEGY NO. 5:
CREATE SUCCESS HABITS

Sometimes, with the best of intentions, parents do their children a disservice. One example of such a disservice is continuously linking the words habit and bad. For example:

  • Quit biting your nails. It's a bad habit.
  • Stop smoking. It's a bad habit.
  • Don't drink so much. It's a bad habit.

Have you ever heard anyone praised for developing a good habit? Not often, and yet, good habits are critically important. The tennis star's consistent stroke, which leads to victories on the court, is the result of a good habit. The student who studies consistently and makes top grades has developed good study habits. In fact, any repetitive pattern that brings success deserves to be recognized and applauded, and should be built into one's system of goals: I will continue this action until it becomes a habit.

Vital habits can be developed to help you maintain your success. For example, in investing, diversifying your portfolio, setting limits on losses, resisting the temptation to get greedy – all are proven goal rules that build both protection and consistency into your goal plan. If you take the time and effort to transform these goals into habits, you will profit substantially from the improved performance of your portfolio and the added protection they give you.

GOAL-SETTING STRATEGY NO 6:
REBALANCE YOUR KEY OBJECTIVES

I hope that, by now, you have been impressed on the importance of values and goals when it comes to your success. You should also understand that while some values may be consistent throughout your life, others may change. When they do, both your goals and your plans to reach those goals need to re-evaluated and rebalanced, in order to get your new value/goal structure into alignment. If you don't rebalance, it will be like deciding to stay on the road to New York after you've decided to go to San Francisco instead. Yes, you're still moving along a path, but you're sure to arrive at the wrong place.

To help you spot these changes as they occur in your life, I suggest that you set a particular time each year to rebalance your objectives. I have found the two weeks after Christmas to be a perfect time for this activity. Business always slows down during that time of year, and the decrease in activity gives you an opportunity to reflect.

Note the consistency in this approach. By consistently rebalancing your objectives at the same time each year, you have made this activity into a habit. While that time might not be good for you, pick one that is, rebalance your objectives, and (if necessary) refocus your life.

GOAL-SETTING STRATEGY NO. 7:
ENJOY, ACTUALIZE, AND REPEAT THE PROCESS

If you incorporate the six strategies, or steps, just outlined into your life, you will find a new sense of gratification and enjoyment. Now that your life is in alignment with who you are, you should begin to feel that you are headed in the right direction – much like the driver with the AAA road maps. Take the time to enjoy this newfound sense of satisfaction.

At the same time, be prepared for that sense of satisfaction to ebb and even disappear. Just as the wheels on your car lose their alignment over time (and far more quickly if you hit a curb), our lives also get "out of alignment" because of life's curbs. It is just a part of human nature: We get caught up in all sorts of things that we never intended to get caught up in.

What's important, though, is simply to understand that we must:

(1) enjoy things when they go well
(2) understand that misalignment will happen
(3) get realigned when we hit that curb (or when life's twists and turns gradually lead to misalignment)

By repeating this process, you will enjoy your life more and continually refocus yourself on the things that are truly important to you. Once you are properly focused, it is easier to let go of those miscues that don't fit into your grand plan.

About JW

JW Dicks, Esq., is a *Wall Street Journal* Best-Selling Author®, Emmy Award-Winning Producer, publisher, board member, and co-founder of organizations such as The National Academy of Best-Selling Authors® and The National Association of Experts, Writers and Speakers®.

JW is the CEO of DNAgency and is a strategic business development consultant to both domestic and international clients. He has been quoted on business and financial topics in national media such as *USA Today, The Wall Street Journal, Newsweek, Forbes, CNBC.com*, and *Fortune Magazine Small Business.*

Considered a thought leader and curator of information, JW has more than forty-three published business and legal books to his credit and has coauthored with legends like Jack Canfield, Brian Tracy, Tom Hopkins, Dr. Nido Qubein, Dr. Ivan Misner, Dan Kennedy, and Mari Smith. He is the Editor and Publisher of *ThoughtLeader®* Magazine.

JW is called the "Expert to the Experts" and has appeared on business television shows airing on ABC, NBC, CBS, and FOX affiliates around the country and co-produces and syndicates a line of franchised business television shows such as *Success Today, Wall Street Today, Hollywood Live*, and *Profiles of Success.* He has received an Emmy® Award as Executive Producer of the film, *Mi Casa Hogar.*

JW and his wife of forty-seven years, Linda, have two daughters, four granddaughters, and two Yorkies. He is a sixth-generation Floridian and splits his time between his home in Orlando and his beach house on Florida's west coast.

CHAPTER 13

HARD GETS EASIER

BY LaNae MAUGHAN

The voice on the phone was strained...

"Dan... Dan has been in an accident."

Those words changed my life forever. Dan, the love of my life, had been run over while fixing our car on the side of a snowy canyon road. The winter conditions were slick and an oncoming car slid on the ice, across the oncoming lane of traffic, off the road, and into the exact spot where Dan was at. It was a freak accident that was not planned by anyone. It was as if the universe conspired against us that day, and the life I once knew would never be the same.

There would be many challenges to face. First, there was the ambulance ride where the medics almost lost him. Then, I could only watch as he was rushed by me into the emergency room, arching his back, fighting for every breath. That scene would be seared into my memory like a brand on cattle. It was hot, painful. A mark that would never really go away.

Receiving the prognosis was hard. Dan might die. He had sustained a brain-stem injury and had lost control of all his involuntary bodily functions. The ability to maintain his body temperature and breathe on his own were damaged. But his heart kept beating as he fought for his life.

Answering the searching question of my five-year-old was hard. "Is

Daddy going to die?" Maybe. It was a possibility that we had to consider. No lies could cover the truth of that moment. We had to face it.

During this time, I clung to the faith of my youth to survive the tsunami of change that was hitting me. Although the sea was rough and the waves were beating against me, I was able to hold on tight through the storm that tested me. And my anchor of faith held strong.

It was not blind faith, though in a way, I allowed it to blind me to the "reality" of the events around me. I couldn't let the terrible things I was seeing and hearing wash me off course. Instead, I relied on my inner guidance in those first few weeks, trusting not what my senses told me, but what I felt deep in my core.

When Dan first started to come out of the coma, he was completely paralyzed. We watched as his sweat glands started to work again, and he eventually began to move the fingers on his left hand. Day by day small improvements came until he could breathe on his own, and then stand up and walk with assistance.

These improvements were miracles from Heaven for which we are forever grateful, and with them came the hope of a full recovery. I knew that if I could just hang on a few more months, he would be back to normal. Life could go on as before and my short stint in carrying this heavy load would be over. And so, I kept moving forward, hopeful for a new day that would be different from the hell I was living. But the new day never came.

Some days the burden just felt overwhelming, and one day I started to unravel. As the feelings of anger and frustration continued to build, I knew I had to get out of the house, or I would have a melt-down in front of the children and Dan. I bolted out the door and headed around the side of the house where I could be alone.

"Why??? Why isn't he better by now?"…the words burst out of me.

I was pacing back and forth with my arms flailing up and down as I walked. "How long do we have to wait? Haven't I done everything I could to help him get better? You promised!" I was angry, and not just at the fact that progress was slow, I was angry at God. I felt betrayed. I had been faithful. I had done my part. Now why wasn't Dan better?

The tears streamed down my face as I continued to wail at the Heavens over the condition we were in. It wasn't fair. None of it was fair, and it wasn't easy either. Eventually, all the pent-up emotion was released like a whistling kettle running out of steam, and I settled down. As I stood there pondering what to do next, I had an impression. It seemed as though God spoke to my heart, "I've done My part. Now it's your turn."

It wasn't really the answer I was looking for, but I could feel the truth in it. I had been praying that God would change our lives, but we needed to change our own lives. The power to improve was in us, and we had been shown there was a way forward; where Dan was once paralyzed, he could walk, and even if it was slow and labored, he did have movement in all his limbs again. We had been given a path, but we needed to take it.

I knew that one step at a time, one day at a time, we could do it. I started to have hope again. Even if the journey ahead was going to be long and hard, there was a chance to overcome our challenges and succeed. We just had to keep moving forward.

Accepting the changes to our path in life was freeing to me. It allowed me to focus on building a new life, rather than clinging to the past. I would have to be able to take care of our family. Now it was up to Dan to teach me what I needed to know about our computer business in order to assume the role of provider. I became the hands that fixed the computers, and the voice on the phone to call for technical support. One computer at a time, I slowly started to gain a proficiency that would carry us forward.

Perseverance paid off. After a time, I was able to get a job at a major technology firm, which allowed me to provide for my family. Our life, which had at one time been a fight for survival, normalized, and those things which were once hard became the new way of living.

Dan and I worked together and raised our four children, including one angel from Heaven sent after the accident. Our family found ways to get around the roadblocks of Dan's disability and enjoy activities together. We learned how to piggy back, fireman carry or arm-chair carry Dan to our desired destination. The main goal was to have fun, and we were not about to let a little lack of ability get in our way.

We focused on the things we could do, rather than what we couldn't. For example, traveling to see the world was easier for us than hiking a back-mountain trail, and so our focus turned there. We have been to the ruins of Mexico and to the Eiger in Switzerland. As Ralph Waldo Emerson once said, "That which we persist in doing becomes easier to do, not that the nature of the thing has changed but that our power to do has increased." For our family, the things we persisted in did become easier because we became stronger in the journey.

I look back on those early days and wonder how I survived. Where did I find the reservoir of strength to move forward? Three key principles helped me face the hard things and strengthened me in the journey:

1. <u>The power to change is within us.</u>

We all face challenges. The key to making them easier is in being open to change. Wishing that our situation will change is not going to make it easier. More often than not, the change that needs to happen is within us.

There were many times that I wished for a different outcome than what I had. If only Dan could walk. Or better yet, if only Dan could talk. Dan's inability to communicate was the worst of the challenges we faced. As much as I wanted a different outcome, the cold reality was that the situation was not going to change. It was me that needed to adapt.

I learned to stop whatever I was doing and focus all of my mental attention on what Dan was trying to say in order to understand him. I turned off the music, quieted the background noise, and honed in on understanding Dan. It was mentally exhausting, but I found as I kept working at it, I became better and better at deciphering his words.

I still interpret much of what he wants to say so that others can understand. Even though he's gone through speech training and vocal exercises, his lips are still paralzed. The hard part never went away, so we became better at dealing with it.

2. <u>Take the next step.</u>

In order for hard to be easier, you need to be willing to move. It doesn't get easier when you stay in the same place. Even if you don't know what the outcome will be, you need to move forward.

Not all paralysis is in the form of a physical disability. Dan's challenges were easy to see, but I needed to ask myself, "How am I paralyzed?" and "What is stopping me from moving forward?"

The thirty-two years since Dan's accident have proven to me that life gets better—as long as we keep moving forward. During times of darkness and despair, I often felt like there was no hope. There were times when I just didn't know what to do. But when I moved forward, even if I didn't know the outcome, answers came. So, even if the way forward is not clear, take the next step. Once you have taken that step, take one more. Life has taught me that the way does get easier as we find the courage to move forward.

3. **Failure IS an option, get up and try again.**

Success seldom comes in the first attempt. We need to be willing to try again when we fail. And we need to allow ourselves to fail in order to succeed.

Dan teaches me this principle every day. Every time he falls, he gets back up. The first time he tried to ride a bicycle after the accident, he tipped over and broke the ball joint in his hip. But he was not deterred. He kept searching for a solution that would work for him. It didn't come overnight – in fact, he had to keep trying for several years before his research brought him to find a recumbent bike which was more compatible with his abilities. Even then, the first few attempts at riding were failures. He ended up in a ditch after losing control of the steering. But Dan went back to the bike shop and after several rounds of modifications, they found a solution that worked for him.

Because he refused to accept failure, he's been able to change his life for the better with the bicycle. If he wants to go to the store, he's no longer dependent on me to take him. He rides his bike wherever he wants to go, including to his children's activities and events. He once rode over twenty miles to watch his daughter play a lacrosse game. He now rides for others, and just recently completed a one-hundred-mile ride to raise money for cancer research.

I'm grateful to Dan for teaching me that true success comes in getting up just one more time than we fall.

Change yourself. Find the courage to take the next step. Get up after you fall. These tools can help you make hard challenges become easier.

Keep on keeping on – and never give up!

About LaNae

LaNae Maughan started her career working alongside her husband, Dan, in their computer retail business. After Dan was critically injured in an auto-pedestrian accident in 1986, he mentored LaNae until she was proficient enough to provide for the family. Since that time, she was able to gain employment in the technology sector and has held various job titles such as Systems Engineer, Global Technical Architect, Project Manager, IT Datacenter / Site Manager, Oracle / Web Application Manager and Business Process Manager. Because of her 'can-do' attitude, she was often given challenging assignments and expected to deliver with minimal supervision.

Her accomplishments include building a network operations center for a major technology firm, delivering the server infrastructure for a major trade show (over 75,000 attendees), and managing teams to deliver global scale, strategic initiatives for the company.

Professional Bio:

- MBA, Marriott School of Management
- PMP, Project Management Professional
- Certified Canfield Trainer in The Success Principles

Life Accomplishments:
LaNae is the mother of four amazing children who have been by her side to not only survive the challenges they faced, but grew to THRIVE in the journey of life. As a family, they have traveled far and wide – from the Alps in Switzerland to the ruins in Mexico, each time finding creative ways to ensure that Dan was able to enjoy the journey with them. Together, they have canoed rivers, kayaked in oceans and climbed the Great Wall of China. They live by the motto that life can be good, even when it's hard.

LaNae is the author of the upcoming memoir about their life journey together. She was also a contributing author in the book, *The Road Ahead*, by Jane Seymour.

You can connect with LaNae at:

- lanae.maughan@gmail.com
- www.hardgetseasier.com
- www.facebook.com/DanLaNaeMaughan

CHAPTER 14

FROM VICTIM TO HERO/HEROINE
HOW TO STOP SELF-SABOTAGING & LOVE YOURSELF UNCONDITIONALLY

BY BARBARA STEINGAS

It's easy to become victim to the circumstances in our lives and feel a sense of helplessness. This is because when we're born, albeit being cute and adorable, we're dependent on everyone for everything. We forget that we are empowered spiritual beings having a human experience and instead come to believe we are limited beings that are flawed. I feel we need this to happen, like the universe's ultimate 'hide and seek' game, so we can discover our innate powers to fulfill our mission and purpose, if we allow ourselves to see beyond the limitations. This usually takes a significant challenge that puts us in an ultimate crossroads of our lives. Just like all the typical hero and heroine stories we've read or movies we've seen. That's why the *Star Wars* movie franchise is one of the most popular in history. Instead of believing this journey is only for the elite few, we need to realize we're all on our own hero and heroine journey. Only then can we stop being the victim character who is self-sabotaging our own goals and successes.

I too was the victim of my story, especially when I was diagnosed with Crohn's Disease at age twenty-two after graduating college. Instead of going out to conquer the world of Physical Therapy and help the patients I was going to be treating, I ended up being a patient in the medical realm of where I was working. The gastroenterologist who diagnosed my condition gave me the grim reality that Crohn's was an incurable autoimmune disease of my digestive tract. Feeling helpless and never having been really ill before, I felt I had no choice but to trust the doctor's knowledge until I hit a "no turning back" crossroads decision. It came several years into the treatment of my symptoms where instead of getting better, I was becoming more ill.

There was a new medication method being tried to help people in my situation: an immunosuppressant drug called 6-MP for short. Basically, it was a chemotherapy drug that would shut off my overactive and out of balance immune system. The doctor was obligated to tell me the dangers of the medication, including how I could catch a cold that could potentially turn into a deadly case of pneumonia, as I would have no defense mechanism to fight it off.

It was then I had an epiphany of thought: I was already on a death spiral weighing only ninety pounds, so I didn't need any extra help in that direction. If my immune system was overactive, why wasn't the goal to balance it out rather than shut it off? It occurred to me that it wasn't any one thing that got me ill. It was a multitude of pieces in a puzzle that came together making this picture of illness, so the same had to be true of regaining my health. I thought how all I had to do was find the right pieces to regain my picture of health. Then it seemed doable.

To succeed I had to find the physical, mental, emotional and spiritual pieces to put me back together again—just like the nursery rhyme character *Humpty Dumpty*. Initially, I found the physical pieces by going to see Dr. Robert Atkins, of the famous *Atkins Diet*. He had a Complementary Medicine Center in NYC. The food strategies he taught me and the techniques he used to eliminate food allergies worked. However, as I started feeling better, I self-sabotaged myself by eating and ingesting the things that fed the yeast/candida in my body that were causing the inflammation in my digestive tract. Finally, after being on that up and down roller coaster so many times, I realized how I was self-sabotaging myself and needed to dig into my mind, emotions and spirit to find out why.

It's the disease in those areas that govern our thoughts, how we feel, and what we believe respectively that is often the cause of our lack of success in any area of our lives. Consciously, we desperately want to achieve our goals, just like I wanted to be healthy again, but our subconscious programs, if not erased and reprogrammed, will continue to keep us in our familiar comfort zone, even if that zone isn't consciously comfortable.

I wanted nothing more than to feel healthy again, so I prayed to God that I didn't want to be sick and in pain anymore. However, I was focused on illness and pain, so I wasn't allowing for a change to occur. This is one of my first success breakthrough strategies: focus on your result and what you want, not on want you don't want. When I began praying to God by giving thanks for my health, then my pieces of health began to come together. Initially, this was difficult because I was experiencing so much pain and ill health. It took time to reap the reward of my new found thoughts and hopes of believing I could heal from this terrible disease.

When we start out a new technique, it's akin to a dirt road that can be easily washed away – compared to the super highway of the underlying subconscious program that has been running automatically for many years. It takes time, patience and practice to create a new super highway. In this quick-fix-and-want-it-now culture we live in today, it's even more difficult. Therefore, we need help to stay committed to focusing on what we want, which seems like a small, distant, slightly-open window in the distance, compared to the big closed door of what we don't want in front of our face.

This leads to the second thing I learned to keep me on track: It has to be a deep down 'must' for you to change and succeed, not just something that would be nice. Even though I thought it was a 'must' to get better, there were things holding me back until I came to the last downward turn on the roller coaster. It was when I weighed eighty-five pounds and was close to death. The pain of where I was, and the fears I had of possibly not surviving, finally outweighed the self-sabotage I was doing. Hopefully, you reach your 'must' before it becomes that drastic, but sometimes we must come to our rock bottom moment before we're ready to fully commit to our goal or dream. This is because it's always scary to move beyond what we know to what we don't know.

We wonder about things like: "What if I fail?" or even "What if I succeed?" What I discovered on my journey is that I was hiding behind the disease as a way not to have to be perfect or be the bad cop by saying "no" to people. These subconscious auto pilot programs were overriding my conscious need to be healthy and out of pain. When I unearthed these patterns, I was able to empower myself to get beyond them and realize it was balance, the very thing I thought of in the beginning of my journey, and not perfection I sought. This allowed me to finally stop beating up the little Barbara in me.

This leads to my third strategy: Think of the hurt and scared little kid inside of yourself and how you want to treat her just like you would other little children. This helped me to stop beating myself up for not being perfect, and to realize that if I deviate off my path to wellness that I can just get myself back on course again, and no longer punish myself for making mistakes. I started seeing things in a gray light, not just in the rigid black and white. Also, this helped me to love myself more unconditionally, just like a parent should.

The fourth strategy I learned along the way was: To ask myself empowering questions rather than victimizing questions. Instead of asking myself, "Why can't I be well?" I began asking, "How can I regain my health and wellness?" Ask yourself how you can succeed rather than why you keep failing. This is an extended version of the number one strategy of focusing on what you want to achieve. As I peeled off the self-sabotaging layers, I realized how I wasn't feeling deserving of being healthy. It was like I was saying to myself, "Who am I to have everything in life I want?" I felt there has to be flaws so I can fit in with everyone and not stand out. Unfortunately, we tend to put ourselves down. Have you ever done that?

Also, being sick was a subconscious way for me to get attention. When we don't get our needs met in a healthy way, we usually end up getting them met in unhealthy and dysfunctional ways. This is because we get taught while growing up by adults who didn't get a manual on how to raise healthy, happy and joyful beings, and they have their own dysfunctions that get passed down to us. We interpret them to mean different things; some empower and serve us, but many disempower us and don't serve us. We believe that there is nothing we can do about it until we come to the realization, usually by a challenge that forces us to, that we can change these habitual thoughts and programs. Then we have a much better chance to achieve the goals and successes in life that we want.

My fifth empowering strategy is: Say affirmations daily, not only once, but several times a day of what it is we want to achieve. "I am" affirmations are the most powerful because they are associated with our identity and what we believe, feel and think about ourselves. Therefore, be very careful with what you say after, "I am…." Listen to your self-talk and begin to identify the disempowering and negative "I am's" you say about yourself. I have a tendency to say "You're so stupid" when I get frustrated. Now I catch myself and change it to "You are a smarty pants." Humor always helps to lighten up and not be so serious with ourselves. Anytime you catch yourself beating yourself up, change it to an empowering one. Write them down so you remember to tell yourself repeatedly during the day. Despite being off medications for over fifteen years now, every morning I still continue to tell myself, "I am healthy!"

To summarize the five strategies I discussed:

1. Stay focused on what you want and on your goal(s) – write them down and look at them frequently – stop yourself when you start to dwell instead on where you are and what you don't want.
2. Make sure the change or goal you seek is a 'must' – no turning back or staying where you are because it has become too painful and outweighs your fears.
3. When you start beating yourself up or self-sabotaging, remember the hurt and scared little kid in you to help you stop. Treat yourself with the same unconditional love and care you would your own or other children.
4. Ask yourself empowering questions that help you move towards your goal and success. To receive positive and helpful answers, you must ask positive and helpful-type questions.
5. Write down and repeat positive "I am" type affirmations that reflect you already achieving your goals and dreams of success.

These strategies aren't the only ones that can help you transform your life, but they are a good foundation. We are all meant to shine our full radiant light and achieve our full potential – no matter what we're taught to believe as we were growing up or even as adults. We all have special gifts and talents that need to be uncovered just like the character Rudolph of the children's story *Rudolph the Red Nosed Reindeer*. May you learn to appreciate your special gifts, achieve many successes, and have radiant health, happiness and joy in your life!

About Barbara

Barbara Steingas is a native of New Jersey. She recently commemorated her 30th year of working at Overlook Medical Center as a Physical Therapist. Barbara graduated Summa Cum Laude with her Bachelor of Science Degree in Physical Therapy from University of Maryland Eastern Shore Campus before attending Columbia Teacher's College in NYC for her Master of Arts degree in Motor Learning.

While attending Columbia, Barbara was diagnosed with an autoimmune illness of the intestinal tract called Crohn's Disease. The traditional medical field deems Crohn's incurable. Barbara followed traditional protocol for several years. When her doctors finally prescribed an immunosuppressant medication, she made the decision to take an alternative path. She started to look at her health as if it were a puzzle that needed solving, and all she simply needed was to find the right pieces.

Barbara set out on a long and winding road until she finally completed her health puzzle. She is happy to be off all medication for more than 15 years, enjoying radiant health today. In addition to having to overcome an "incurable" illness, Barbara has also had to deal with a great deal of personal loss, including her late husband who crossed over in 2008 from a sudden heart attack. It was his unconditional love that helped her glue together the pieces of her health puzzle. She was fortunate enough to find love again several years later with another wonderful man. After three years together and on the verge of becoming engaged, the second love of her life passed away suddenly from diabetic ketoacidosis (fatally high blood sugar level).

Wanting to help others find their own radiant life and put the pieces of their own puzzles together quicker and more easily, Barbara has written several self-help and inspirational books. These include *The Healing Puzzle*, which won Honorable mention in the self-help/inspirational category of a global contest, *Solving the Crohn's & Colitis Puzzle*, which is an Amazon best-seller, and G*ermans Are Funny, Too*. Her newest book *Solving The Grief & Loss Puzzle* is published by Balboa Press.

Barbara is a popular motivational and inspirational speaker. She is also a Radiant Life Coach, Certified Convention Speaker and is listed on the Las Vegas Convention Speakers Bureau.

She chose the word "radiant" because it represents health, happiness and joy. It encompasses her passion of helping others who are dealing with loss, health issues, and other challenges to optimize their physical health, mental and emotional happiness, and spiritual joy.

Barbara not only uses all that she's learned through her own life challenges and her experiences in her coaching practice, she also complements it with healing modalities. She is a Reiki II Certified Healer and is trained in a Crystal Chakra Energy Balancing technique. Barbara incorporates her knowledge and skills from her many years of Physical Therapy experience, as well as specializing in eliminating pain from soft tissue issues.

You can connect with Barbara at:

- Barbara@barbarasteingas.com
- www.barbarasteingas.com
- 908-391-4463

CHAPTER 15

WHEN ONE DOOR CLOSES...

BY SHERRY McCOOL

I bet you've heard the phrase...when one door closes another one opens... countless times. When I first heard those words, I thought they were a promise I'd see another door open right in front of me with something better and more wonderful than what I had before.

But, my experience has been when a door closed it usually was not fun. Naturally, I wanted prompt deliverance from my pain and if it didn't happen in a timely manner, I became frustrated, depressed, resentful and angry.

I often added to my discomfort by making the assumption it was my fault the door closed - I must have done something really bad and totally unacceptable to have caused the door to close. Therefore, it was my responsibility to make it reopen.

At other times, a door closed in my life because something I knew I could not change happened – someone died or an event occurred that I understood was beyond my control. Intellectually, I knew the door was closed and I couldn't reopen it, but knowledge of those facts didn't necessarily make me ready, willing or able to want another door to open. Even though the door was closed it gave me comfort to look at it, solace to lean against it and reassurance to grip the door handle because I wasn't ready to let go and move on.

Both Alexander Graham Bell and Helen Keller are credited with the wise observation, *"When one door closes another door opens; but we so often look so long and so regretfully upon the closed door, that we do not see the ones which open for us."*

Decades ago, I was going through a sad, overwhelming, fearful chapter in my life when a friend called and asked how I was doing.

I recounted in great detail the events of my current situation and how I had bought a *"when one door closes another one opens"* refrigerator magnet because people were constantly saying that to me. According to my refrigerator, I was waiting.

My friend chuckled, "Have you let go of the door handle of the door that closed?"

I grimaced, "I'm thinking about it…but…honestly, I don't really want to let go – this door is all I have left of the way it used to be."

Calmly, my friend asked her favorite questions which she learned from Hale Dwoskin at a Sedona Method[1] retreat:

"Could you let it go? Yes or No?"

"Would you let it go? Yes or No?"

"When?"

I gave each question serious consideration. I was desperate for some relief - I took a deep breath, I gathered my courage and answered each question without my usual excuses and rationalizations.

Could I stand up and let go of the door handle? YES!

Would I stand up and let go of the door handle? YES!

When would I stand up and let go of the door handle? NOW!!

---

1. *The Sedona Method* by Hale Dwoskin (www.sedona.com)

Answering YES! YES! NOW! immediately gave me hope. That hope was quickly replaced by my awareness I couldn't see any doors...I was surrounded by darkness.

Upon hearing my "poor me" sigh, my friend shared, "If it's dark, turn the light on."

I rolled my eyes. "What makes you think there is a light?"

A patient response. "I've been there. I promise, there is a light – find the light switch and turn on the light."

My friend seemed so confident. "OK...what have I got to lose?"

Another chuckle from my friend, "Good point, call me back when you find it."

I don't remember how many times I sat back down feeling alone, sad, and frustrated because I could not find the light switch. But, eventually as promised, I found it and when I flipped the switch...there was light. In that moment I knew where I was, and I felt relieved.

I called my friend, "You were right - I FOUND IT!!!

My friend laughingly inquired, "Have you figured out where you are?"

My appreciation was evident, "Yes, thank you! When I turned it on I realized I'm in a hall and there are doors of all sorts, different sizes and colors randomly spaced on both sides of the hall far beyond where I can even see. But the doors are closed."

My friend, "That's right! You are in the hall and that is where you wait for another door to open. I promise waiting doesn't mean life stops, it's just part of life. I have also learned it is best to avoid getting invested in being angry, fearful, frustrated, resentful or generally negative...none of those make waiting easier. Do your best to be grateful, look for ways to be of service to others, be a willing learner and an eager student of life as you wait to see what adventures come

141

your way."
The words on a refrigerator magnet and guidance from friends gave me a new design for living as I waited in the hall for the next door to open.

And, it did!

Doors opened and closed, and my life moved on.

For 34 years, my life included a career with Marriott International. Eventually the time came for me to close that door. I gave the decision to retire thoughtful consideration. Because I planned for that door to close I fully expected the transition to the next door to be effortless and without much delay. My intention was to do business and human resource consulting, write for children and spend time with my husband.

When the retirement festivities ended, I settled into living life without the necessity of multi-tasking my way through the day. I had time to do fun things, help my husband build a patio and learn how to drive our John Deere tractor.

My husband, an antiques dealer, was just home from a two-week trip to Maine for summer shows. It was a lovely day to do something outside, so I volunteered to work in the garden with him. We discussed plans to look at a condo in Florida and considered making an offer on a small cottage he had seen in Maine.

Our discussion about real estate was diverted because he was replanting a bush that required him to get some "good" dirt from the back yard. While I pulled weeds and thought about the cottage in Maine...a door unexpectedly closed.

- How could he die just getting dirt from the back yard, he was trim and fit and only 54 years old?

- How could he die, we were going to buy a cottage in Maine?

- How could he die without saying good-bye?

- But, he did. On the way back to the front garden with the good dirt he had a massive heart attack and he died while I performed CPR.

- That door slammed closed with no warning. One minute it was open and the next I was in the hall.

Thankfully, friends and family reached out to me; they helped me, encouraged me, included me and were 100% there for me. They gave me the usual advice, "You need to get a dog and don't make any major changes or decisions for the first year." That, I came to realize was just another way of saying...avoid being self-centered while you patiently wait for another door to open.

On a Sunday evening about nine months after my husband died, I attended an event at Unity Church. Jack Canfield was the speaker; he was there to talk about his book, *The Success Principles – How to Get from Where You Are to Where You Want to Be*[2].

That event would profoundly change my life even though I didn't realize it at the time. What I knew immediately was I liked Jack's positive energy and how he shared his talents, skills and abilities with others. I valued his message about:

• taking 100% responsibility for my life
• knowing it was my response to an event that determined the outcome

---

2. *The Success Principles* by Jack Canfield (www.jackcanfield.com)

(E+R=O)
- deciding what I wanted and taking action
- making the choice to continue to continue to continue

I bought his book and more important, I read it...while I continued to wait for another door to open.

Watching TV one Sunday night, I saw a public service announcement for the Peace Corps. It immediately got my full attention as I could not recall seeing a Peace Corps announcement since the 1960s. It brought back an old memory of when I was a freshman in college and wanted to join the Peace Corps but was told to finish my degree. By the time graduation rolled around I was more concerned about my husband's lottery draft number for Vietnam than joining the Peace Corps.

For over 30 years, that dream had been tucked away when a public service announcement I just happened to see gave my Peace Corps memory life. And, encouraged by Jack Canfield's words, "take 100% responsibility for your life," I decided this was an incredible opportunity for me to pursue making that old dream my reality.

I gathered information about the Peace Corps, did informational interviews and decided to submit my application. I excitedly shared my intention to join the Peace Corps with family and friends...everyone did their best to be supportive.

The next eighteen months was a rigorous process of medical reviews, gathering decades old information and completing numerous medical exams - multiple times.

My volunteer assignment would require two years plus six months of training, a mortgage payment for a home filled with antiques on two plus acres in Maryland did not seem financially prudent. It was time to take action and do whatever was necessary to let go and get ready to move on. Sounds simple, but it was not easy!

There were days when I sat on the bottom step of the stairs leading up to the bedrooms wondering if I had the physical and emotional energy to climb them one more time. But, climb them I did, motivated to do whatever had to be done to make my Peace Corps dream reality.

When I told my Mother and Grandmother I was moving to a foreign country to help people build a sustainable business...they asked I make one promise. Without hesitation, I promised I would not accept an assignment to a country where there was war or insurgence in the near vicinity.

Eventually, the house and everything except the dearest personal possessions were sold. My assignment had not been finalized so friends gave me temporary housing in an apartment above their barn.

And, there I waited some more. My Peace Corps placement counselor finally offered me an assignment but after thoughtful consideration I turned it down. I felt it would cause hardship for my Mom and Grandmother to know I was assigned that near to countries with active genocide.

Turning down that assignment prompted my counselor to suggest I take thirty days to reconsider my commitment to the Peace Corps. It seemed to him, I was being overly influenced by my family.

Initially, his suggestion angered me because I felt I'd done everything asked of me to meet all of the Peace Corps requirements and had fully prepared myself to be out of the country for at least two years. But, I got past my ego driven anger and I didn't push back.

I waited, unsure about what I should do to move things forward.

One morning, a few weeks later just as I opened my eyes, I heard the words, "WHY ARE YOU GOING TO A FOREIGN COUNTRY TO TAKE CARE OF STRANGERS? THERE ARE PEOPLE HERE WHO NEED YOU."

Startled by the calm firm voice, I replied, "WHAT?"

The voice simply responded, "YOU HEARD ME."

The message to walk away from my dream was not what I expected. However, I meditated, prayed and thought about it for three days before mentioning it to anyone.

Then, I shared it with a friend who let me know she would be greatly relieved if I moved to Texas to be with my Grandmother and Mom. She, like others, had wanted to be supportive of my Peace Corps dream but really thought being with my family was the better plan.

The old dream re-awakened by a public service announcement had been my motivation to take action far beyond what I would have thought possible. But, listening to my placement counselor and the still quiet voice is what gave me a breakthrough opportunity. I decided to choose a different door and withdrew my Peace Corps application.

As I drove to Texas, I remembered my dear departed husband always had thought Texas was a foreign country.

I am forever grateful I did not miss the chance to share my Grandmother and Mother's last days and to know when each of their doors closed there was nothing left unsaid between us.

Experience has taught me, **what happens while I'm waiting in the hall is life**, and it's my responsibility to make "waiting" an awesome fun adventure.

PS: Experience has also taught me there might be a time when I just need to break through a wall and build a door for myself…but, that's a story for another time. ☺

About Sherry

Sherry McCool brings vibrant energy to any situation and enjoys working with clients to achieve greater success and breakthrough results. She offers a variety of business, human resource and leadership development programs including: talent assessment, assessment training and executive coaching.

As a management consultant, Sherry provides customized team development, transformational training and large-scale organizational change events enabling individuals and groups to more effectively use their talents, skills and abilities to deliver improved results with a shared vison and cohesive effort.

McCool held numerous leadership positions during her 34 years with Marriott International including multiple General Manager/Market GM assignments. She also served as Regional Director Human Resources, Vice President Human Resource Development and Vice President Human Resources North America Lodging Operations.

Sherry created McCool Consulting, LLC in 2004. She continued to support the talent assessment and development process with Marriott International and Marriott Vacation Club. She also consulted with Financial Industry Regulator Authority (FINRA) on talent assessment, development and succession planning.

McCool is a Certified Canfield Success Principles Trainer with a bachelor's degree in Education, a master's degree in Human Resource Development and a wide array of human resource and talent assessment certifications.

Her book, *Lessons Learned Waiting In the Hall*, is expected out early 2019.

CHAPTER 16

LEAN INTO PASSION AND CHANGE EVERYTHING

BY BREESE STEVENS

"So, you're here to save the world. What do you say to that?"

There I was in the conference room, seated opposite the owner of the company and his number two guy, attempting to come up with intelligent-sounding answers to their fiery questions. I felt like Neo in The Matrix when his colleague asked him the question above.

Six months prior, I had come on board as a computer programmer because the company was struggling to keep up with its rapid growth. Little did I know that things got lost in translation after the interview. The questions I was being asked in the conference room were way beyond my expertise, and my elementary answers must have sounded like someone attempting to speak French by pronouncing English words with a French accent. Because this is what happened next: the two men looked me straight in the eye and laughed me out of the room!

I felt bewildered, humiliated and small. It was obvious that they thought I was there to be the saviour of their IT department. And I thought I was there to be a member of their IT team. I felt crushed, bruised and stepped on. "Has the work I've done so far meant nothing to them?" I felt like an idiot; worse, I felt like a fraud. "So that explains the 45 percent increase in salary from my previous job!"

Doubt crept in. "Am I good at programming or just imagining it?" "Is programming even what I am meant to do in life?" I felt confused and unsure about myself - and about life. The programmer in me reached for the keyboard in an effort to find answers. I actually Googled "What is the meaning of life?" Many spiritual links popped up in the search results but seeing the words 'life coaching' somehow triggered me.

Suddenly, my mind took me all the way back to my preparatory work for university. I was ticking the required computer classes off my list when it happened: I fell in love. Brain, Mind and Behaviour was my introduction to Psychology, and I was hooked. I even switched my major on the spot.

But doubt crept in as I compared the two majors. "What kind of money does a Psychology career offer?" "What will my family think if I tell them I am no longer studying Computer Science?" In a hurry, I switched back to Computer Science.

Staring at the Google search results, I clicked on 'life coaching'. The more I found out about it, the more I realized that I still loved learning about the mind-behaviour link. My old love had resurfaced. That's the thing about love, isn't it? You can bury it all you want, but it doesn't die. The conference room incident had awakened a regret about not having pursued Psychology as a major.

I decided to immerse myself in a yearlong coaching training program, and before I knew it, I tumbled into the world of entrepreneurship. My inner turmoil seemed to intensify, which is not what I had signed up for. I felt as if my mind was being taken over by aliens. Weird book titles, like *Think and Grow Rich*, were flung at me. Concepts that made no sense to me like 'choose your response'. Annoying questions like "What is your reason 'Why'?" made me clench my fists. And frightening ideas that encouraged profit and making money.

When my head eventually stopped spinning, the 'alien' stuff slowly began to sink in. I could appreciate the purpose of setting goals. I had been put in situations that made me step outside of my comfort zone. I learned that change requires work. Self-belief and confidence emerged from somewhere deep within my soul. My creative juices started flowing. And I began to give myself permission to change old beliefs. "Was I becoming one of those aliens?"

However, self-imposed financial pressure eventually made me abandon entrepreneurship and run back to the familiarity of the programming world. I looked the corporate part in my charcoal grey suit dress and long-sleeve pinstripe shirt - with silver cufflinks. Then I heard a voice: "Is this it? Is this all there is to me?" With my fingers frozen and hovering above the keyboard, I wondered if anyone else had heard that voice. It spoke again: "What am I doing here?"

By month eight of this strained relationship with programming, I had gathered enough evidence of living a life I didn't love. The whole world was telling me that I had an impressive career with equally impressive pay, and they were right. I had worked hard to earn my computer science degrees and build up my programming skills. I was doing a type of programming that few people know how to do, and my skills were in high demand.

But freedom is priceless. I wanted to feel comfortable in my own skin and add value to the world in a passionate way. So, I took off my cuff links and stepped into the 'big unknown', crushing the protests of the voice of doubt in my head. This gave me the courage, confidence and clarity to lean into my love of the mind, and I discovered my passion for writing. I went from living a lie to working alongside my desires, skills and talents in a field I love.

Based on what I learned, here are seven ways to be comfortable in your own skin, live from a place of passion and get results.

1. Invest in your self-development.

Investing in yourself is the biggest investment you can make in life. That's because when you invest in yourself, you are investing in something that cannot be taken away from you. Even if you lost all your external investments, you can apply yourself to begin again or start something new.

You also don't know what you don't know. Just think of useful things you know now that you didn't know five years ago. Things that have helped you improve your life in some way. Imagine where your life could be five years from now if you gained new knowledge. Your mind is wired for learning, and it is your responsibility to keep developing it.

Go as small or as big as you want with self-development but create the habit of doing it daily. Read good books; follow personal development mentors; attend workshops, seminars or webinars; take courses. These resources exist for your benefit.

2. Learn to forgive.

Not forgiving is like walking around with a big weight hanging from your neck. Not only is it heavy and uncomfortable, it is also an inefficient way to get around. And you will not reach new heights in life this way.

Forgiveness means that you are willing to think differently about the other person. They may still need to be held accountable for the consequences of their actions, but you are declaring that what they did to you no longer has power over you.

Equally important is the other half of the equation: atonement. This is where you look at you. If you believe you played even a small part in the situation, be willing to admit it to yourself and seek to make peace with your heart.

3. Accept others the way they are.

It's easy to love others when they behave the way we want them to behave or the way we think they should behave. Wanting to control others feels as natural as breathing to many of us, so there is work involved here.

Come up with something to say to yourself when you feel yourself go into control mode. "Hands off wheel" is what I use, because it reminds me to get my hands off the wheel of someone else's life.

Allow yourself and others to make mistakes. Build in a buffer to catch small mistakes and to leave them there. The shop attendant charging you one dollar extra; your spouse putting the hand-wash-only dish in the dishwasher; you buying the wrong paint colour.

Contrary to what your mind tells you, it is not a requirement in life to have others agree with you on everything, and vice versa.

Recognize that others may have an opinion that is different from yours and learn to live with that.

4. Recognize the importance and value of hard work.

Results come from consistently doing the work. So, if you are not seeing results, are you doing the work? Just because you want something doesn't mean that it will magically appear.

Beware the lure of distraction. You know the one: you start something, do the bare minimum, conclude it doesn't work and switch to something new. Or tricking yourself into believing that you have all the time in the world, so you will do it later. Here is how to kill distraction: decision. Author Napoleon Hill has said that, "indecision is the number one cause of all failure." You must learn to make decisions and stick with them if you are going to go after results.

5. Lean in: go from resistance to flow.

If you had a choice, which would you choose: for life to feel like you are pushing a boulder up the hill, or feeling like a bird with its wings spread out, gliding along, carried by the drift of the wind?

Learn to accept what is. Recognize what you have control over and what you do not have control over. No matter how hard you resist what has already happened, it will not change. The only power you have is to change how you see the situation.

Practice being in the room. Everything you need to help you with what you are doing is located somewhere close by. The right book, person or opportunity are constantly around you. But unless you pay attention, you will not spot them.

Activate your internal guidance system. It has the answers to your deeper questions, and it is connected to your truth.

6. Give yourself permission to change your beliefs.

Why do you believe what you believe? Almost everything you

believe was given to you by someone else. When you are a child, you blindly accept beliefs given to you. But as an adult, you are responsible for the things in your head.

Learn to form your own opinions and to think for yourself. As you go through life, chances are that not all beliefs you adopted as a child hold true for you now. This is not difficult to spot. But worrying about what others may say if you choose to change a belief is what makes it feel difficult.

Once again, it comes down to what you say to yourself. Choose something that you can say to yourself in order to move forward. "I can live with that" is what I use.

7. Connect with your highest purpose.

No matter how much you try to avoid it, at some point you will come to realize that spirituality is the heart and soul of why your life matters. And if you want to live an amazing life, you must bother with it.

Spirituality is not religion. While religion may lean on spirituality, being a spiritual person means recognizing that there is more to you than meets the eye. You believe that there is a higher force at work in you than just your physical being.

Your perception of life extends beyond the physical world, and you choose to recognize a spiritual dimension to your existence. A visible world and an invisible one. One you see with your physical eyes, and the other you see with your mind's eye. Your aim becomes to be in the world but not of the world; to be fully engaged in life but have your thoughts operate on a higher level.

Basic confidence is one of many things that comes from knowing the spiritual part of you. But perhaps the biggest benefits come from receiving a sense of who you are and why you are here.

About Breese

Breese Stevens helps her clients understand how to create lasting change in life. She creates content that becomes a source of reference for her clients. Her material inspires people and connects them to their truth. Breese provides her clients with practical tips, tools and techniques that they can apply directly to their own lives. Her philosophy is that people already have the knowledge within; they just need to reconnect to it. People want to know how to go from standing still to seeing results; how to create momentum. Breese draws from her ongoing self-development and shares her knowledge and wisdom with her clients.

As a previous computer programmer, Breese helped her clients by building systems for them to make their tasks more efficient and their results more effective. She helped them improve their performance and get better results. As a writer, Breese is able to help people globally with moving toward personal freedom. She helps her clients gain clarity about what it is they want, make decisions, and understand that they must take responsibility for creating change. As a result, they feel more comfortable in their own skin and become inspired by their own lives. They live from a place of passion which impacts everything they do.

From her own experience with creating content, Breese has discovered her passion for writing stories and books. Her stories inspire, educate and entertain, thereby walking her readers through their own journey of rediscovering truths long buried within their hearts. Her goal is to inspire her readers to step into courage and listen to their hearts. Breese uses a unique technique when writing stories, drawing on her skills of writing computer programs. This technique guarantees the authenticity of the stories and the effectiveness of storytelling that has her readers play out the stories in their own minds.

Breese is a graduate of the University of California at Davis, where she earned a Bachelor's degree in Computer Science. Breese also holds a Master's degree in Computer Science from the University of California at San Diego. She is the author of the book *Mind Myths: 50 False Beliefs You Don't Know You're Obeying As Truth.* Breese's personal development journey began in 2011 when she hit an unexpected snag at work one day that made her question everything about her life. She has read many books, attended numerous workshops and seminars, and put herself through several intensive training programs. She is studying under the guidance of Jack Canfield to become a Success Trainer.

Breese was born and raised in South America and emigrated to the United States as a teenager. She lived in the United Kingdom for the past decade and relocated to Paris,

France, last summer. She is learning to speak French - and not simply pronouncing English words with a French accent.

You can connect with Breese at:

- Breese@HeroesDoor.com
- www.facebook.com/BreeseSandraStevens
- linkedin.com/in/BreeseStevens
- www.instagram.com/Breese.Stevens

You can also enjoy reading Breese's blog at:

- www.BreeseSandraStevens.com

CHAPTER 17

LEADERSHIP INSPIRES SERVICE AND REAPS SUCCESS

BY NICK NANTON

Over many years of working with successful people, I have observed one thing they all have in common. They are certainly intelligent, have a good work ethic, and yes, they may even have gotten a little bit lucky! But more noticeable than anything else, people who experience Successful Breakthroughs have one fundamental thing in common: the ability to lead. Time and time again, it simply comes down to this one simple truth: great leaders eventually experience success breakthroughs. While it can take time, a great leader will lead his or her team until they breakthrough to success. They serve others around them and do what needs to be done. I had an incredible opportunity a few years ago to learn the importance of leadership, and this learning experience came from an unexpected place.

There I was, walking with my squad. My feet ached from the 10-mile extreme terrain hike we were on, and my back was throbbing from the 30 lb. pack I carried. On my body was just about everything you would need to survive in the wilderness, and slung over my chest was my AR-15 rifle. I was the point man, and it was my job to keep a lookout for any potential threats or targets for my team. The success of our mission was of utmost importance, and it had been drilled into me that it was my job to make sure our team succeeded. Also, despite the fact that I was in physical pain, in a fairly stressful situation, I had no idea what was waiting for me around each corner; if I'm honest, I was having the time of my life.

No, I've never been in the military, and up until this time, I had never lead a squad or rifle team into combat or trekked through enemy territory (that changed about 6 months after this, but you'll have to read about that later!). My experience comes from one of the most intense leadership training experiences that you've probably never heard of just short of actual military training. It's called "Downrange" and it is one of the most innovative and interesting leadership and team building experiences I've ever been part of. *Downrange* brings teams of people to the Water Valley Ranch in Wyoming for a 3-day experience where they take part in various military training exercises. The idea is to put people in military situations and allow their natural leadership abilities to come to the surface. The experience consists of training in firearms, military maneuvers, combat tactics, and team strategies. It all culminates on day three with a night hostage rescue mission that you and your team carry out. Imagine taking your team from your normal office job and having to carry out complex military operations as a unit. Trust me when I say it brings you together, fast! But even more important than the military training, *Downrange* taught me what leadership is really all about.

One of the most common things I hear discussed in the business world today is the topic of leadership. Everyone wants to be a leader. We see high profile CEO's like Steve Jobs and Mark Zuckerberg lead their companies to untold success, and there's something in all of us that thinks: "I wonder if I could do something like that someday?" But therein lies the quintessential problem with most people's picture of leadership: it's always in the future.

We're often more concerned with the leader we're becoming than the opportunities to lead we have *right now*. We're like the guy who dreams of running a marathon someday but won't get off the couch and go for a walk. We always view our opportunity to exercise our leadership abilities as something that will come to us in the future. And we keep thinking about our future chance at being a leader so much that we miss the fact that we have an incredible opportunity to be a leader right now.

The truth is, every single one of us is a leader. All of us are in some position of leadership. You could be the CEO of a company or managing a team; you could be a professional practice owner or an entrepreneur; or you could be a father or mother or an active member in your community.

Either way, all of these positions come with a certain expectation of leadership.

I think the reason we get caught up thinking about the big, future chances at leadership is because our definition of leadership is flawed. We think of leadership mainly in cliché ways. We think of things like taking charge, making decisions, casting compelling visions, etc. And, for certain, leadership definitely does involve those things. But those are not the heart of leadership. If we want to get to the core of leadership, I think we need a new definition, and I want to tell you about the single greatest definition for leadership that I've ever heard. It was told to me by a friend of mine and one of the best leaders I know, during one of the most interesting experiences I've ever been a part of. His name is Keni Thomas.

I met Keni a few years ago through our mutual friend, Brent Maher. I was in Nashville to do some songwriting and I was introduced to Brent. Brent told me that I needed to meet an up-and-coming musician that he had recently signed. (Brent has produced and engineered six Grammy-winning albums, he discovered the Judds, and produced all ten of their albums and wrote many of their hit songs…so when Brent tells me I need to meet someone, I listen!) As if his recommendation wasn't enough, Brent's description of Keni made me do a double-take. It went something like this: "Keni is a talented singer/songwriter, excellent guitarist, and he's good looking…oh, and also he was one of the US Army Rangers involved in the Battle for Mogadishu, otherwise known as *Black Hawk Down*." So, suffice it to say, I had to meet this guy!

Meeting Keni completely lived up to the hype, too. Here was an energetic, fun, unassuming and compelling guy who had all the makings of a great country music star, but also was a decorated war veteran with combat experience in one of the most influential military encounters in the last 25 years. We instantly bonded over our shared love of music, Nashville, and the Florida Gators. I also knew that Keni could be really helpful to me in motivating and inspiring my clients with his story. At the time, I was putting together my big annual conference for Best-Selling authors and I needed speakers. The good news: Keni was known, not just for his musical talent, but he had also traveled the world speaking and sharing his story from his military experience and some of the leadership lessons he learned during his service. So, one day I called Keni up to ask if he'd be willing to come and speak at our upcoming event. Keni told me that he would love to come and speak, and that he would even do it for free. Now, I've been around this world enough to know that there's no such thing as "I'll do it for free."

So, I responded, "Great! What's the catch?"

Keni laughed, "Well, there's no catch, but I *do* want you to come up to Wyoming with me for my new *Downrange* experience and film it."

"Alright, I like adventure," I said, "so I'm in."

I agreed to come up and film the experience. So, I asked two of the guys I work with a lot, Carlo and Shawn, to come with me. My crew and I flew out to Colorado and met Keni at the airport. He showed up in a cheap rental van to take us the five and a half hours to the ranch in Wyoming. During the drive, let's just say I was a little unnerved. I'm not sure if you've ever been to the middle of nowhere, but there are lots of bends, hills, mountains and snow. And this guy drove like a complete madman...or an Army Ranger on a mission...you decide! We were driving around bends in the mountains way faster than I thought this old van could handle. But at the same time, I felt this strange sense of trust in Keni's capabilities. I knew what he had been through, and I knew that he had the experience and training to handle much worse than some drive through the mountains. And so, over the course of the drive, I found myself beginning to relax because I felt confident in his abilities. Oh, and I asked him like a hundred times, "are you sure this van can take this speed, in the snow, around the curves, with all the people in the back?" At some point during the drive, I got to hear more of Keni's story.

Keni was a college graduate when he signed up for the US Army Rangers. In 1993, he found himself stationed in Mogadishu, Somalia for a peacekeeping mission codenamed "Operation Hope". On the afternoon of October 3rd, on a day when he was actually scheduled to have off, he was brought along on what would wind up being one of the most influential military engagements in the last 25 years. The next day-and-a-half of combat would forever be known as "Black Hawk Down". Early on in the fighting, Keni's squad leader was wounded by enemy fire, and

Keni found himself in the position of having to take charge of a squad. So here he was, at 22 years old, in the middle of a firefight, heavily outnumbered, and suddenly placed in charge of three other soldiers. Keni knew that he was trained for just this situation, and he vowed to do everything he could to make sure the three men in his squad made it home from this conflict. And they did, all of them.

During our drive, as Keni was telling me about his story, I kept thinking, "Man, this sure is different from my path to get here!" To put this in perspective, at about the same time that he was in the middle of the Battle of Mogadishu, I was a 13-year-old running around my neighborhood chasing girls and trying my best not to get into too much trouble. But towards the end of the drive, Keni mentioned his definition of leadership, and it has stuck with me ever since: "Leadership is the example you set for the people you serve."

That was his definition of leadership: it is an example you set for the people in your life that you are responsible for serving. It is incredibly simple and at the same time incredibly profound, just like the country music that Keni loves so much. And when I heard this definition, that is when I realized that the experience that Keni had in Somalia was a universal experience that everyone goes through. Not that we've all been in combat, but that we've all been in places that were unknown to us and have had to lean on the people we're with. One of the things that Keni will always talk about is that when the bullets start flying, the only thing that matters is the people to your left and to your right. It's the people that are with you that you are meant to serve and lead.

I learned from Keni that leadership is not something you are preparing to experience someday in the future. You shouldn't be looking ahead wondering when you're going to get your chance to lead. Leadership is simply the example you set *today* for the people you serve *today*. For one, leadership is about serving those around you. It is not about using power to get people to do what you want. It's about coming behind people and helping them be the best they can be, so that you all (as a team) achieve the goals you hope to achieve. And secondly, leadership, at its core, is about setting an example. Leadership is not telling people what to do, it's about doing what needs to be done.

In this way, every one of us can take leadership, no matter where we are in life. We have to lead ourselves. We have to do the small things that must be done, and in so doing we will set an example that people will follow. We also need to see ourselves primarily as servants. Leaders exist to help those under their care to succeed. And if we all succeed, then the mission succeeds.

Of course, we ended up getting to the Water Valley Ranch safe and sound, thanks to Keni's driving. We filmed the *Downrange* experience and ended up producing a documentary short called "Downrange." That weekend was a profound experience for me, but not only because of the experiences at the ranch. What Keni told me on the drive up there has stuck with me ever since. I learned that leadership is not something that I am working towards in the future, but simply a choice I make every day whether or not I will set a good example for the people in my life that I'm called to serve. Whether it be my wife, my kids, my team, or my clients, my job is to serve others and set a good example. And that is something that every single one of us has in common. And, if we do that, if we set an example for the ones we serve, if we actually lead people, then eventually we will experience a success breakthrough. So, take that with you, avoid the bullets, and lead on.

About Nick

An Emmy Award-Winning Director and Producer, Nick Nanton, Esq., produces media and branded content for top thought leaders and media personalities around the world. Recognized as a leading expert on branding and storytelling, Nick has authored more than two dozen Best-Selling books (including the Wall Street Journal Best-Seller, *StorySelling*™) and produced and directed more than 50 documentaries, earning 5 Emmy wins and 18 nominations. Nick speaks to audiences internationally on the topics of branding, entertainment, media, business and storytelling at major universities and events.

As the CEO of DNA Media, Nick oversees a portfolio of companies including: The Dicks + Nanton Agency (an international agency with more than 3000 clients in 36 countries), Dicks + Nanton Productions, Ambitious.com and DNA Films. Nick is an award-winning director, producer and songwriter who has worked on everything from large scale events to television shows with the likes of Steve Forbes, Ivanka Trump, Sir Richard Branson, Rudy Ruettiger (inspiration for the Hollywood Blockbuster, *Rudy*), Brian Tracy, Jack Canfield (*The Secret*, creator of the *Chicken Soup for the Soul* Series), Michael E. Gerber, Tom Hopkins, Dan Kennedy and many more.

Nick has been seen in *USA Today, The Wall Street Journal, Newsweek, BusinessWeek, Inc. Magazine, The New York Times, Entrepreneur® Magazine, Forbes, FastCompany,* and has appeared on ABC, NBC, CBS, and FOX television affiliates across the country as well as on CNN,FOX News, CNBC, and MSNBC from coast to coast.

Nick is a member of the Florida Bar, a member of The National Academy of Television Arts & Sciences (Home to the EMMYs), Co-founder of The National Academy of Best-Selling Authors®, and serves on the Innovation Board of the XPRIZE Foundation, a non-profit organization dedicated to bringing about "radical breakthroughs for the benefit of humanity" through incentivized competition, best known for its Ansari XPRIZE which incentivized the first private space flight and was the catalyst for Richard Branson's Virgin Galactic.

Nick also enjoys serving as an Elder at Orangewood Church, working with Young Life, Downtown Credo Orlando, Entrepreneurs International and rooting for the Florida Gators with his wife Kristina and their three children, Brock, Bowen and Addison.

Learn more at:
- www.NickNanton.com
- www.CelebrityBrandingAgency.com

CHAPTER 18

YOUR RETIREMENT INCOME SHOULDN'T FALL WHEN THE MARKET DOES

BY STEVE JURICH, AIF®,
IQ WEALTH MANAGEMENT

When the market fails, retirees shouldn't be left to worry about whether their portfolios can continue to support them.

Most investors try to accumulate as much money as possible to alleviate the worry of running out of it one day. And why not? The more assets you have, the less you should worry, right? If only that were true! Most retirees – even a good portion of the nation's 11 million millionaire households – worry about the possibility of running out of money fairly often. And if you ask people who retired in 1999 or 2007, prior to two of the biggest bear markets ever, they'd tell you that those worries are justified.

Of course, when the market is hitting new highs and people are on the verge of retirement, they may feel quite justified in expecting a return of 8% to 10% on their investments from now to forever. This may in turn cause them to believe that they can withdraw 4% or 5% for life from a non-guaranteed account with no worries.

Unfortunately, markets don't always cooperate – they fall from time to time. So, it could be a bad bet to fully rely upon stocks sitting at all-time highs or bonds at all-time lows. If you lean heavily on risk-based assets to provide permanent income, you should probably expect a rocky ride.

Again, consider the period from 2000 to 2009. In that time, we saw the Millennial Crash from 2000 to 2003, which was a slow train wreck resulting in a swoon of almost 50%. Then, after the real estate refinance boom from 2003 to 2007, investors were treated to another once-in-a-lifetime crash of nearly 57% from peak to trough starting in the fall of 2008 to the spring of 2009. Result? For that 10-year period, the broad market recorded a net-negative return. So much for the idea that stocks always make 10%.

That kind of situation is the last thing you want to deal with in retirement. As a financial adviser who counsels retiring, affluent professionals, I have learned that many retirees who are taking steady withdrawals from accounts – while those accounts are losing value to the market – often experience real emotional distress.

Plus, as you move into your 60s and 70s, you will become less risk tolerant. Younger investors can look at market downturns as an opportunity to buy even more stocks. But that's not the way it is in the real world of retirement. Many of my clients, who were once fairly aggressive investors, suddenly – and fairly – don't want to lose any money once they retire.

ARE *BOND MUTUAL* FUNDS THE ANSWER?

Unfortunately, because interest rates on quality bonds have fallen to historic lows, bond funds will likely not be going up in value during your retirement, especially as interest rates are expected to go on a steady uphill climb. It is very important to remember that existing bonds lose value when interest rates rise. This is why bond mutual funds are at risk today. As the economy expands and the threat of inflation returns, interest rates are expected to rise in response.

Those rising rates might cause you to believe that you will soon have more money come into your fund. Unfortunately, the world of bond funds does not work that way. As new bonds are issued that pay higher interest rates, the bonds already in your fund lose market value. Your older bonds paying lower interest can't keep up with the new bonds. Therefore the value of your old bonds inside the fund goes down. Your account value goes down. And your stress level may go up.

The moral is, you can't rely on the old, dusty textbooks about retirement investing anymore. They were written when bonds were paying 6% to 8%. Today, those same bonds are paying only 2% to 3%. What this means to you is that bonds cannot support the amount of income most retirees need. You could say the investment world has flipped for the ten thousand people a day who are retiring now. Whereas 20 or 30 years ago, bond rates were so high that risk averse retirees could leave the stock market completely and simply "live off the interest," today's bond rates don't offer that luxury.

IS THERE ANY SUCH THING AS A WORRY-FREE RETIREMENT INCOME?

Most people retiring today look forward to living off a combination of social security, investments, and perhaps a pension.

Pensions help retirees simplify their investments because the income is steady, unaffected by markets and designed to pay for life. Unfortunately, fewer people are retiring with pensions. Pensions, in fact, are getting to be a thing of the past, being replaced by 401(k)s, 403(b)s and other employer-sponsored retirement plans.

Here's the problem: Many retirees find themselves retiring with a sizable income gap. Your income gap in retirement is the difference between your income and living expenses. For many retirees today, their social security benefits will simply not cover all of their living expenses and their plans for travel, hobbies, etc.

Without a big pension to fill the income gap, those retiring today are justifiably worried that poor investment outcomes caused by bear markets could lead to a spend-down of their retirement money.

SUMMARY

Bank accounts and bonds are at historic low rates and therefore offer little refuge. Real estate is overpriced. That seems to leave the stock market as the only solution. But markets are far too unreliable. Trying to outrun bear markets while withdrawing enough money to live on could be a disaster. Ask anyone who retired in 1999 or 2007 who stayed heavily invested in stocks.

Retirees today know they cannot rely on their investments alone to provide the steady income they need. This is why you are seeing strong demand for retirement annuities, especially fixed index varieties with income riders.

Offering a lifetime guarantee of income, not affected by stock or bond markets—like a pension—annuities are becoming quite appealing. Indeed, annuities should command viable consideration for anyone feeling squeezed by low interest rates and risky markets.

Every year, Americans are buying approximately $200 billion in annuities according to LIMRA, the recognized life insurance marketing association.

It's a surprise to most people to learn that annuities are so popular. You wouldn't know it because the information available on the internet from mostly young journalists is often lacking. That shouldn't stop you from exploring the facts for yourself. If you get the right annuity, you can enjoy principal protection 24/7/365, very strong income guarantees and growth potential without market losses.

Remember that annuities are not just investments, nor are they just insurance—they are a combination of the two. An annuity is a contract with a licensed, audited insurance company to watch over your money, pay interest, and pay you an income for life, based on the institution's financial strength and claims-paying ability. Annuities can be used for 401(k), 403(b) and IRA rollovers, to replicate many of the benefits of a pension. This may help alleviate the rational, math-based worry you may have about running out of money.

If you worry that bear markets and unkind interest rates could ruin your retirement, you are not alone. And, you are not irrational. We really could see another "2008" financial crisis one day, and it could come at just the wrong time – when you need your money most..

This is a crazy world. Retiring can be exciting, but investing should probably get less so. Annuities may sound boring, but boring is beautiful when it comes to the money you simply can't afford to lose. In real estate, the motto is "location, location, location." In retirement, it's "income, income, income."

By making sure you have more income than you can spend coming in every month for the rest of your days, your retirement can be more fun and worry-free. Rather than placing your retirement dreams into a "hope-so plan" on Wall Street, consider the guarantees of a quality annuity for your IRA rollover. Rather than a "hope-so plan", you can finally own a "know-so plan."

You will never regret owning more safety, security, and income as the future unfolds.

About Steve

Steve Jurich is an Accredited Investment Fiduciary®, a Certified Income Specialist™, and founder of IQ Wealth Management, a Registered Investment Adviser in Scottsdale, Arizona.

He is the popular radio host of *Mastering Money*, heard daily on Money Radio and on podcast at: www.MasteringMoneyRadio.com. Steve's book, *Smart is the New Rich,* is an Amazon best-seller. His comments have appeared on Bloomberg, TheStreet.com, MarketWatch and CNBC.com.

The many challenges facing retirement-age individuals and those planning for retirement require a skilled professional with a commitment to a fiduciary duty. Steve and his firm are dedicated to putting the needs and goals of his clients in first position and keeping them there.

His clients range in background from engineers, teachers, and medical professionals to business owners, government workers, and accountants. With nearly two decades of personal retirement planning and investment management experience, Steve can offer reliable guidance.

In Steve's words:
"I enjoy growing as a professional and growing as a person — both are processes that never stop. But my passion is helping my clients achieve the clarity, focus and relief from anxiety that comes from having reliable financial outcomes."

To reach Steve, please call:

- His office: (888)310-1776 or
- Email him: Steve@IQWealth.com.
- Website is: www.IQWealth.com

CHAPTER 19

SUCCESS IN THE AGE OF THE NEW HUMAN

BY SHEILA CASH

Early on in my private practice of evolutionary consulting, a middle-aged sales manager named Bob contacted me with some trepidation. He was hopeful, but distraught and without answers. We got off to a slow start working together and then before too long the proverbial dam broke open. Now we were talking!

Bob loved his wife but couldn't bear the thoughts of going home after work anymore. Having been immersed in a conservative culture all his life, he felt shame when considering telling his family and parents about his decision to divorce. He had been raised with the philosophy that you demonstrate respect by staying by your family's side, no matter what. Secretly, Bob blamed his family for tying him down. His church community echoed the expectation that he and his wife stay in their marriage until death.

In addition, he was feeling squeezed by his job in the family-owned business and had recently been to his doctor for chest pains. Bob shared with me that he had been considering finding a new career, but he didn't really feel qualified to make it somewhere else. He had always viewed others out in the world as being more capable than himself. He also believed that change was frivolous, irresponsible, unstable - the future was to be viewed with great caution.

So, he stayed focused on the paperwork on his desk and how he could solve immediate problems. Though other employees in the business resented his familial ties with the company, he was mindful to quell his reactions, and not rock the boat. He followed his company's standards for resolution in business and stayed in his comfort zone "inside the box."

But Bob's inner voice was screaming out to him to choose to listen to his deeper knowing. His gut sense told him to make changes – many changes, and to get out of the old conditioning that was closing in like a vice – to breathe into new potential, the potential he'd felt as a young man.

Bob was willing to open up to a fresh way of seeing life. Over the ensuing months after his eventual divorce, he discovered that specific meditation practices can shift one's cellular chemistry to empowerment. We practiced visioning changes in his life and creating clarity for new intentions that would bring balance and inspiration. *As he took responsibility for his circumstances, the perceptions that had previously kept him locked in shifted into an empowered state.* Bob learned to be consistently proactive in making choices. One day, he remarked on how shocked he was to realize how his default pattern had been to adjust rather than make a new choice, and to react rather than choose. He told me that for the first time in his life, he finally understood that he was here to make his own meaning.

From there, transformation came fast and freely. It's hard to say whether he let go of his old programming first or whether it simply slipped away as he empowered himself with the gift of choice – using his senses to discern the most balancing and meaningful choices every step of the way. Little by little, bit by bit, his sense of who he truly was, who he'd been as a young man, who his most authentic self was, arose. The Bob I currently know and love is an inspired, radiant, peaceful and jovial man on a mission!

*****

Our rapidly changing world has created the need for an entirely new way of life. Success strategies must be approached from an evolved consciousness that is accordingly adept. Thought leaders within the field of conscious evolution have recognized the need for us to step into a visionary level of consciousness within humanity. *This is being identified as the New Human.* Discoveries in the fields of quantum physics and energy economics have shown us that our thoughts and actions have a far-reaching impact. Additionally, the advent of artificial intelligence that permeates our lives has also dictated that we broaden our understanding of what we can contribute alongside its burgeoning frontier. The time has come to expand and deepen the scope of our strategies accordingly. Technological advances bring information, but you bring the wisdom.

Welcome to the age of the New Human!

*****

The following eight insights will bring transformative breakthroughs on your path to a successful life:

1. Align with the Bigger Picture

In our daily lives, we often become fixated on the little picture – on what's happening in this moment, what our reactions are and what feelings are taking over. Looking at the universal perspective can bring us a sharper strategy for success by looking at all viewpoints possible. An integral view, with all angles being accounted for, is a balanced, whole perspective to draft from. Much of life is organized around thinking that is considered to be right/wrong, black/white, conservative/liberal, etc. When we polarize our views this way, we miss out on the value of an integral understanding that brings much greater insights than any one myopic position could.

In this age of the New Human, information comes in leaps and bounds now.

<u>Takeaway #1</u>
Wisdom results from cultivating the skill to put all the fragments of available information together into an integral composite to include comprehensive possibilities and permutations.

2. Align with Relativity

In the old world, we were trained to think in absolute terms. Classic teachings often guided us into a fixed reference point on any given subject. Concrete definitions on explicit concepts make us feel, subconsciously, that we are sheltered from ignorance and are therefore more in control. But *adaptability of cognizance* is what is needed for progress in our high-tech culture.

In the new world of quantum thinking, the scope of possibilities has amplified exponentially. There is always simultaneously *more than one correct answer* to any question. Each perspective has its own merits. But decisions based in the absolute can stagnate or even paralyze an optimal outcome. Your own progress forward into a life of achievement will be well-served by learning to perceive in relative terms rather than attaching to a need for absolutes. This will keep you open to ever-newer information.

Takeaway #2

If you remember that there are always more options, expanded opportunities will be available to you for every strategy.

3. Align with the Mirror

On an evolving path forward, a valuable tool for refinement is to see people and circumstances as mirrors. You can ask yourself, what about this person or situation feels negative *within me?* The answers can be quite surprising. For example, you might identify someone in your workplace as egotistical and self-serving and you feel repulsed when near them. You may think, "I'm not like that, so there is no mirror there for me!" However, the mirror may be that you actually feel taken advantage of and would like to have a more balanced workload like that person seems to have. The mirror technique can reflect areas where taking action on your own behalf will bring ease and balance to your life. It shows you where to shift your thinking and what needs to be harmonized with and transcended.

We can learn the most from people we understand the least. They bring opportunities to learn acceptance, cooperation, humility, compassion, forgiveness, and unconditionality. Often overlooked, these attributes bring true success in the long run through the security and benefits of inner peace and fulfillment, without which we end up hopping from job to job and relationship to relationship. These are qualities that will also create a solid trust in you from others.

Takeaway #3
See the people and circumstances of your life as mirrors to your own state of consciousness in order to make valuable discoveries about how best to navigate your future.

4. Align with Choice

The ability to make choices proactively is an often-overlooked tool, believe it or not. Be mindful that you always have more choices. Never limit yourself to some idealized version of perfection. Every choice is a learning experience that will ultimately carry you forward to your greatest self-actualization in vocation, relationships and success in life.

Ambivalence can become a comfort zone. Begin choosing and leave indecision behind. *The point is...to choose.* That's where you find the outcomes all along the way that will be most "right" for you. Every choice will bring advantages as you pay attention to learning how each moment, person, or situation can bring the greatest clarity to your life.

Refining your individual preferences, day by day, creates the direction of your future. You and only you are responsible for every single choice you make. No one else is going to live your life for you. Enjoy the process knowing that every choice will bring you one step closer to your greatest fruition.

Takeaway #4
Ultimately, the quality of your life is based on the choices you make in each moment.

5. Align with Intuition

We are connected to the universe at quantum levels. Those who have practiced higher consciousness techniques such as meditation, understand through experience that one can "open" to knowledge. It is highly empowering to practice developing the senses that awaken your own untapped magnitude of consciousness that will effectively direct your choices and understanding in life.

Your human senses are valuable tools for processing. We are each born as perfect antennae, tuned to the universe. Your senses give you a foundation for assessing every circumstance. Through your senses, you can comprehend patterns and connections to develop an integral picture of the universe that informs you beyond the filter of your common beliefs. Sensory development offers fresh insights to life conflicts and *can deconstruct a strategy that may have been charged with indecision and fear.* The more information we have to help us navigate, the easier decisions about life are to make. Understanding this phenomenon will expand the brilliance in all areas of your life. This is truly a worthy path in the pursuit of success.

<u>Takeaway #5</u>
Exploring and developing extrasensory and multidimensional skills leads to discoveries that raise your game to a new level.

6. Align with Authenticity

Your personal gifts, insights and even personality are your unique path to success. *You bring what no other on earth can bring to your strategies for success.*

Being aware of what is not authentic in our lives is as important as recognizing what is. We do this by being who we are rather than trying to be someone that we're not. Remember that you change from year to year. Don't default to the assumption that you are the same person. Be sure you continue to reassess who you are and who you have become each year. Consider what values you may still retain in your subconscious that may no longer align with your life, and further could be throwing you way off track. Then let those go and move on.

Align with your own creative impulse and take the lid off of your exponential potential - this is now your quantum contribution. As you create, give particular notice to what draws your attention and speaks to your heart. Align people, places and circumstances with your uniqueness for the most prosperous and fulfilling life.

Takeaway #6
Your most authentic values in life are intimate cues to your
own greatest potential.

7. Align with Empowerment

True empowerment is not loud. It is not about controlling. It is about cultivating the courage to align your own authentic beliefs and conduct with your highest consciousness. Empowerment holds empathy and the capacity for equality. Empowerment is courageous, responsible and mature.

We need a lot of courage in our lives. Facing your fears allows you to refine your alignment with courage. Resolve to be fearless in recognizing hypocrisy, contradictions, and separation in each circumstance.

Being empowered means being accountable for your decisions and circumstances. Claiming your empowerment means being capable of owning your actions. Stepping into empowerment means not crediting others as being better than you are, as that is a reflection of the fear of trusting yourself. Projections disempower us.

Empowerment is mature and is about being self-governing in your discernment and decision-making. You no longer need to look "out there" for answers. You will gain valuable experience in empowerment when you use your inner authority.

Takeaway #7
Success comes when we stop trying to make others
accountable for our conditions.

8. Align with Meaning

A truly successful life is one that contains personal meaning. One of the greatest gifts of consciousness is being able to create meaning for ourselves. We discover, create, and expand meaning as we live our lives. It emerges through the actual processing we do along the way. That sense of meaning eliminates floundering and feelings of being ungrounded or unworthy — issues so many of us have faced.

177

Meaning is not a landing place. It's not static. It's not a destination. It is a dynamic, symbiotic process of realizing why we're here.

You are entitled to the privilege of making meaning. Proactively stepping into this privilege will make the difference between a meaningless, confusing, and painful life and a life that is filled with ease, understanding, and purpose.

Takeaway #8
*Decide what is truly most meaningful to you and
arrange your life around it.*

*****

The New Human creates from a future orientation rather than the old conditioning of the past. Outdated and stagnating programming which are now purposeless are unloaded, and no longer block the pinnacle of success. Silencing yourself and limiting your thoughts is antithetical to your proactively evolving life. The decision to let go of all that which holds you back becomes a conscious one.

Seeking a bigger picture and intuiting expanded perspectives reveals choices that had previously seemed hidden. You now choose to filter your life through a consciousness aligned with the unlimited capacities of who you authentically are and how you want to be in this world. You openly embrace true empowerment. You are now ready to cross the threshold of your own personal inner revolution.

May you be inspired to live your life anew on the road to success!

About Sheila

Sheila Cash is the author of the #1 Bestseller, Evolve Your Life, and is the CEO of Evolve Your Life, LLC, a company specializing in evolutionary consulting in the 21st century. She is an international teacher, speaker, and facilitator in the fields of human potential and conscious evolution. She has founded numerous groups on expanding consciousness and her Transformational Empowerment Process based on epigenetics and neuroplasticity. Using an integrated blend of ancient and contemporary modalities from quantum physics, psychology and new biology, she guides clients into innovative strategies for navigating their most successful lives. A visionary and original thinker, her teaching is dynamic in accordance with evolutionary shifts in cultural consciousness.

Facilitating and teaching for over two decades, Sheila coaches groups and individuals to uncover their own deepest and most profound knowing, coming to the essence of their truest authentic selves in order to see how all parts of their lives integrate seamlessly into a whole and purposeful life path. She guides people to put the puzzle pieces of their life together and relate it the bigger picture: why we are here, what our purpose is, and what life is really all about. Her evolutionary teachings transcend standard how-to instructions and self-help manuals to awaken a deeper understanding of how our collective evolutionary path can bring practical alignment to our individual lives. She operates on the rationale that the truth of your life is not stagnant – but rather evolves day-to-day, minute-by-minute.

Sheila studied closely with many thought leaders in the field of conscious evolution including Barbara Marx Hubbard, Patricia Albere and Craig Hamilton. Her coaching is centered on her philosophy that the more you expand the picture, the easier it is to get to your authentic decisions that will serve you best both in the short term and the long haul. Her goal is to help her clients *align* with their most authentic goals.

Sheila believes that our new consciousness in this age of AI and high tech demands an up-leveled degree of skill in expanded consciousness as well. She redefines success in a comprehensive and integral way for the people she works with. Lifelong success entails creating your own meaning.

In the unfolding of the deeper truths of who you are, a new understanding of success is synthesized, illuminating authenticity and purpose in the process. Sheila navigates with unconditional acceptance and sees the humanity in all those she encounters. She delights in the increasing unfolding of our global community, and in the connections with people she makes every day.

For information on current courses with Sheila, go to:

- www.sheilacash.com
- https://www.facebook.com/groups/394757947648124/
- https://twitter.com/sheilacash

CHAPTER 20

HOW TO FALL IN LOVE IN 7 DAYS

BY RON JOHNSON

My wife and I have been married for 7 years. When we met back in 2011, I was on a holiday when I ran into her. I was flying back to North America in 7 days and the night before my flight, I proposed. She said "yes" and the rest as they say, is our beautiful history. Every time we share this story at a party or a dinner, people are amazed and have this exasperated look on their face which screams, YOU ARE CRAZY. I agree you have to be a little crazy to pull this off. The crazies don't believe in impossible. If either of us had given up after our series of heart-wrenching and soul-crushing breakups, if I had given up after my divorce and my depression, we wouldn't have met each other and there would be no space for this beautiful human being in my life.

I still remember the first time I met Isabella in 2011. I recall seeing her in the distance, and the first thing that hit me was her smile. I have always been a sucker for smiles. This was a smile that beat all other smiles. She radiated energy that could light up a room. We greeted each other with a warm embrace like long-lost friends happy to see other. We walked up to her car, and as we drove away in her black, sporty, stick-shift automobile, I remember thinking to myself, "Boy, does she know how to ride that stick!" This was Day One.

We went back to her place. We sat down to have breakfast and shared our life stories. We talked about our life journeys, what we did after high school, the choices we made, the people we fell in love with, the places we had visited and our hopes and dreams for the future. Both of us had interesting stories to share. We were genuinely happy for each other and proud of what we had accomplished so far. By now, it was time for lunch, and she had a specific chicken dish in mind to cook. I volunteered to help her in the kitchen as we continued our animated conversations sprinkled with giggles and laughter.

As she got out the ingredients and we divvied up our tasks, I asked her if there was any way we could listen to some music. If I am in the mood to cook, I like to dance to some music too. I also recall her telling me that she studied dancing professionally while she was in Texas, and I definitely wanted to see that for myself. She rushed upstairs and brought down a radio, and to my surprise, there was an FM station that played some really good English music. I was in charge of the gas stove, and all things were burning hot. She chopped up the ingredients following the recipe 'to the T' and dropped it in the frying pan. Both of us found ourselves dancing to the groove of the music while the kitchen filled up with the aroma of the fresh ingredients and spices. I looked over my shoulder, watching her sway to the music and thinking to myself, "Damn, this girl can dance!" I stretched out my hand and took hers in mine as we danced what looked like a combination of salsa and jive. We were having fun as we spun around in each other's arms until the song was over and I had to return to my duties as master of the stove.

Both of us loved psychology; we craved adventure, we had similar tastes in music and clearly loved to dance. Later that evening, we decided to catch a movie. It was quite a romantic experience for me. We were holding hands; her head rested on my shoulder as we took in the whole movie experience. Five months later, on our honeymoon, Isabella shared that she felt protected when she was walking with me that evening at the theater. My presence and body language communicated to everyone: "Back off. She is mine." I did not realize I was doing that until she told me after we were married! It is amazing how the subconscious works.

It was the end of Day 1 of our 7-day adventure and I knew in my gut right then and there that she was 'The One'. How did I know that? It took Isabella three more days to acknowledge what I was feeling. The heart knew what the heart wanted, but the head was holding her back because of a couple of beliefs. On Day 3 she decided it was worth giving it a shot and she put forward three conditions. She wanted to meet my friends. She wanted me to meet her friends and this had to take place in a different city. Lastly, she wanted to meet my parents. I had three days left and we travelled through three cities and on Day 7, under a starlit sky, with the ocean breeze caressing our bodies and music in the air, with food and drinks worthy of kings and a tropical resort that was purely magical, I got down on one knee and she said 'yes' in 7 days.

I have written an entire book about the 7-day adventure and the 7 challenges I offer my readers.

THE 7 CHALLENGES THAT HELPED ME FALL IN LOVE IN 7 DAYS

1. Peel the Onion

This by far is the hardest challenge. As my marriage crumbled apart, I had to take a hard look at myself—looking at myself in the mirror and figuring out what needs to change in my life. If you aren't able to find the answer, the easiest way is to ask someone who is close to you. It may be a best friend or a family member. Siblings are blessed with the gift of telling you exactly what is wrong with your life! If you really want a life partner and you haven't been able to find someone in almost 7 billion people on the planet, there definitely is something that you aren't being honest about in yourself.

Yes, it does require you to be vulnerable. As I am writing this chapter, I am on a 6-pack challenge with my buddies from the around the world. We have an aussie, a brit, a canuck, a yankee and a couple of desis all wanting to lose weight and be in the best shape of our lives. We were athletes as kids and we reconnected after 20 years, to hold each other accountable as we faced our worst selves. Face your fears, face your worst self, come to terms with it and then adopt a strategy that will work for you.

2. Disempower the Victim

I call this the mind-jedi challenge. I blamed my divorce for the longest time. I blamed the women who broke my heart. There were a lot of people I blamed, and that kept me exactly where I was, single and depressed. The moment I realized that there was a lesson in it for me, the moment I realized that this heart-wrenching experience was a moment of learning and not a moment of complaining, that's the moment my life turned around. I disempowered the victim in me.

The question that really needs to be asked is, "How do I attract the right person in my life?" The first step to do that is to stop complaining and take 100% ownership for everything in your life. What do I do from this moment, so that my past doesn't repeat itself? What do I do from this moment that I am surrounded by positive and uplifting people?

3. Show me your friends

This challenge is the most fun, and no, it is not making a list of all your friends although that is a great exercise to do every couple of years. Prior to meeting Isabella, I dated women from around the world. I call this my world tour phase. I dated women from England, from Germany, from South America and Canada. I fancied a German Jew who had her PhD and could speak 4 languages and the list goes on.

How many of you are scared to talk to someone just because they are taller than you, broader than you, talk louder than you, look different from you? How many stay away from people with long beards and turbans because of the negative stereotypes created by the media? Are there people in your life who are racists, sexists or homophobic even though you don't consider yourself to be one? How many of you can catch the biases that run deep in your subconscious mind?

So here is the challenge. While you are waiting at a bus stop or riding the subway, talk to someone you wouldn't normally talk to. If you are American and you don't know any Muslims, get yourself a Muslim friend and appreciate their strengths. If you are Israeli and you don't talk to Palestinians, find one and make an effort to connect with them. You never know what might happen? We have to work on our internal biases, overcome them and see the beauty and humanity in all mankind. There is beauty everywhere, and if you train your eyes to appreciate beauty in all its forms, colors, and sizes, it will broaden your horizons and energize you.

4. Choose Happiness

This is the easiest challenge but requires discipline to practice. How do I choose to be happy when the express highway is packed with bumper-to-bumper traffic in non-peak hours in one of the best cities in the world? Are there things in your life that drive you up the wall? How many pet peeves do you have? How many of you agree that the things that irritate you the most, reveal the most about you?

Happiness is key to attracting the right kind of people and things into your life. If I am miserable, I attract miserable people and things to my life. The choice is mine and yours. How many of you have heard the song, "Don't Worry... Be Happy"? I love that song. I have to constantly ask myself: "Alejandro, is it worth losing your joy over this incident?" If I forget, my accountability partner (my abundantly joyful wife) loves reminding me about it.

5. Old is Gold

There was a time in my life when I didn't want to meet any of my friends and family. I was ashamed of myself and how my life had turned out to be. I considered myself a failure. How many of you dread going to your high school reunions? How many catch yourselves avoiding emails from your alma mater inviting you for an alumni meet? How many of you make an attempt to stay connected to people you were once close to but somehow lost touch with along the way?

One thing I notice, no matter where I go in the world — and I have spent a considerable amount of time in these beautiful places, picking up five languages along the way — single men and women are always looking for new partners to date! Why not reconnect/ reach out to people whom you enjoyed spending time with from your high school or university days? Check in on them and find out how they are doing? Are they single? Do they have kids? Are you okay dating single parent with kids?

Facebook helped me reconnect with Miss Gorgeous after fifteen years! She had to go through her journey and experience life on her own. I had to travel my path and figure s--t out, and when we finally met after fifteen years, we were ready for each other. All this happened because we didn't say no just because we knew each other from our past.

6. Hack your dating mindset

In my twenties, I had a very narrow window of choice when it came to a life partner and most of it was under the influence of my surroundings and the culture I grew up in. In my thirties, I started questioning all my beliefs about what kind of woman I really wanted in my life?

How many women out there believe they need a really tall man to accommodate their heels? How many men out there believe their partner should be the most gorgeous woman they know? How many times do we give physical attraction and sexual attraction the number one priority when it comes to selecting our partners? When I met Isabella, both of us had to be open to the new possibilities of the human being in front of us and not compare him/her to our past. Physical attraction is critical; however, it shouldn't come at the cost of connecting spiritually and having similar life goals.

7. Go Big or Go Home

I must confess this is my favorite step. This is where you seal the deal. This is when you put a ring on it. How many of you have met a remarkable person whom you fell madly in love with but refused to say anything until it was too late? How many of you, while visiting another city, felt an incredible connection and knew deep down inside that this individual was good for you but hesitated to talk about it and now find yourself regretting not saying anything?

Take action. No matter how many books you read, seminars you attend, or mentors you have, none of it will matter if you don't take action! Do the work needed to transition from where you are to where you want to be and don't be shy to get all the help that you need!

About Ron

Coach Ron Johnson is a Life Transition Consultant based out of Toronto, Canada. He is a certified Canfield trainer in the Canfield Methodology. Ron considers himself a global citizen. He was born in India, raised in Kuwait and spent the rest of his life in multiple cities around the world picking up 5 languages along the way. He even spent some time as a refugee in a UN peacekeeping camp in Jordan during the first Gulf war.

Experience maketh a man, and Ron sure has some interesting international experiences to draw from...a recruiter, a banker, an entrepreneur, an author, a coach, a public speaker, a martial artist, a bollywood dance instructor and a philanthropist. Ron believes true empowerment requires a journey that is as much internal as it is external and facilitates people to get on to the path of success and self-discovery. Ever since he was twelve years old, people consistently told him that when he grew up, he should become a counselor, a shrink or a priest because he was great with people. People loved talking to him and he had the innate ability to make them feel good about themselves. His global multi-cultural background has enabled him to appreciate and respect multiple contradictory perspectives. Ron ultimately took the advice seriously and found his calling in helping people help themselves.

Ron has an undergraduate degree in Engineering, an MBA specialising in Human Resource Management, and a Masters in Spiritual Care and Psychotherapy from Waterloo, Canada. He has over ten years of experience coaching individuals and teams throughout his corporate career and he has also spent over a year working at a counselling centre helping people cope with challenges related to work, school, relationships and family. He finds it extremely fulfilling engaging people from all over the world.

Ron is the author of the book, *How to fall in love in 7 days*, in which he captures the nail-biting story of how he and his wife got engaged in 7 days while holidaying and travelling through three different cities in South Asia. Ron uses his book to teach people how they can use love to attract success in their lives and the secrets of listening to their gut.

Ron cares deeply about children. He is the founder of the Abundance Loves Children Foundation. The foundation aims to support 100,000 homeless children from kindergarten to their undergraduate degree and end female infanticide in India.

You will find out more about his book, *How to fall in love in 7 days* on the website:

- howtofallinlovein7days.com

To contact Ron and avail his consulting services go to:

- rjsuccesscoaching.com

CHAPTER 21

REPROGRAMMED FOR SUCCESS

BY SHERRIE LEWIS-MASSIE

As we focus on Success Breakthroughs, have you ever found yourself wanting to make changes in your life, wanting to improve your situation, but for some reason you seem to be stuck and can't move forward? Have you looked at other people who seem to be having great success, who seem to be having breakthroughs and wonder how they do it? What is their secret and why does it seem to elude you?

There are probably a number of reasons why we feel stuck or unfortunately even sabotage our own success. In this chapter, I would like to introduce you to a little secret weapon that we all have that can help us get unstuck. Unfortunately, many of us don't know about this power. Or, if we know of it, we haven't intentionally set out to use this wonderful power for our own good. As we teach you ways to tap into this secret weapon, you will begin to realize that you have been given the power to change almost every situation in your life.

Let me introduce you to RAS, the Reticular Activating System. The Reticular Activating System (RAS) is located in your brain and is only about two inches long. RAS is really a complex collection of neurons in the brain that start close to the top of the spinal column and extends upwards around two inches into the brain. Because of the location of RAS, you will probably never get to actually see him. However, you really should become better acquainted with his workings, because RAS has ultimately been setting the course of your life.

You may have noticed that I have been referring to RAS as having a gender, versus just being a complex mass of neurons. For me, it helps to see RAS as this tiny entity housed in my brain. I envision him as being placed there by our creator to help us to become successful. By giving RAS an identity, I have found that I am better able to relate with RAS and thus become better positioned to help him do his job in a way that benefits me.

RAS has a very big job. If you would like to read more of the science behind RAS, just Google the Reticular Activating System. You can find massive amounts of research and complex explanations of his workings. However, for our purposes, we will keep the description of RAS in plain language and leave the more detailed scientific description for another time.

Simply put, RAS gives your brain the ability to sort through all the information around you. Studies have shown that there are about 2 million bits of information coming at us every second. These stimuli comes through all our senses—what we see, hear, touch, taste, and smell. As you can imagine, we would not be able to handle being consciously aware of 2 million bits of stimuli at any one time. Therefore, our RAS breaks down that massive number of stimuli and only permits about 120 bits per second through to our conscious mind.

That means that only a very tiny fraction of the information you have been exposed to actually make its way into your conscious mind. The question that should be at the forefront of your mind right now, is "where does that other information go?" It is redirected to your subconscious mind. You didn't lose it, it is there. You just are not conscious of it.

RAS sorts through this massive amount of data and in a split second he redirects the majority of it to be stored in your subconscious mind. These are things that RAS has deemed as not important to you at the moment. RAS only lets in the important things. . . the things that you need to pay attention to at this moment. For example, have you ever been walking down a busy, noisy street and then above all the noise you suddenly become aware that someone across the street is calling your name. Above all the noise, you become aware that your name is being called. Why is that? It's because RAS has deemed that your name is important information to you, and therefore should be allowed to come to your conscious mind.

That is the job of RAS. He acts as a gatekeeper of sorts, deciding what is important enough to let in and what should be redirected to the subconscious. So, how does RAS know what to let in? You've told him. "When did I do that?" you may be asking. Simply put, you tell RAS what is important to you by what you focus on.

I have a funny story that explains how RAS works and how we ultimately program him and tell him what is important to us.

RAS, WALMART, and BOILED PEANUTS

Personally, I do not like boiled peanuts. As a result, I have never really paid too much attention to where you purchase them. Yes, I may have seen the signs along the highway when taking road trips. But, since I had no desire for them, I never stopped and, therefore, could not tell you exactly in what city I had seen the signs. Last Thanksgiving, my friend's family was in town visiting. Her grandmother and mother expressed a desire for boiled peanuts. My friend began the scavenger hunt of finding boiled peanuts in Atlanta, Georgia.

I happened to be speaking with this friend while she was on her hunt. We talked, trying to determine which little town was close that might carry the boiled peanuts. We both had a lot to do, so I wished her good luck and hung up. I was *en route* to Walmart to pick up a few items before I could return home.

I walked into Walmart and went straight to the aisle for the nuts and snacks. I was in search of unsalted cashews (one of my favorites). Walmart carries them, but often, to my chagrin, they are out of stock. Many days, I would rifle through all the cans of the various nuts on the shelves before I could find one can of the unsalted cashews.

On this day, I walked up the aisle and came to the place for the cashews and guess what I see, right there on the same shelf as the cashews? You guessed it, boiled peanuts. Not only does Walmart carry boiled peanuts, but they are also stocked on the same aisle I visit very often looking for my beloved unsalted cashews, and not once had I seen them before. So, did Walmart just decide that day to stock boiled peanuts? No, this is RAS at his best. I'm sure that I have overlooked these boiled peanuts a number of times. Because they were not important to me, there was no need for them to register in my conscious mind. I did not need to be aware of them.

However, because I had been focusing on them while trying to help my friend, RAS now decided boiled peanuts must be important to me, so he opened the gate and allowed the boiled peanuts into my conscious mind. I am now aware of boiled peanuts. He changed my tape. Now, whenever I go into Walmart in search of my unsalted cashews, I also see boiled peanuts.

This is a funny example of how RAS uses your focus to help determine what he will allow to come to your awareness. I am sure that you have experienced your own version of this story. You may have experienced buying a brand-new car and then on the way home from the dealer, you see this same make, model, or even color everywhere. Did everyone all of sudden decide to buy the same car? No, but because you were intent on purchasing a car, you began to focus on the details of your car. The act of focusing your intention actually reprogrammed your RAS. He changed the tape and now added this data as being important to you. It is his job to help you, so he allows this data to flow to your conscious mind. This is where you can make conscious decisions to act upon what you see and hear. I think you can see by these examples that we may need to get a better understanding of RAS and how to get him working for us instead of against us.

So, how can we intentionally program RAS to work for us? Can we actually change the tape? Yes, my story with the boiled peanuts is a prime example of my reprogramming my RAS. We reprogram RAS through what we focus on, what we are watching or seeing with our eyes; also, by what we are listening to through our ears, and what we are speaking through our mouths.

If we want to utilize RAS as a powerful partner working on our behalf, we need to become intentional about our focus. One of the greatest tools for reprogramming your RAS, and thus changing the tape, is visualization.

Visualization works because it helps you to see what you want. As you spend time getting a clear picture in your mind of your desired outcome, you are actually reprogramming RAS; you are in essence changing the tape. Thus, RAS begins to open up and allow this data to come into your conscious mind so that now you can use it to line up your current life with the vision you saw.

This is the Law of Attraction at work. We've heard a lot about the Law of Attraction in recent years. *The Secret*, both the movie and the book, has brought a lot of attention to the Law of Attraction. Basically, the Law of Attraction states that we attract what we continually focus on. If you focus on the positive, you will attract the positive. If you focus on the negative, you get the negative. After our discussion about RAS, I think you can understand why this is true.

Visualization is one of the best ways to reprogram RAS. As you visualize, you are focusing. The more detailed you are in your visualization, the more success you will have in changing the tape and reprogramming your RAS. Because, when you can see it in your mind, it is the job of RAS to help bring it to your awareness.

Go ahead and try a quick visualization experience right now:

1. Sit comfortably in a chair and close your eyes.
2. Get a clear picture of what it is you want. What are you doing?
3. Don't just see it, create a mental movie. Allow your other senses to get involved:
   - What are you hearing? What are the sounds around you?
   - What smells are in the air?
   - Are you eating anything, . . .chewing gum, . . .having a mint?
   - What are you feeling? What emotions are you experiencing?

The more intense and clear your vision, the better. Allow all of the emotions of the vision to overwhelm you. You may even find yourself smiling or crying depending on the vision you just experienced. That felt pretty good, didn't it?

The great part about visualization is that it is available to you at any time. So, use it. Now, over the next couple of weeks, keep a record of the coincidences you will experience. Maybe you will just happen to bump into a person you needed to speak with. Or, maybe you will just happen to see an advertisement connecting you with the very item that you needed to complete your project. Coincidences are oftentimes RAS at work.

Determine to add visualization to your arsenal as a tool in your breakthrough to success. It is a great gift. It costs us nothing to be able to visualize and to get a new vision of the life we want. Using visualization to help reprogram your RAS will be a one-two punch for a success breakthrough. The possibilities are all around you. You simply are not noticing them, or worse, you may be self-sabotaging, because they don't line up with the vision that you have programmed in your mind.

It may be time to reprogram your mind through visualization. Start today, intentionally enacting your secret weapon, RAS, and let him help lead you to the life of your dreams.

About Sherrie

Sherrie Lewis-Massie touches her client's hearts and ignites their spirit to go after their dreams and to live their life on purpose. Sherrie is an Empowerment Coach and holds firm to the belief that we each have the power to live our lives to our full potential. Sherrie is the Managing Director of The Massie Team, a small coaching and training firm in Atlanta, Georgia. Sherrie and her partners help individuals begin to live their lives on purpose. After holding leadership positions in both the private sector and government for over 30 years, Sherrie decided to step into the role of entrepreneur where she could more directly help influence a change in people's lives.

Having grown a team of thousands of independent agents that expand into international markets, Sherrie believes that entrepreneurship is the only way that we can truly determine our own destiny and to leave a legacy for our families.

Sherrie is also the Founder of WOW (Women of Wisdom). WOW is made up of over 1,000 women. Its focus is to provide opportunities that position its members to enjoy true wealth. Sherrie believes true wealth is wholeness in every area of your life (spiritually, mentally, physically, and financially). WOW hosts Women's Conferences that challenge its participants to unleash the greatness within them, to enjoy their unique beauty, talents, and gifts, to take back their power, and to live life to the fullest.

Sherrie is a Certified Speaker, Trainer, and Coach with the John Maxwell Team. Through her unique coaching and empowering strategies, she aids individuals in personal and professional growth. Using proven leadership methods, she assists individuals and organizations in moving towards their desired goals.

Sherrie is a graduate of Oglethorpe University in Atlanta, Georgia, where she currently resides with her husband (Arnold).

You can connect with Sherrie at:

- www.massieteam.com
- Sherrie@massieteam.com
- www.facebook.com/SherrieLewisMassie

CHAPTER 22

WHY BEING NICE LEADS TO SUCCESS

BY CYNTHIA LETT

It is a common understanding that we want to do business with people we like. Think about it. If you had bids from two companies who offered basically the same options, but one of the vendors was represented by a really nice, respectful professional who showed that he likes you, which company would you hire? Most likely, the nice guy would be chosen. So, how can you be sure you are the "nice guy"? Knowledge and practice of proper business etiquette will help.

In business today, the complaints about others' behavior outweigh the delight in working with them. There is cursing, ignoring conversations, not making introductions, weak handshakes, not wearing name badges where we can read them, cell phone conversations that interrupt face-to-face communication, texting during meetings and conversations, lousy voice-mails, having to listen to others' iPods at their desks, being interrupted while concentrating on work, and a myriad of other rude pet peeves. No wonder we are stressed out by our work and workplaces. We know you don't want to be "that guy." Avoiding a bad reputation is not hard if you pay attention to the relationship you have with others rather than your own needs. "But", you ask, "how do I get what I want?" You will be amazed how much more recognition and opportunity for success you will have when you pay more attention to others' needs than your own. It is so unique in today's workplace that even being a "little nicer" can reap great benefits.

Here are some practices that will set you apart from all others – especially your competition in the workplace. You will be happy to know that if you practice these skills everywhere with everyone, your social life will improve as well:

❖ Smile at everyone, whenever you can.

❖ Listen to whoever is speaking to you and acknowledge them.

❖ Validate others' points whether or not you agree with them. Everyone has a right to their own opinion – they and you.

❖ Greet everyone you come into contact with – even if you said "Hello" yesterday, it's a new day – say "Hello" again.

❖ If you say "Hello," say "Good-bye" when you leave their presence.

❖ Shake hands firmly, but not with bone-crushing strength. Three seconds is the typical U.S. handshake.

❖ Don't use foul language with anyone for any reason. You WILL offend someone, but you may never know whom. They won't tell you, they will just leave you alone.

❖ Speak up – don't mumble. If you believe you have something to say, say it so the person(s) with whom you are speaking can hear you.

❖ Always try to make a great impression on everyone you meet. That means you wear clean clothes that are appropriate to where you are, stand up straight, brush your teeth, comb your hair, wash your face and don't have an offensive smell (use deodorant and don't overdo the fragrance). Look like you are happy with YOU. If you do, others will be too.

❖ Don't make your cell phone more important than the person standing in front of you. If you must check who is calling, ask permission by saying, "Do you mind if I take a quick look?" Don't answer it and talk to the caller, just see who called. Let it go to voicemail for retrieval when the others are not right in front of you. The exception to this is if you are expecting an important call and you ask permission in advance to answer it from those with you.

❖ If you need to check your messages, excuse yourself from present company for no more than three minutes – check, return the calls necessary and get back to your company quickly. Then apologize for stepping away once you return.

❖ If you are going to get something for yourself, like a drink at the bar, dessert at the cafeteria or more paper from the supply closet and someone is standing with you, offer to retrieve something for them as well. Think about them and show their time and comfort is important to you.

❖ Don't gossip. Gossip is defined as anything that you personally didn't witness. You will most likely get details wrong and could put someone in an unflattering position if you are taking what someone else says happened as truth. If someone asks you about it, just tell them you weren't there so you can't comment.

❖ Don't take items from other's desks without permission.

❖ Don't use a speakerphone if you can see that anyone else can hear the conversation.

❖ If you do want to use a speakerphone, always ask permission of the others on the other end. When using it with more than one other listener, identify yourself each time you speak.

❖ Always be on time. When we are late, we waste other people's time and there is no excuse for this. If the unforeseen happens and you must be late, call and make sure it will be convenient for the others to wait for you.

❖ Make requests, not demands. This is a basic etiquette rule and one that is ignored constantly. Use words like *"May I?"* and *"Do you mind?"* and *"If you can..."* rather than barking orders. We all believe we should choose to act, not be demeaned to react.

❖ Always speak to people with respect and concern. No matter the position you hold, you are no better than others nor are they better than you. If they don't know it, show them with your actions, not snide remarks.

❖ Learn how to introduce yourself and others. Consider the order of precedence (where one's position falls on the list of importance). Always remember that the Client or Guest, if there is one present, will have the most important position.

This is a relatively short list and there are SO many more considerations to developing respectful and professional relationships that will help you get ahead in your career/business. Start here, master this list, practice these skills every day and you will undoubtedly be considered the "nice guy" amongst your competition.

Then... find out what more you can do to make the other person's life easier. This will reap its own benefit for you.

About Cynthia

Cynthia W. Lett has been teaching professionals for over 30 years how to set themselves apart from their competition and advance their careers and social lives. She is an international speaker, consultant and coach to Fortune 1,000 executives, government agencies in 30 countries and savvy professionals worldwide.

Cynthia is the director of The Lett Group and Executive Director of the International Society of Protocol & Etiquette Professionals. She is the author of *That's So Annoying: An Etiquette Expert on The World's Most Irritating Habits and What to Do About Them* and *Lett's Talk ... Real Etiquette Dilemmas and How to Solve Them.*

As a recognized media expert, her commentary on workplace/career issues is regularly featured on TV and radio, in newspapers and magazines.

For more information:

- Call: 1+843-800-6002
- www.cynthialett.com
- www.lettgroup.com

CHAPTER 23

TAKE 100% RESPONSIBILITY FOR YOUR LIFE

BY VICTOR DEDAJ

You cannot control your circumstances or what happens to you, but you can change yourself and how you react to those circumstances. We often believe that someone is responsible for giving us a great life and giving us opportunities because we exist. The truth is that all of this depends on one person, and that person is yourself. You are responsible for your success, income, relationships, and everything else that happens to you.

People prefer to blame their parents, friends, teachers, the economy, the weather, and anything else we can find to blame. The one person we normally don't blame is ourselves. This has been going on since the fall in the Garden of Eden. Adam blamed Eve and Eve blamed the the serpent. Since then people want to blame everyone else for their problems and lack of success instead of themselves.

I used to blame other circumstances and people for whatever happened to me. If I did not get a good grade, it was the teacher's fault. If I was not making more money, it was the fault of the company, my boss or my boss's boss.

Later on, I learned something. In some of my annual job reviews, they would tell my boss that I worked hard and did whatever assignments they asked me to do and would get it to them promptly. They also mentioned that they would also like me to give them extra information when I performed assignments.

One area for improvement that they said was while it was nice I always did everything I was asked to do and did it promptly, they would also appreciate it if I wrote some commentary on the reports I ran for them to give my opinions on them. I realized that I needed to give more value to the people I was working with. While I worked hard, I was not giving them extra value, and that affected me at year-end. That was no one's fault but my own. I was giving only what was asked of me. Not providing extra value and only providing what I was asked for cost me promotions and raises over the years. Now, I always go above and beyond to provide people with extra value.

I later also learned that lesson when I went to work as an entrepreneur. When you're dealing with prospects, you need to give as much value as possible, and overdeliver on it. It will make you more successful and make you more money.

I thought that I would do the extra work after they paid me more for it. What I did not realize was that I would have to do the extra work in order to get the extra raises, bonuses, and promotions.

The difference between the extraordinary and the ordinary is that little extra you give. It makes all the difference in the world.

Successful people always try to provide 'way more' than the value expected of them. You need to overwhelm people with value and make them feel that they got 'way more' than what they asked for and what they paid you for. If they feel you did not give them enough value, they will feel cheated, won't work with you again, and won't recommend any of their friends to you.

When I started taking responsibility for my life, everything changed. I felt more powerful and in control. When I blamed my problems on other people or circumstances, I felt weaker and incapable of changing my situation. I felt I had no control over my life, and that external events and people would be responsible for what happened to me, and that I had little control over whatever did happen to me.

Realize that if you arrive late for work, it's not the traffic or the trains that made you late. You were late because you did not give yourself an extra 20 or 30 minutes for your commute to work. If you leave early enough, you will get there on time.

I live in New York City, which is a commuter city. People take the subways most of the time. I have learned that in dealing with the subway system, all kinds of things can go wrong. There can be train delays, a passenger can get sick on the train which will force the train to stop, etc. On the weekends the trains also don't run as frequently in New York City. I often deal with people who estimate on web sites like Hop Stop, how long it will take to meet up with me, and they wind up being late, and they blame the subways. I tell them that the subways are not at fault, and that they should have given themselves extra time to get there. If you miss a train just as it is leaving, the next one may not come for 10 or 15 minutes. Then you may need to switch trains, which may mean more waiting. If you leave a little earlier, you can avoid those problems.

I am always on time for my appointments. One reason is that I always budget enough time to get to them. If you are late for a job interview, it is your fault that you are late. If the company deducts points for the interview because you were not on time, it is not their fault. You should have allowed more time to get there. The other interviewees got there on time, so there is no reason you could not.

One of my mentors, Jack Canfield, wrote a fantastic book called the *Success Principles*. It has 67 principles of success. The very first one he discusses is taking 100% responsibility for yourself. Successful people always take 100% responsibility for whatever happens to them.

When I left the corporate world and became an entrepreneur, I struggled in the beginning because I expected my sponsors to do everything for me. Jim Rohn used to say you can't hire someone to do your pushups for you.

When people did not join me in my online businesses, I often would make an excuse as to why they didn't join. I would say that they were too cheap, too scared, too lazy, not motivated, not understanding, etc. The problem was that I did not look at the part I played in the exchange. The one common factor in each situation was me. Then it hit me that maybe there was something I needed to change.

Once I realized that I was the main factor in my lack of success, I stopped blaming others and worked on myself. I focused more on how I could serve and help them, and solve their problems and needs. Once I changed my focus, I started seeing more success.

I looked around myself. There were people who were not as smart as I am, with less experience than I had, who were more successful than I was. It seemed unfair to me, but then I started asking myself, "Why is that?"

One reason I discovered was that successful people took 100% responsibility for their own success. Yes, bad things happen to you. You can control how you respond to them. I often used to wallow in my misery and say, "Woe is me." That did not help me make more money. I stopped feeling sorry for myself and started taking responsibility for my actions and reactions.

I realize that I expected a lot of people to do things for me, such as my mentors and sponsors. I came to the realization that I had to take 100% responsibility and realize I was responsible for my own success.

Realize that you are in control as to how you react to each person and each situation. There are many different people who will react differently to the same event or the same person, so it's not the person or event that is the cause. It is how you choose to react.

We all have things that happen to us that are not good. We can't control those things. What we can control is how we react to those events. If there is a traffic jam, some people may get furious, while others are relaxed and enjoy the music in their car. The difference is how they react to the same event. The happier people take control. I have learned to do that. I used to be reactive, but now I am proactive. Bad things can happen, but I still choose how to react to them.

I realize that when I expected other people to take care of things for me, it weakened me. I was dependent on them. It gave me an external locus of control instead of an internal locus of control. I felt everything outside me controlled what happened to me. When I took control over what happened to me, I realized that I had an internal locus of control. I could control my reactions to events, and thus, what happened to me.

When I left the corporate world and became an entrepreneur, I no longer had bosses and companies to blame for not getting promoted. I found other things to blame instead. I could blame my upline for my not succeeding in my business opportunity, or blame the compensation plan for my not making money.

As an entrepreneur, I started out by relying on the training of companies I belonged to. The problem was sometimes the companies would go under or the government would shut them down. I also fell into the habit of relying on my sponsors too much. What I didn't realize was that my sponsors could help guide me, but they could not succeed for me. I had to put in the effort myself.

I was in a network marketing company where you could sometimes get spillover from your sponsor's downline. There were six people in a matrix, and when it got filled, any extra people would get passed down to you or someone else in your sponsor's downline.

My sponsor deactivated himself and left. But he was still listed as my sponsor, even though he was inactive. I would not get any spillover recruits credited to me. I requested to have my sponsor changed since he was no longer active. The company refused to do so, and I felt it was so unfair. They told me that I had to do the work and build up my downline and not depend on a sponsor.

That made me angry, so I left the company. Of course, I realized later on that I should have focused more on developing myself and building my business with that company. If I had focused on recruiting people instead of hoping for spillover, I would have made more money.

Even though I was upset, they were right. I was not taking 100% responsibility again. I realized that ultimately it was up to me, and not to any sponsor or mentor for me to succeed. I had to do the work, follow the company trainings, and work on my personal development.

Jim Rohn used to say to work harder on yourself than on your job. If you work hard on your job, you can make a living. If you work hard on yourself, you can make a fortune. When you develop yourself, it does not matter if the company or business you are in goes bankrupt or gets shut down. You can take your talents somewhere else and succeed.

Many successful people have become bankrupt and became millionaires again because of their personal development. If you have a million-dollar mindset, even if you go broke, you'll eventually get back to a million dollars.

I've worked very hard on myself in terms of personal development, and know that I can take my talents anywhere now because I worked hard on myself and can succeed no matter where I go.

I also used to make excuses. Making excuses prevented me from seeing things as they really are, and they prevent you from doing the things you need to do to have a better and more successful life. They say you can create results or excuses. What you choose will determine the kind of life you'll end up having. Excuses rob you of control.

Excuses allowed me to escape the responsibility of not becoming more successful in life. It was easy to blame another person or outside circumstance and believe that there was nothing I could do about it. I could complain to people and get sympathy from them. But nothing was changing or getting better. When I focused on getting results and taking responsibility, my life got much better. I felt empowered and in control, and wound up becoming more productive and more successful.

You can make an excuse for everything, but you won't get far in life. Or you can change the way to respond to what happens, and you can change your life. You need to gain control of your thoughts and behaviors. If you don't like your outcomes, then you need to focus on changing your responses. We make excuses so we don't look like we failed and messed up.

We are very creative in making excuses why we are not succeeding, but shut off when looking for reasons to succeed.

Since I began taking responsibility for my life, I have become a successful entrepreneur, coach, speaker, and author. I have also hosted two events, and am looking forward to accomplishing many more great things in the future.

About Victor

Victor Dedaj is a lifelong New Yorker, born and raised in the Bronx. He is a Certified Canfield Trainer in the Success Principles. He is also a coach and motivational speaker. Victor loves helping people succeed and inspiring them to achieve great things with their lives. Victor utilizes his corporate training in much of the

[Photo credit: Christopher O'Hare]

work he does as an entrepreneur.

Victor has built businesses in affiliate marketing, network marketing, digital products, cryptocurrency, paid advertising and e-commerce. He is also a social media expert. Victor is a big believer in having multiple streams of income. You can find Victor at events all around the world hanging out with other successful entrepreneurs.

He worked in the corporate world in finance for nearly two decades, mainly as a performance analyst. Victor later transitioned into the world of internet marketing and entrepreneurship in 2013 after leaving the corporate world. He truly enjoys being an entrepreneur and being able to travel the world and meet great people.

Victor Dedaj is the author of the book, *You Can Become Successful.* He is also a contributing author to Mark Hoverson's book *The Million Dollar Day: Proven 24-Hour Blueprint Reinvents Your Future With Radical Productivity, Profits & Peace of Mind.*

Victor believes that the more people you serve and help become successful, the more successful you'll be in life. Victor believes that you should focus on helping people. They want to know that you care about themselves first. Once they know that you care about them and have their best interests at heart, they will want to work with you in whatever business you are in.

Victor enjoys the freedom, flexibility and lifestyle he now has as an entrepreneur, as well as being able to work from any place in the world. He is also a Travelling FreedomPreneur and FoodPreneur. As a foodpreneur, Victor enjoys sampling all the great cuisines of the world. His view is "Food determines mood."

Victor is also an active and devoted Catholic.

You can connect with Victor at:

- victordedaj@victordedaj.org
- www.facebook.com/victor.dedaj.3
- www.twitter.com/victordedaj
- https://www.instagram.com/victordedaj

You can also visit his web site at: http://victordedaj.com
Or his YouTube channel at: http://vicdedaj.com

CHAPTER 24

BREAKTHROUGH TO HEALTH

BY TONI CAMACHO, Ph.D.

On December 2004, I was diagnosed with adrenal fatigue and PTSD. A lifetime of stress, anxiety, overworking and neglecting my body had finally caught up with me. My condition was severe, the activity of my adrenal glands was so diminished that I had difficulty staying awake for more than a few hours per day. My body was significantly affected, and I had many other symptoms such as weakened immunity, sleep disturbances and an inability to handle physical or emotional stress. I saw many Doctors, and all told me that there was no solution for this condition. Not being a person who is known for quitting easily, I decided to look for an answer in natural medicine. Through my journey to health, I learned about the mind-body connection, the power of compassion, and how the food we eat and the thoughts we think affect our physiology.

I applied these principles to my life, and thirteen years later, you would not even suspect that I had suffered from adrenal fatigue. This experience taught me that real healing is multi-dimensional. It was not easy or fast, it took about a year to heal, and I did it with herbs, a whole food nutrient-dense diet as well as meditation and improving my emotional condition. There is always an opportunity to heal. My desire is that you will find on these pages hope, new possibilities and ideas that will spring you forward into health.

Understanding the Problem

I wish my story were unique, however, according to the CDC, chronic diseases and conditions—such as heart disease, stroke, cancer, Type 2 diabetes, obesity, and arthritis—are among the most common of all health problems in the US. And they predict that by the year 2030, the number of Americans living with a chronic disease will increase by 37%. Moreover, the prevalence of both autoimmune diseases and allergies has been increasing since the 1950's; the National Institute of Health estimates that one in five people are currently suffering from an autoimmune disorder. That is 20% of the US population (65,353,349 people)!

The most common symptom of an autoimmune disease and other chronic illness is inflammation. Inflammation is part of the body's immune response. It can be beneficial when, for example, your arm is hurt, and tissues need to be repaired. Though, when inflammation sticks around more than necessary, it causes more harm than benefit. Many factors can trigger chronic inflammation. However, the source can be narrow down to toxicity and deficiency due to emotional and physical stress, poor diet, and exposure to toxins.

The Solution

The good news is that by taking some simple and inexpensive measures, such as consuming high-quality herbal supplements, watching what you eat and what you drink, these disorders are preventable, and in many cases, reversible. It sounds too simple to be true but is not. This approach has been applied successfully by Eastern traditions for centuries, and in the late twentieth century, the value of herbs, a proper diet as well as the interaction between psychological processes and the nervous and immune systems began to be recognized in the West as well. For this reason, when I work with clients, my approach is multidimensional. I take into consideration their physical symptoms and their emotions as I personalize a health plan. Nevertheless, there is a core protocol that adapts to each individual's needs. let's review it.

I. <u>GENTLY CLEAR TOXINS WHILE NOURISHING</u>

Americans eat an average of 3,393 calories per day; it is almost double the number of the recommended daily calories. Unfortunately, even though Americans overeat they are undernourished because of *what they eat*, the Standard American Diet is mostly comprised of fattening foods that are devoid of nutrition. It lacks in vitamins, minerals, enzymes, and antioxidants, while being high in refined sugar, refined grains, table salt, toxic protein, cholesterol, saturated fat, preservatives and artificial flavors and coloring. These elements create chronic inflammation and consequently illness.

Many symptoms of chronic illness, as well as autoimmune disorders, can be linked to an impaired digestive and detoxification system. Proper nutrition, a well-functioning digestive and detoxification system are essential to maintain a healthy weight, reduce your risk of chronic diseases, and promote your overall health. Therefore, to improve your health, no matter what condition you have, you will need to nourish and gently cleanse your body with food and herbs.

Herbal medicine aims to return the body to a state of natural balance so that it can start healing itself. Plants have been humanity's primary medicine for centuries and herbalism has been practiced to remedy or alleviate many conditions, such as allergies, asthma, eczema, PMS, migraines, menopausal symptoms, chronic fatigue, IBS, and cancer, among others. A significant benefit of herbal medicine is that it is safer and sometimes even more effective than synthetic pharmaceuticals. On the other hand, according to the Journal of American Medical Association adverse reactions to medicines are the fourth leading cause of death in the United States. Herbal supplements do work and are highly effective, but only if you are using high-quality ingredients that are *given in the right quantity*.

All herbs may be purchased and consumed individually. However, it is more practical and effective to use a formula that was designed for you or your specific condition, that is why a personalized herbal supplement is a valuable service I provide to my clients. Always buy organic and from a reliable company such as Herb-Pharm, Gaia Herbs or my brand Moongazing Herbal Apothecary.

a. Cleansing Herbs

Take daily herbs that gently accelerate the cleansing process while supporting the liver and kidneys in flushing ingested and environmental toxins from the body such as:

- Dandelion
- Burdock
- Red clover
- Milk thistle
- Schizandra

b. The Diet

I believe that no one diet fits all. In my practice, I customized my client's diets based on their condition, constitution, personality and emotional issues that they may be experiencing. Yes! You read correctly; you can choose foods that will benefit you based on your makeup and emotions. This concept is based on eastern medicine where one of the fundamental principles is that we should eat according to who we are. Therefore, there is no such thing as a universal 'right' diet. Each person will have a different constitution and needs, consequently different nutritional needs. However, the following is a base diet that anyone regardless of their health condition can benefit from. You can add and remove foods based on your individual needs.

Buy organic produce whenever possible to limit your exposure to pesticide, GMOs and other environmental toxins. Additionally, organic fruits and vegetables are considerably more nutritious than non-organic.

What to eat?

- **Eat plenty of soups:** Soups are full of nutrients and are easier to digest.
- **Eat anti-oxidant, anti-inflammatory, detoxifying and nutrient-dense foods:** foods such as beets, cabbage, broccoli, cauliflower, leafy greens, kale, and turnips, radishes, carrots, brussels sprouts, sprouts, seedlings, chlorophyll, turmeric, garlic, onions and other medicinal spices.
- **Cilantro and Fiber:** Excrete toxins and excess hormones.
- **Green smoothies:** These juices should be made of primarily green vegetables with a little fruit like green apple for flavor.
- **Fermented foods:** These are full of probiotics that support gut and the detox process.
- **Berries:** Berries contain phytonutrients and antioxidants and are low in glycemic index.

How to eat?

Suggested meal times:

Time	Food
When you wake up	A cup of **Miso Soup** or **Lemon water**: Squeeze ½ a lemon in a cup of water, add honey or maple syrup to taste.
8:00 am	**Breakfast smoothie:** 1 cup of mixed greens, 1 carrot, ½ an avocado (or another source of good fat such as almonds or cashews), 1 stick of celery, 1 cucumber, a few basil leaves, 1 cup coconut milk, ½ a beet, ½ cup of mix berries, 1 scoop of pea protein powder.
10:00 am	**Green smoothie** of your choice.
12:00 pm	**Soup/Salad:** With plenty of good fats, fiber and clean protein.
3:00 pm	**Nutritive herbal tea:** Tea made with herbs such as nettles, oats, and alfalfa. Or **Chai Maca Latte:** Mix 1 tablespoon of maca, 1 tea bag of caffeine free chai, 1 cup of hot coconut milk. Add honey to taste.
6:00 pm	**Dinner:** Include organic meats and vegetables or soups.
8:00 pm	**Detox juice:** 1 bunch of cilantro, 1 cup of coconut water, honey to taste, juice of ½ of lemon. Blend ingredients.

Things to avoid

- **Gluten:** Stop eating gluten, only if you have an autoimmune disorder or if you are sensitive to it; otherwise eat organic gluten. This includes wheat, barley, and rye.

- **Dairy:** All cow milk products should be avoided, replace them with:

Dairy	Options
Milk	Coconut, almond, hazelnut, rice, hemp or cashew milk
Butter	Coconut oil, ghee
Yogurt	Coconut, or almond yogurt
Whey protein	Pea protein
Ice cream	Coconut, cashew or almond-based ice creams
Cheese	Cashew and other nut cheeses

- **Sugar:** In addition to table sugar, avoid foods that contain sugar or high fructose corn syrup. Use stevia, honey, maple syrup, agave as an alternative. Remove completely from your diet artificial or modified sugars, such as Splenda, aspartame and saccharine.
- **Caffeine:** Eliminate caffeine products as much as possible. If you have been using caffeine for a while, you might want to wean yourself off instead of going cold turkey. Use a coffee substitute such as Dande-blend or Teeccino's Dandelion Dark Roast instead of coffee.
- **Alcohol:** Leads to blood sugar imbalances, liver backlog, leaky gut and overgrowth of bacteria in the small intestine.
- All canned, jarred, boxed, smoked, bottled and otherwise preserved items.

II. <u>RESTORE GUT HEALTH</u>

Gut health is essential for your well-being. People with chronic illness, auto-immune disorders and allergies often have a leaky gut, or "intestinal permeability." A condition caused by toxins and infections in which the lining of the small intestine becomes unhealthy and may have cracks or holes causing undigested food particles, toxic waste products, and bacteria to "leak" through the intestines and go into the bloodstream. Consequently, causing an autoimmune response in the body including inflammatory and allergic reactions. Moreover, the intestines will not produce the necessary enzymes for proper digestion. As a result, the body cannot absorb essential nutrients, which can lead to chronic illnesses, hormone imbalances and a weakened immune system.

a. Herbs to restore the lining of the intestines:

A few of the best-known herbs to restore the lining of the intestine are:

- Marshmallow
- Licorice
- Plantain
- Chamomile
- Peppermint

Drink two cups of tea made with these herbs every day. Make with ½ oz. of herb for 16 oz. of water. Simmered on low heat for 20 mins (covered).

b. Balance the flora in your gut:

One of the leading causes of intestinal permeability is imbalanced flora in your gut including an overgrowth of yeast and candida. Several studies confirm that gut microbiota is engaged in a dynamic interaction with the immune system. When one or more steps in this interaction fail, autoimmune or chronic diseases occur. Therefore, improving your gut flora will enhance your health. Thus, *it is essential to add to this regimen a good probiotic supplement* and *antimicrobial herbs such as barberry, oregano, goldenseal or Oregon grape root.*

III. <u>MINIMIZE ENVIRONMENTAL TOXINS</u>

Identify chemical and metals you are being exposed to and eliminate them as much as possible:

- Replace teflon, stainless steel, and plastic cooking utensils with less toxic options, such as glass dishes, ceramic-coated pots and pans, and cast-iron skillets.
- Use wood utensils to cook instead of plastic-coated or metal utensils.
- Use Chlorine-free parchment paper instead of aluminum foil.
- Replace your plastic food storage containers with glass containers. If you use plastic, use BPA-free plastic (including storage bags).
- Remove chemicals such as fluoride and chlorine from your water.
- Add air-cleaning house plants to your home such as aloe vera, spider plant, dracaena, ficus, peace lily, Boston fern, snake plant, and bamboo palm or use an air purifier.
- Minimize your use of conventional personal care items such as shampoos, lotions, cleansers, makeup, antiperspirants, and perfumes and replace them with clean brands.
- Use EMF protection devices.

IV. <u>IMPROVE YOUR EMOTIONAL HEALTH</u>

Your emotional health plays a role in the health of your body. Scientists are now discovering that changes in our consciousness produce changes in our bodies. Each thought and feeling releases a particular set of biochemicals in our organs. Each experience triggers changes in our cells. Chronic stress and negative emotions such as worrying over mortgage payments, work stress, or keeping up with a packed schedule have an enormous negative impact on your health. Short-term stress can usually be dealt with, and as such, does not adversely affect our bodies. However, when stress is chronic, it begins to disrupt the natural process of the body, and the immune system begins to become impaired. Cortisol, a hormone produced by the adrenals when you are under stress, negatively affects the digestive and immune system. Therefore, accumulated stress can lead to allosteric overload where serious health problems can result.

There is nothing wrong with experiencing negative thoughts and emotions like anger, resentment, and personal need. The problem is with habitual negative thinking that goes on day-after-day, it creates stress and causes an imbalance in your body that contributes to disease. *Studies have linked chronic stress and negative emotions to headaches, infectious illness, cardiovascular disease, diabetes, asthma, gastric ulcers, high blood pressure, and high cholesterol.* Stress can also have an indirect effect on a person since people may use unhealthy coping strategies to reduce their stress, such as overeating, drinking, and smoking.

An essential step towards healing is to learn how to manage stress and negative emotions. Researchers have found that the simple process of journal writing about stressful incidents improves immune function. Moreover, there are hundreds of different techniques, including yoga, guided imagery, qigong, and meditation. Likewise, there are many ways to maintain good emotional health such as EFT, the Sedona method, the work from Byron Katie, CBT, CFT, Gestalt therapy, NLP and many more. Find the technique that works best for you and try to work on improving your emotional health daily.

Moreover, you can use herbs to help you manage stress and anxiety. Nervine and adaptogen herbs are nutritive and directly benefit the nervous system. Moreover, herbal nervine therapy increases our ability to cope with the stress of daily life. If you are under chronic stress, you may benefit from taking nerve tonic herbs on a regular basis such as:

Adaptogen	Nervine
Ashwagandha	Skullcap
Ginseng	Wood betony
Eleuthero	Chamomile
Reishi	Ca. poppy
Holy-Basil	Valerian
	Hops
	Lavender
	Oat straw

If you are wondering how long you should follow this protocol, the answer is until you are healthy again. Please note that it took years to get to where you are, therefore even if you feel better it might take years to recover fully. I have seen with my clients; treatment usually takes between three and six months. Assuming they follow this protocol every day. However, people with serious conditions may take between 18 and 24 months to fully recover. If you are healthy, or once you recovered you can follow this protocol twice a year as a detox program.

About Toni

Toni Camacho is a Holistic Health Practitioner (HHP) & Registered Herbalist (RH) in San Diego, California. She holds a Ph.D. in Psychology, an Herbalist Certificate and is a certified Canfield trainer on the Success Principles. In private practice as an HHP for over 13 years, she has been influenced by a variety of clinical modalities and orientations, and by the diverse life experiences of her clients.

Toni's approach to healing is multi-dimensional. In her work, she integrates the principles of Eastern and Western nutrition, herbololgy, energy medicine, energy psychology, Buddhist mindfulness and personal counseling to assist others in working through their physical or emotional blocks to attain optimal health, achieve their goals and dreams and improve their quality of life.

In addition to her private practice, Toni founded Moongazing Herbal Apothecary in 2013, with the vision of making accessible and affordable organic herbal health and skin care products, which can be used as alternatives to the toxic medications and skin care products that exist today. Moongazing's goal is to create the finest products free of synthetic materials from ethically-grown and harvested ingredients, as well as to improve the overall lifestyles of its clients by education and example.

Moongazing's products and Toni's practice support health in the areas of: immune support, cold/flu relief, Irritable Bowel Syndrome (IBS), cholesterol management, blood pressure regulation, hypothyroidism, blood sugar regulation, seasonal allergy relief, women's health (hormone balance, menopause symptom relief, fibroids, etc.), and men's, including detoxification and digestive tract cleansing, among others.

In clinic, Toni also guides and supports her clients to create a life filled with peace and joy, manifest romantic relationships, heal food and body image issues, clear financial fears and create abundance in every area of their lives. Consultations can be done at distance via Zoom, Facetime, Skype, or phone. Herbal supplements can be shipped.

You can contact Toni at:

- Toni.Camacho@MoongazingApothecary.com
- https://www.facebook.com/moongazingapothecary/
- https://twitter.com/MoongazingHA
- www.DrToniCamacho.com

CHAPTER 25

PLANNING FOR THE FUTURE IS THE KEY TO SUCCESS

BY ALEXANDRA JACKSON

Lawyers call planning for the future "estate planning," but it is really just personal planning for how you want things to happen when you are no longer able to handle them yourself. We all know that planning is king. No football team operates without plays and no army marches without tactics. Despite that, many do little planning for the future.

Let's take a look at Melanie. Melanie is a doctor in her mid-fifties, not yet ready to retire but thinking about it. She's married with one adult daughter. Her husband David is five years younger and works as an architect. They live in the same house she bought before marriage. Their daughter Charlotte is in her late twenties and just bought her own home in the same town. She works as an accountant. After her recent knee surgery, Melanie spent some time thinking about what might happen in the future and laid out her plan, which ultimately left her with better peace of mind and her family in a better financial situation. Here are some tips for replicating Melanie's success:

1. Know Who You're Trying to Benefit

The heart of every good plan is knowing your goals. If you aren't sure where you're going, it's hard to get there. The heading specifically says "who" (I have yet to meet anyone who wants their grandmother's wedding ring passed on to their daughter because they think the ring will enjoy it). Directions on what you want done are about relationships - the people (or pets) you like, and the ones you don't. Take gifts to charity, for example. Someone donating money to the Red Cross usually shows an interest in supporting blood drives and disaster relief, efforts to help people. Giving to a school shows someone wants to support educating the next generation. Knowing who you want to help, whether it's your family, your friends (or even your pets), or a charitable organization is the key to success.

Prioritize. Ideally, everyone would have enough resources to do everything they want in their future plan. However, most people don't. Knowing the goal is important and being able to prioritize goals to match your resources is critical. Sometimes, there is a tension between providing for a spouse versus passing an inheritance to children. Some planning tools, like a single-family trust, can create a tension when the trustee administering the trust has a duty to take case of both spouse and children. Be willing to compromise, or consider more complicated arrangements, to meet all your goals.

Remember, not all of your resources are tangible ones. Time is a resource too. If you want a trustee who will send out weekly reports on the trust, but you named your daughter who works full time and lives overseas as the trustee, consider whether having weekly reports or having your daughter in charge is more important.

Melanie knows she wants to protect two people in her future plan – her husband David and their daughter Charlotte. Melanie wants to protect her husband first, and her daughter second. David is older – retirement is creeping up, and there is not enough time left for him to recover if something goes badly wrong economically. Charlotte is young and has time to plan for the future. Since Melanie doesn't have unlimited resources, David will have to come first in her plan.

2. Know What Plan You Will Get If You Fail to Plan

The most overlooked part of future planning is that everyone has an "estate plan." Anyone who doesn't do their own planning will get (without any choice) their state's plan. Every state has laws about intestacy (dying without a will) which contain a series of assumptions about who gets what. In most states a person's spouse will receive part or all of their estate, on the assumption that is what you would have wanted (yes, even if you die in the middle of a bitter divorce). For some people, these default plans work. If you are one of them, great! Look no further, but make a mental note to later re-evaluate your plan. The two big things you need to watch out for going forward are: 1) changes in your circumstances and 2) changes in your state law.

If you are not one of the people these laws will work for, consider which parts of your goals and priorities don't line up with the state's default plan. Think of it like buying clothes – sometimes things fit right off the rack, and sometimes you need them altered. This same process applies if you have an estate plan but have not updated it recently – look at your plan and your current goals and make the same comparisons.

Let's go back to Melanie. In her state, if she dies with no plan, her husband would get everything. Her assets combined with David's assets should be enough to support him, but he would have to manage them well. Ideally, Melanie would like a plan where someone else manages, or at least assists David with his finances, in case he has health problems or his career does not go well.

3. <u>Consider Your Path</u>

Blacksmiths don't use a hammer where they need pliers, and neither should you. Consider whether what you want is best for the people you want to benefit. If you have a family business, a trust that keeps your business out of probate court and running smoothly may be more effective for protecting your family than a will. If you want a trust to avoid the time spent in probate, but you're a minimalist renting an apartment, consider whether a will would suffice without the costs of a maintaining a trust. If you want a will because it's less expensive, but your spouse is in full time care with dementia and will lose their Medicaid coverage if they inherit from you, a trust is more appropriate than a will. To quote Peter Drucker, "There is nothing so useless as doing efficiently that which should not be done at all," so take your priorities into consideration.

Common Estate Planning tools:

(i). Wills: The most familiar future planning tool for most people, this specifies the disposition of your property at death. Wills go through probate, which can be more or less lengthy and costly to your estate and your beneficiaries depending on how busy the Probate Court in your area is and whether anyone is trying to contest your will. Wills are still usually simpler to create and use than a trust, and cheaper, but not as flexible as trusts. Wills can also include guardianship provisions that dictate who will care for your minor children in case something happens to you.

(ii). Trusts: The other common estate planning device, these are more flexible but usually more complicated. They typically have more ongoing requirements for maintenance than a will and cost more (both in money and manpower). However, they are often more protective and can better suit more complicated family situations. Trusts can also allow assets to move without passing through probate, which can be very useful for planning for family businesses.

(iv). Insurance: Usually life insurance; this can be used in a variety of creative ways, including funding various other planning tools. Be sure to keep track of when your coverage(s) expire and what beneficiaries you have designated.

(v). Powers of Attorney and Living Wills: These flexible documents can allow trusted individuals to manage your assets – like property or accounts – as you lose interest or the ability to do so or become unable to make health care decisions for yourself. Although they don't always spring to mind immediately, for most people these are important and useful tools for successful planning.

Melanie's plan:

Melanie loves David, but Melanie always managed the family accounts because David has never met a set of golf clubs he didn't need. When he was a bachelor, he lived month-to-month without much thought for the future. Melanie is concerned that David will have a hard time in retirement, when he has more time to spend money and less to spend. Charlotte, on the other hand, has Melanie's frugal habits and a keen head for budgeting, but Melanie doesn't want to just give her the house and hope everything will go smoothly. The option that would give Melanie the most peace of mind is to create a trust for her husband with Charlotte as the trustee. The trust can be as broad or as narrow as Melanie wants and is able to fund.

4. <u>Clarity is King</u>

Nothing frustrates people you have appointed to key roles in your future plan like lack of clarity. If your will says you want your sister to receive the painting of water lilies in your living room, and you moved it to another room five years later and never changed that language in the will, the executor of your estate is in an awkward position. Likewise, if you have a trust, be clear in the language what the trustee should be doing. Directing that a trustee should pay for anything "necessary to the happiness" of a beneficiary is very different than directing them to pay for "school tuition, school books, and room and board in campus housing only." If you have a goal, say it. Flexibility is wonderful, but you don't want your plan to be so flexible it is aimless, either.

Melanie's decision to appoint Charlotte as trustee gives her some relief because she knows Charlotte will look after her father. However, there may be areas where Charlotte would be more lenient than her mother, or Melanie may not want to put Charlotte in the position of having to say no to her father. For example, Melanie is worried primarily about providing David with a place to live, so she puts language in the trust directing the trustee, Charlotte, to pay David's housing expenses, including his utilities. However, Melanie knows that David has been angling for a hot tub for ages, so she explicitly directs Charlotte not to pay for any costs related to installation or maintenance of a hot tub. Being clear about what is and is not a housing cost helps Charlotte take care of David and avoid friction by taking the decision out of Charlotte's hands.

5. Tell Key People About Your Plan

The most successful plans are not surprises. If everyone in your family knows your plan, and it's consistent over time, it is unlikely to be contested. Proof that your family knew about your plan and said nothing well before you died, makes it hard to contest.

Always tell people who are key to your plan (such as guardians for your children, or trustees) that they are part of your plan. Ideally, always ask before naming anyone to roles that require time or effort. Some may not want to take on that responsibility. You should also name backups.

You are often best served by selecting someone who shares your views and would choose similar things, particularly with people who have the power to make health care decisions for you. Research shows that people often make the decision they think is personally best, not necessarily what they think the person they are deciding for would want. If you are explicit enough in your directions, this is rarely an issue, because your directions create a basis for other people to object to decisions against your wishes. But it's better to pick someone who won't be up at night if your wishes go against their moral compass.

If you're in a situation where you feel unsafe or uncomfortable telling someone about your plan, by all means, don't, but take appropriate safeguards. Leave copies of important documents in safe places where the people you are concerned about will not be able to reach them, like your doctor's office (for health care directives) or attorney's office (for your will or similar document) and in a safe deposit box with the second key with someone you trust.

At the end of the day, the key is this: methodical planning will get you much further than haphazard planning or no planning at all. Do it right and revisit it regularly, and you will never leave your family stranded in a time of need.

About Alexandra

Alexandra Jackson has literally grown up with the law. She has been surrounded by lawyers her whole life (including her father, uncle, and cousin), to the despair of her social worker mother. She started working in her father's law office at the age of 14 as a part time receptionist and worked there through summers in college and law school.

Alexandra attended Smith College in Northampton, Massachusetts. During college, she majored in East Asian Languages and Cultures with a concentration in Japan. She learned Japanese and spent her junior year in Kyoto, Japan, where she attended Doshisha University. She was on the Dean's list each year she was in Northampton and earned a Liberal Arts Commendation in addition to playing in the Handbell Choir and participating in the Creative Writing Club, among other activities.

Because of her successes at Smith, Alexandra was offered a merit scholarship by the University of Maine School of Law, where she graduated *cum laude*. While at Maine Law, she also made time to participate in the Transactional Law Society and the Women's Law Association. During law school, Alexandra attended several national seminars by the National Organization of Veterans Advocate as a student member, and upon graduation became a full time supporting member in addition to her membership in the American and Maine Bar Associations. She is admitted to both the Maine and New Hampshire bars as well as the bar of the Court of Appeals for Veterans Claims.

During law school, Alexandra determined that in addition to practicing Veterans Law part of the time, she wanted to combine her parents' interests in law and in working with families to develop her own specialty – focusing on planning for families and businesses. To that end, she extensively studied business and tax issues, including estate planning for families, small business owners and elder law. She recently attended the prestigious Heckerling Institute of Estate Planning to hone her skills.

When not practicing law, Alexandra loves to travel, particularly to Japan. She has been to five continents and vows to get to South America and Antarctica to complete her sweep of all seven. When home, she enjoys creative writing, playing video games, and spending time with her cats.

CHAPTER 26

WOMAN TO WOMAN

BY GERI MAGEE, Ph.D.

There is no better time than now! As the world celebrated the 2nd International Women's Day on March 8, 2018, I found myself reflecting back in amazement at the women who inspired me to keep going, to keep trying, and to never give up.

Many of my inspirational mentors are gone now, which I realized now leaves me to be an inspiration for women around the world. Through my hard work, and dedication to numerous national and international organizations over the years, I have gained great insight into various realms of cultural union and division. Seeing diversity with open eyes and heart has encouraged me to still keep going under adverse situations and ill health that I am overcoming in my own life.

I have watched and participated in, with adoration, the multi-woman marches around the globe in honor of women over the past two years. Being able to be a part of such a movement, for each of us to care for the other in compassion, love, sincerity and pride, has touched me to the depths of my heart. I have such great admiration for women around the world. I love that we have had a chance to have our voices heard. However, there are still many who do not even know they have a voice or cannot speak up because of persecution by societal norms.

As women, we need to continue to push forward. We have now shown the world we are bonded, and we can obtain unity of sisterhood, no matter what or who stands in our way. It does not mean you need to be a radical. But consider becoming a successful agent of change instead, not only for ourselves, but for the future generations that come after us, both female and male. I am feeling honored today in writing this chapter – a beautiful gift that the universe has given me to share my strength, wisdom and knowledge with the world – which has always been my personal successful endeavor.

I am a firm believer in the Laws of Attraction. Jack Canfield has written *The Key to Living the Law of Attraction*, one of his recent publications, which I truly enjoyed reading. I attended Jack's appearance in Seattle and in my life in August 2017, when I attended "One Day to Greatness." I had the opportunity to attend the VIP luncheon and was able to introduce myself to Jack as his next business partner; needless to say, the room cracked up. So here I am on that journey alongside him, co-authoring this book along with other successful individuals like myself.

As I have gone through life's journey from the unknown to the known. I watched and learned from my family, friends, colleagues and acquaintances, the lessons of life. However, the biggest lesson of all that I observed and I continue to learn for myself, is the knowledge that knowing one's self is the essential part of success.

- How do I communicate?
- What are my likes/dislikes?
- What are my needs vs. my wants?
- How do I define this, and above all, be able to have the finesse to be successful in the world?
- How do I set boundaries as well as respect others' boundaries?
- How do I assert myself for the wellbeing of all?
- Do I respect and consider myself, as well as others who are around me?
- Do I practice on a spiritual path that brings me to the awakening of enlightenment, joy and happiness?
- Am I content that I can share my strengths with others on my life's path?

Many look to the universe to find solace within the scientific and metaphysical world with amazement and awe. Other questions we need to ask ourselves as complete individuals:

- Who am I as a sexual being?
- Do I take comfort and express myself to my partner?
- Is it in a healthy, open fashion to create that special intimate bond between two people?
- Do I talk about what arouses me and what does not?
- How have I developed my most intimate relationships with myself and others both personally and professionally?

These were questions I asked myself throughout my life's journey. My mentors have asked these of me as well, along that exuberant, bumpy, exhilarating and very eventful ride of life.

We are here for one another. The more we know ourselves, the more we grow and can share our lives with others, we find that balance is not an easy feat. Growing up, my mother always said, "Well, life isn't fair." True, I agree, but I also believe we have choices on our life's path to choose to see through various lenses. So why not choose lenses that help you see the light at the end of the tunnel as well as the variance of a colorful life. We are a reflection of the life around us, so choose who you associate with, that keep you in that heart-and-mind frame. The lenses I have chosen have aided me in surviving this confusing world. This alone keeps me essentially whole of heart and open minded. I choose to find solutions around me or in me. I continue to grow and advance essentially because my system is continuously growing, changing and adapting. And so I must, if I want to keep the state of mind, body and soul that has allowed me to flourish in life itself.

Now, I am here to share a small part of my journey with you. From GED to PhD, the many lessons I have learned are not from a degree but from a Godly/universal direction. However, especially in today's workforce, education is needed to move forward to sustain one's own life. I have been a mentor to both women and men through my two careers. I predominantly worked in an all-male environment that was, and still is, driven by men. This is where I learned fortitude and discernment.

I learned about human nature, through ironic and comical ways of life, to help aid individuals, couples, families and businesses as a financial planner, banker, mentor and later as a therapist and theorist, during my second major career shift in mid-life after completing most of my educational goals. This gave me great insight. Two-thirds of my clients were women that I educated and aided in regards to finances as well as therapeutically, in order to find the freedom and be able to find balance and an enjoyable life. I believe that by fortifying myself in advance through a male-dominated career. I was able to bring insight to many women and men as I worked and played in life. I found there is a karmic balance of fairness for one to keep going, learning and growing one's self in the miraculous balance of life. As I traveled to cities, states/provinces and countries for either work or pleasure, I gained insight into the larger systemic world around me. I share this journey for those that wish to listen. As I have listened to those who have taught me in the past, now I bring that knowledge, love and compassion to the forefront of the current world we live in.

As I continue to develop myself, I bring both the female and male aspects of my characteristic traits with the multitude of hats I wear on a daily basis. Each day is a new adventure of life in knowing one's self and sharing yourself with others. Even though many days may have been hard, I look back into my own life to see the karmic balance. It's amazing how we, as humans, can obtain so much knowledge from the world and universe around us, which keeps us sustaining the pressures of life and every day challenges. But diversity is where we grow the most.

I firmly believe that the 'school of hard knocks' is where our fortitude comes from as an individual and a participant in a very large, universal system. However, as I mentioned earlier, in today's world, education is a must. It gives us the foundation and basics of human development with insight into ourselves, as well as the various environments and their systems in which we participate daily, for us to interact with the equilibrium bringing us to the homeostasis of the norm with which we are to engage with others. However, I believe there is relevance to bring all of one's authentic self to each of the variances, so we can remain whole and balanced in our individuality, while participating personally and professionally in life. Not all have the opportunity to attend school. So then we learn by each encounter and endeavor we participate in. That's where we all diverge from others to become our own individual self, mind, body and soul once more.

Is an education needed? ... many ask. My answer is what have you learned from life? Life itself is an educational experience. Not all have the opportunity to sit in a classroom or have access to the internet or books for self-educating. But they still exist and grow. That's when the systemic community around them is one's own classroom of experiential teaching from society's norms and expectations. Prior to my degrees, I learned by doing, watching and listening. Like many women did in my era, we all watched in awe the advancement of women on the global societal platform.

Ironically, my own advancement came from helping others, to the benefit of myself, my family, my friends, my colleagues and my communities – both small and large – all with which I learned to be the kind, compassionate leader that I am. My goal was to educate myself while I was learning, to give as I was given, and to advance to the best of my ability. Without my degrees, I was unable to advance to certain levels that I knew I was more than qualified for, based on my years of experience. I was 'ceilinged' out, continuously. By being one of the first women in the development of insurance products, policies, procedures and technological advancement of applications in various industries aided me in being able to feed my family, put a roof over our heads and have some luxuries in life that many women still cannot do in the societal demands and roles women must play/endure to survive.

I developed myself through life with the aid of multiple communities, self-help and inspirational books, lectures and meetings, as well as various associations with people, businesses and organizations. All were predominantly symbiotic relationships in aiding each other in endeavors to reach the highest potential at each point and time in life.

Because of my personal need for insight, enlightenment and self-advancement for myself as an aide for all around me, I was granted a great opportunity to carry a message to others. I held onto that dearly precious gift that the universe bestowed on me. That gift of motherhood and grandmotherhood is one of the most precious gifts that I treasure.

Being able to share the gift of knowledge through womanhood from childhood to adulthood is a blessing. I can now share these things with those that choose to be enlightened and are looking towards advancement of themselves and their systems through the various messages I received from the universe – to help woman/mankind through understanding and utilization of the Universal Relationship Pyramid™ – primarily as a public speaker, educator and mentor.

As I became ill, I found myself in bed for long periods of time. I had time for reflection. I used this basic pyramid tool as a thought process to aid me in the multitude of systems in which I participated in life to find balance and wholeness once more. I developed the Universal Relationship Pyramid™ theory years ago, prior to my dual degrees in Business Globalization/psychology Bachelors and Masters in Systemic Therapy/Business Organization and PhD in Diversity. Along the way I have added to it to help myself and others. All that participated in my life unknowingly helped aid in the development of the Universal Relationship Pyramid theory – a brick-by-brick breakdown formula to see where you are in your relationship with yourself, your higher power and others. Take it one day at a time.

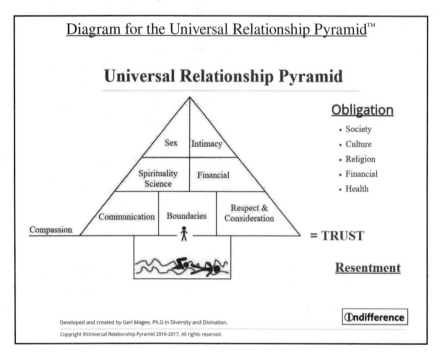

236

About Geri

Geri Magee, Ph.D. is an honest, direct, and assertive woman whose life journey has helped both women and men from around the world achieve their potential. She has developed herself as a business woman/proprietor, a public speaker, educator, therapist/mentor, contractor and employee for Fortune 500 companies.

Throughout Geri's life, she has held many different roles; her best is that of a single mother. Her success is not something she did alone but with the help of the community around her.

Geri started as a Financial and Estate Planner at age 23. She later made a midlife career shift after earning a Bachelors and Masters Degree both in Business Globalization/Organization Development and Systemic Therapy and a PhD in Diversity. Geri believes you don't need to be aggressive with people. She has observed in her life that aiding others multiplies success. Geri helps others to stand up and work together to achieve their goals. That's true teamwork in motion! Leaving someone on the sidelines was never her 'cup of tea'. She looks for the potential of each individual around her and couples it with her own to make the world better.

In 1992, Geri first started her career in the insurance industry, and become an expert in the field of asset allocations and preservation of assets within two years. She worked mainly with women to develop secure investment strategies for financial freedom. At that time, she was one of the few licensed women in the industry. Top banking and insurance companies recruited her to develop their insurance and financial divisions.

It wasn't easy for women in the industry to accomplish, but her 29 years of successfully creating multiple products and programs aided her in working and contracting for major companies such as Allstate, AAA, Hartford, Safeco, NY Life and Mass Mutual, managing multiple locations simultaneously through multi-tasking and adaptability.

Geri's received several 'Woman of the Year' awards both professionally and personally. She has background as a p/t radio host and has been on *Good Morning America, Sacramento* magazine and is a member and multiple-award winner of IWLA.

Geri specializes in solution-focused and experiential therapy practices, coupled with degrees in business organization. She owned two practices in Western and Eastern Washington until 2014. Then she became ill but is now beating all odds and statistics. Geri remains healthy and positive about life, an inspiration to all that meet her.

Geri created the "Universal Relationship Pyramid" with theories she used for over twenty years in both profit and non-profit organizations. She states that utilizing the "Universal Relationship Pyramid" is easy to do if you break the pyramid down brick by brick. You can create the life you want. First by understanding who you are and secondly by how you choose to react and resolve the various situations and environments around you. After ten sessions most clients never return, successfully resolving situations in their own systemic world. Clients/Patients learn multiple skillsets from the Universal Relationship Pyramid to move from the unknown into the known.

CHAPTER 27

YOUR ENERGY MATTERS!

BY LARI WARD

My client was visibly upset as she said: "I am so tired of the doing the same thing over and over again; same job, similar man-just a new name, same lack of money. I feel like my life story is on a merry-go-round. I repeat mistakes, say 'yes' to wrong relationships and make and lose the same amount of money. WHAT IS WRONG with me? Why do I repeat the same self-defeating patterns over and over again? I'm smart, I should know better. I am SO stressed by this. I try to change and I can't." My client had big dreams and great ideas, yet something always seemed to get in her way of feeling successful in all areas of her life.

It is often the positive thoughts and dreams we *don't* act on that shape our lives. We create positive intentions and then wonder, "Why can't I follow through; why isn't this working?" The reason positive thinking often fails is because it is a thin veneer over the negative messages that have become embedded in your subconscious mind. Your life stories, beliefs and habits are created from the messages you heard from parents, teachers, siblings, friends, church, school. It would be great if all you heard was encouragement growing up and how wonderful you are, but sadly this is not the case for the majority of people.

Each and every single one of us is living a story that is only partially ours. You may be living your mother's insecurity or embodying your uncle's anger. You may also have the compassion of your grandmother and your father's ingenuity. Many of the beliefs about yourself are created by the time you are 5 to 7 years old. From the time you are born, your experiences and what you hear are repeated in different forms every day until they become embedded in your subconscious and, some believe, in your cells and DNA. They affect your self-concept, becoming habits and beliefs which then can block your innate gifts. Unfortunately, this storyline, which most of the time is not true, defines how you feel, think and ultimately act each day. How can you move towards success when you feel stuck and living with limiting beliefs that are not yours?

Our thoughts and beliefs are a form of energy, which we transmit out to the world via the morphogenic field. Think of this field as the 'world wide web' of energy that is constantly moving around and out from you. Your thoughts are like magnets and attract back to you that which you send out, all without you even being aware of it. If you feel unworthy you will be transmitting this lower vibration and find yourself never receiving what you truly want. Growing up, my client constantly heard: "You are not good enough. Why do you always settle for second best? Why would you want to do that? You will never succeed, you're too scatterbrained." Memories such as these are frequently called into action, resulting in you doing the same things over and over.

John, another client, was approaching the review of his contract with a prestigious consulting firm. He wanted to increase his consulting salary and negotiate better terms but he couldn't get up the nerve to talk to his CEO. He believed he wasn't as good as others and felt powerless. During my work with John, he discovered a distant memory of coming home from school when he was 10 years old to find his mother had given his dog away. He was devastated. As part of his personal story, he believed that he had no power or choice in things that mattered the most to him – and that people in authority always prevailed. By working with this limiting belief, John was able to move forward and negotiate a very lucrative contract with the company. He shifted his belief of being powerless and not good enough to one of confidence and influence.

All of our encounters are recorded as experiences, and these experiences influence our way of being, thinking and acting. Every encounter has the opportunity to trigger a deeply embedded pattern or emotion. Such as with John. He was highly successful, yet felt powerless. When there is an unresolved emotion such as fear, anger, panic, worry or grief, the body's cellular memory keeps you repeating the pattern until the emotions and beliefs surrounding the original experience(s) are shifted out of the body's subconscious. Our mind is our greatest ally as well as our biggest trickster, as it likes to ruminate in the past, keeping us on the same merry-go-round, even when we are tired of the ride. Success is just a concept and our beliefs as well as judgements about ourselves come well before we understand what success even means. Our lifelong patterns are rooted in our energy and mind. To evolve and change we have to disrupt and reframe them.

Through the use of Energy Medicine, I began to look at my client's personal stories in a different way. Thoughts, feelings, beliefs and habits are all just energy. They have a life and vibration of their own. Thoughts create your reality. Happy one day, upset the next, moving forward on a project and then sabotaging or distracting yourself. You attract people, events and circumstances into your life that validate your stories and beliefs. You may fear success, feel you are not good or worthy enough, or don't deserve to be highly successful in all areas of your life. You continue to have the same type of arguments, meet the same type of people, or have ongoing issues with money, work or love. Same scenarios, different times.

It's frustrating, especially when you want to shift to a new paradigm. So why do you end up in the same place over and over again, despite your best efforts? Because *anything outside your comfort zone is not yet programmed into the cellular energy of your subconscious.* Your mind is designed to keep you safe in the here and now. Any change from what you know or are comfortable with causes a *stress response* in your body. When your body/mind tries to shift out of a limiting belief, the sympathetic nervous system activates the fight, flight or freeze response at a primal level, which overrides your positive intentions. It is the mind's role to keep you safe. This means that even a negative familiar pattern is safer than a positive new pattern.

Our sympathetic nervous system cannot discern between a Tyrannosaurus Rex walking into the room and a fear of being rejected, or any of our other limiting beliefs. To evolve beyond limitations, to create new life stories, all you have to do is calm your primal response, which will shift the body/mind energy! This creates a new normal, allowing you to evolve into a higher sense of being.

"Seriously? All I have to do is release the stress caused by unresolved emotions and limiting beliefs?" The answer is a resounding *"Yes!"*

Stress is the emotional and/or physical response to a psychological, physical, or environmental state, either real or imagined. The mind perceives a stressor as an emergency and sends the majority of the blood from the forebrain to the chest and extremities. The body/mind is placed in an instant "fight, flight or freeze" situation. We can run but we can't think clearly!

This stress, which can be triggered by limiting beliefs and emotions, can keep you in a constant state of alert. What happens then is that you can feel fearful, anxious, depressed, worried, or angry and unable to let go of repetitive patterns. Change or even the desire for change creates more stress and since your energy is designed to keep you safe you go back to the known pattern, behavior and story. Maintaining the status quo is easier; pushing through requires a new belief, mind-set and energy.

You can change your life by changing your energy, which will shift you to empowering patterns and will subvert unresolved limiting beliefs and emotions. Using simple energy techniques, you can tap directly into the sympathetic nervous system while you are focused on the unresolved emotions and beliefs. This then resets the emergency stress response loop and eliminates the triggers of unresolved issues.

These three easy *Energy Interventions* are your power tools of transformation. Use them for everything. Begin by saying, *"I have the **energy** of stress, I am **not** the stress."* Once you recognize that you just have the *energy* of stress then you are open to shift it.

This following technique reduces the symptoms produced by the fight, flight or freeze response and brings a sense of calm and reduces fear, by quickly re-programing the body's sympathetic nervous system.

RELAXING IN THE MIDST OF CHAOS

1. Place the palm of your hand on your forehead.
2. Put the other hand on the back of your skull right above where the head curves into the neck.
3. *Drop into your thoughts, limiting beliefs and stress.* There is no need to feel or think positive thoughts as it's better to sink into your feelings of the moment while you are holding the points.

4. Hold this position, stay focused and breathe gently until you feel a pulse in the palm of your hand on your forehead or for 2-3 minutes, whichever comes first. For deep shifts hold up to 20 minutes or longer.

Once you feel the pulsing in your hand, shift to a positive image or thought and hold for a minimum of 2-3 minutes. Longer is better for lasting change. Joy and radiance shift deeply-embedded patterns.

In Chinese medicine, the hand on the forehead is over points that bring the blood back to the forebrain and the back hand is over points that reduce fear. When you bring the blood back to the thinking portion of the brain (forebrain) while being in the stress, the mind will begin to no longer recognize the thought or situation as stressful and won't react in the future. You are reframing your limiting beliefs.

TRANSFORMATIONAL TAP

This powerful energy technique, also known as the Temporal Tap, was developed by Dr. George Goodheart in the 70's and revived by Donna Eden, has been found to dramatically shift our habit fields. Myself, as well as many clients have attracted money, relationships and jobs into our lives just by doing this frequently. This energy intervention taps into the portion of your brain and nervous system that works to maintain core beliefs, behaviors, habits and attitudes. It calms the brain, opening it to receive new information, thereby establishing new habits and emotional responses. It is as if you are updating your computer's operating system and installing positive new programs. Use this for EVERYTHING and watch how your limiting beliefs and life stories change.

Identify the thought, feeling, habit or belief you want to change then reframe it and create a new intention. For example, you choose to shift from feeling not good enough to believing you are successful. Your intention could then be: *"I am relaxed, focused and successful in all areas of my life."* Now combine this with the transformational tap.

TRANSFORMATIONAL TAP TECHNIQUE

Note: If you are left-handed, reverse this process: Around the right ear tap the negatively-worded positive statement. Around the left ear tap in the positive statement.

1. Begin by tapping firmly with the pads of your fingers in front of your left ear and continue tapping on the temporal bone around and behind your ear. Repeat the tapping sequence three to five times saying a negatively-worded positive phrase such as, *"I no longer worry about not being good enough."*
2. Tap around your right ear beginning at the temple in front of your ear. Repeat your positive intention such as, *"I am relaxed, focused and successful in all areas of my life."* Or, *"I am successful in all areas of my life."* Create your own and **always** phrase it as if it is already a fact. Tap around your ear three to five times while saying your intention.
3. Repeat the entire sequence three times, beginning with left ear then right ear.
4. After each sequence of affirmations, stretch the lobes of your ears by pulling them outwards. Begin at the bottom and go all the way around to the top.
5. Repeat the technique several times a day.

Be patient with yourself. You have been wired with these limiting beliefs most of your life. It will take time for them to resolve and create new patterns. TRUST and stay with the process. Once your mind integrates your affirmation/intention and your sympathetic nervous system no longer activates the stress response, you can create a new intention to work with.

ACTIVATE YOUR RADIANT IMAGINATION.

Do what is fun and brings you joy as you move into this phase of evolution and change. My acronym for JOY is **J**uiced **O**n **Y**es. Say YES to life. When you activate joy, you leave behind self-judgement and blame. To energetically tap into your innate radiance, cross your arms and put your hands underneath your armpits with your thumbs against your chest. Visualize in great detail and color what you want in your life; make it big, happy, and in present time. Sit with this for a few minutes and do daily. You are raising your energy vibration which will then attract like energy to you.

As your energy evolves, so will your business, relationships, and all other areas of your life. If you own a business, these same strategies will help evolve the company.

As you begin to shift your old stories just know that success begins in the heart, not in the mind. Accept yourself as you are: insecurities, old stories, things you have labeled as failures. View them as a blanket over your life. They have held and covered you, but they don't define you. You are not your past, nor are you how people have seen or judged you. You are not the trauma, the fears or the limiting beliefs. Neither are you your accomplishments or someone else's perception of who you should be. You have survived and thrived on the bumpy roads you have taken and you are gloriously alive. Your greatest success is really loving the essence of who you are today.

Use the Energy Techniques to bring your heart and mind together to expand your brilliant essence into the world, while letting go of your limiting beliefs. Allow your energy to radiate, rather than contract. It is time to throw off the blanket, turn the page and write a new chapter. Are you ready?

I think so….. *just go for it* and remember…

YOUR ENERGY MATTERS - and you have the power to create a new normal.

About Lari

Lari Ward, R.N., EEM-AP is an Eden Energy Medicine Certified Advanced Practitioner, highly-intuitive facilitator, mentor and teacher. She guides people through their own personal renaissance to shift old stories, patterns, and beliefs using the power of energy medicine and energy psychology tools.

Lari's passion for transformational energy work helps people re-calibrate their lives for clarity, vitality, abundance and joy. She has been credited as being the catalyst of change for individuals, entrepreneurs, small businesses, major healthcare corporations, and even a high school sailing team.

For the past 48 years, Lari has been helping people create better lives. She has provided powerful mentorship to entrepreneurs and emerging leaders that are ready to breakthrough boundaries and embrace abundance in all areas of their lives. In her private energy medicine practice, she has compassionately guided people back to living healthy lives.

Lari graduated from St Paul's School of Nursing in Vancouver, BC, and attended the University of Washington post grad. She is a consummate learner and always curious about new ways of being and growing.

After being an ICU nurse and watching the disempowerment of patients and staff, she created an innovative management consulting firm. For 28 years, Lari worked with major healthcare systems, clinics and physicians to create pioneering and progressive solutions to problems and new forms of business. For the past 15 years, she has been dedicated to mentoring entrepreneurs, teaching and practicing Eden Energy Medicine. Lari is a senior faculty member for the Eden Energy Medicine Certification Program.

Lari has taught and worked in the USA, Canada, UK, New Zealand, and Australia. Her most exhilarating experience was teaching children in Kenya how to balance their energies. Her workshops are always fun, enlightening and transformational.

A small town in Washington State with a dynamic view of the Olympic Mountains is where Lari calls home. She loves life, being in nature and travel. She is also an award-winning photographer and has two grown sons. New adventures or a good book both bring radiance to her life.

Lari's transformational work will guide you to access your ageless wisdom and leave behind limitations, so you can live with heart, spirit and abundance. She asks: "Is now the time to be all that you are?"

Remember: **Your Energy Matters!**

Lari can be reached at:

- Tel: (360) 697-5999
- Email: lariward@earthlink.net or lari@lariward.com
- Mailing Address: 24400 Rhododendron Lane NW, Poulsbo, WA. 98370

For more information, visit:

- www.lariward.com.

Acknowledgement
Author's photo by: INGRID PAPE-SHELDON PHOTOGRAPHYP.O. Box 77624, Seattle, WA 98177
EMAIL: ingrid@pape-sheldon.com OFFICE: 206-985-9978

CHAPTER 28

ENVIRONMENTAL INFLUENCES

IS YOUR ENVIRONMENT DRIVING YOU TOWARDS OR AWAY FROM SUCCESS?

BY LAUREEN GABRIELLE

You are a product of your environment.
~ W. Clement Stone

Becky ended her call with a mix of pride and dread.

Becky was just informed by her local newspaper that she was selected to be featured as one of the small business owner success stories. The feature requires the business owner to submit an article along with a case study of their approach to success. As a Coach, Becky was proud to have been selected by the town's people, and happy that the press coverage would boost her business. The timing couldn't be better as she had hoped to expand her part-time coaching practice into a full-time career.

However, she was overcome by waves of fear as she relived stressful memories associated with having to write papers during her college days. She'd rather 'shoot herself in the foot' than create a literary piece of work. There was a lot of negative self-talk swirling around in Becky's head. Ironically, Becky was experiencing the very same negative self-talk she coached her clients to overcome. It was obvious to Becky that she had a lack of self-confidence when it came to writing.

Becky fell into coaching through a series of serendipitous events, and since she did so well with growing her business, she didn't invest the time to be formally trained or obtain a coaching certification. Part of Becky's anxiety with writing about her success was that she didn't have a manual from which she could draw upon to explain her approach to coaching. All of the tools and practices she used with her coaching clients were driven more by her intuitive nudges than proven theory.

Becky's entire town, as well as the surrounding community, would now have the opportunity to peer into her approach to coaching. The more Becky thought about the situation, the more exposed and vulnerable she felt. The same thoughts played over and over in her head, "Could I really write a good article? How will my approach to coaching be perceived by others? What if people find me inept due to my lack in coaching credentials? How should I decide on what case study to include in the article?"

The following day, Becky didn't feel any better as her anxiety level increased. She contacted her own coach, Jane, to get some guidance and input. When Becky explained the situation to Jane, she saw immediately that Becky needed to begin the session with some stress relief techniques.

Jane then coached Becky through a few PSYCH-K® Balances to address the limiting beliefs that were causing Becky's negative self-talk and anxiety. Becky recently learned about PSYCH-K® and was considering getting trained to provide the same practices to her own clients.

PSYCH-K® is beneficial for addressing limiting subconscious beliefs by enabling the right and left-brain hemispheres to communicate allowing for a "whole brain state". This state empowers an individual to move beyond resistance and/or limiting beliefs in an accelerated way to successfully achieve goals. For Becky, the current goal was to feel a sense of confidence with writing her article in a creative and intelligent manner. Becky's session with Jane was wrapped up with some can-do affirmations.

Between the stress relief exercises, PSYCH-K® Balances and positive affirmations, she practiced with Jane, Becky felt unstoppable! Becky was reminded of the value and importance of getting coached by Jane and felt grateful to have a partner in this situation.

With this newfound sense of confidence, Becky decided 'to strike while the iron was hot' and began to think of ideas on how to approach her article and case study. As she took some time to reflect back on her coaching practice, she could not think of a single most influential aspect of a person's ability to achieve success, than their environment. The light bulb went off! That would be the focus of the content of her article.

Broadly speaking, a person's environment – the people and situations they encounter on a daily basis, as well as the thoughts and emotions that comprise their emotional environment – plays a major role in their ability to achieve success.

Throwing all caution to the wind, Becky plunked herself down at her computer and began to type…

> We each interface with multiple environments. A person's external environment includes people, places and things in a home environment, work environment or elsewhere. Internally, we have thoughts and emotions that drive our behavior. At a fundamental level, our internal environment is based on our beliefs. We have beliefs for which we are consciously aware such as our beliefs about religion, politics, etc. We also have subconscious beliefs for which we may not be aware. Subconscious beliefs could span generations of old thinking habits, patterns and behaviors.
>
> Even more important than the environments in which we intermingle is our perception of those environments. Two different people could experience the same exact environmental conditions and come away with two entirely different perceptions. These perceptions are strongly based on a person's inherent belief patterns. An individual prone to a negative belief pattern can perceive particular environmental conditions as being obstacles and barriers. Whereas an individual with a positive belief pattern can perceive the same exact environmental conditions as beneficial opportunities.
>
> Now let's evaluate your situation. Since we have both external and internal environments, let's start with the most physically pronounced, the external environment. Think about your home, are you comfortable being there? Do you find it to be a place of refuge where you can recharge your batteries before going back out into

the world? Now, think about your work environment. Is it cluttered or open and airy allowing space for you to think and be creative? Your work environment can have an immense impact on your productivity. It is important to know what kind of work environment suits you and brings out the most of what you have to offer. Then, there is the actual work that you do in that environment. Do you enjoy it? Do you find it meaningful and fulfilling?

People have a profound effect on an environment. According to Harvard's 75-year longitudinal study, nothing has a greater impact on someone's health, wellbeing and overall success in life than their relationships with people.[1] Do you feel a sense of love and connection with the people in your life? Do you enjoy spending time with them? Think about the stressors you experience in life, and whether they are associated with your relationships with people. The easiest way to tell the impact people have on your life is to evaluate your emotional state while spending time with them. Do you feel happy and relaxed or on edge and irritated? Do they lift you up or drain your energy?

Let's face it; it's not always easy or even possible to remove people from an environment. Ultimately, the only thing you have control over are your thoughts. If you are unable to make changes with the people in your life, you must realign your thinking and stressful reaction towards those people.

Nothing has more of an effect on your life than your mindset. Your internal environment, which includes your beliefs and thoughts, are generated from both your conscious and subconscious mind. Your conscious mind is used for logical thinking and reasoning. Then there is the subconscious mind for which you may not even be aware of when it is in use. However, it controls a whopping 90% of your behavior. Yes, you read that correctly. Imagine not even being consciously aware of the behavior pattern you default to day-in and day-out due to your subconscious mind?

To better explain the subconscious mind and how it works, think of a time when you were learning a new task such as how to drive a car. You were aware of every move your body had to make to turn the car, accelerate the gas, press down on the brakes, etc. If you have driven for some time, you can likely attest that it requires very little conscious thought to operate a car. Why? Because your subconscious mind stored these memories as a program. This program in your subconscious mind is then engaged while you drive so your conscious mind does not need to be.

Here is another example of your subconscious mind in action. Recall a time when you were going about your business and a particular song came on the radio that you hadn't heard in a long time. Immediately, out of nowhere, you were transported back to a certain event or period in your life as if you had effortlessly stepped back in time. This is an example of the remarkable power of the subconscious mind. All along, it has stored the memory of the song with the attachment of that particular event or period in your life. Have you given conscious thought or effort to storing that information in your memory? No. The subconscious is always working on your behalf behind the scenes.

Here's the kicker, the subconscious can work for or against us – making the difference between success and failure. Studies have shown that many of our subconscious beliefs were formed between the ages of zero to seven. Seriously ponder that. What was going in your life during those formative years? What messaging did you receive from your parents? Was the messaging healthy or harmful? Objectively assessing what your environmental conditions were as a child offers great insight to your current behavioral and thinking patterns.

While your subconscious beliefs play a huge role in your life, they are not always easy to identify as they may be completely incongruent with your conscious beliefs.

Let's break this down. For example, you may consciously believe you deserve to earn a good living, but if you have an unknown, subconscious belief of unworthiness you may never succeed with finding a job that provides you with a good living.

A surefire way to know whether your beliefs are serving you is to simply evaluate your environment, both internal and external. Do you find yourself challenged with the same situation or circumstance time and time again? This is a sign of an underlying, limiting subconscious belief. What do the conversations in your head sound like? Do they lift you up or bring you down? Are your days filled with stressful and worrisome emotions?

Beliefs generate thoughts that create emotions. Our emotions fuel our energy. Notice when you feel happy or enthusiastic, those feelings are often accompanied with a spike in energy. Similarly, when you feel unhappy and sad, you likely feel much less energy or interest in activities, a common occurrence with depressed people. If your subconscious beliefs are congruent with your goals, you will generate the energy required to take action to achieve success.

Both success and failure leave clues, there's no doubt about it. Take the time necessary to seek out any subconscious beliefs that are not serving you and replace them with beliefs that will drive you toward success. You can do a lifetime of personal development work, but if you have unknown limiting beliefs stored in your subconscious, you will continue to feel stuck and frustrated.

What does your environment say about you?

With a sigh of relief, Becky was happy to have finished the first draft of the article. On her next draft, she would weave into her personal experience of how practicing stress relief techniques and PSYCH-K® Balances enabled her to overcome the disempowering beliefs about writing the newspaper article. Her own experience would make a great case study for the benefits of using a coach. Becky thought there would be no better ending for her article than with the way she ends all of her coaching sessions - with a call to action!

Here are three steps to move you towards success:

Step 1:
Since your mind is the most important asset you have towards achieving success, start there. Assess your internal environment and the conversations that go on in your head. Ask yourself, "Does this inner dialogue serve me?" Do the emotions you generate from the thoughts you have on a day-to-day basis give you the energy required to move you toward success?

Step 2:

Assess your external environment simply by looking around. Proximity is power! What do you see? Does it reflect where you thought you'd be at this point in your life? Do you have a genuine interest in the activities and people in your life? Be honest, do the external environments from which you engage move you toward or away from success?

Step 3:

The answers to Steps 1 and 2 will help you realize if you are on the right track or moving in the wrong direction. If you haven't already created a vision for your life, do this now. While using what you learned from your answers to Steps 1 and 2, create goals that are aligned with your vision along with a clear action plan to get you there. Remember, a vision without a plan is nothing more than a day dream.

If you feel uncertain or stuck with any of these steps, seek the support of a coach to help guide you through the process and accelerate your progress.

Becky was thankful to draw upon her tools as a coach and muster the courage to overcome her limiting beliefs associated with writing. Becky chose a quote from one of her favorite authors to end the article.

The only limits you have are the limits you believe.
~ Wayne Dyer

Closing note:

As busy as we all are moving from one task to the next in our daily lives, it is easy to lose sight of what is right before us. Doing the work to evaluate your environmental influences is key to success. For some, this will be a matter of simply becoming more aware of environmental influences. For others, it will require digging deep to identify and overcome limiting subconscious beliefs. Either way, I assure you, it will be well worth the time and effort.

I can speak firsthand of the benefits of doing this work and working with a coach to facilitate the process. It never ceases to amaze me how valuable a third-party perspective can be to propel a person forward which is why I find coaching to be so fulfilling. It is a coach's highest honor to hold a vision for their client and help empower them to expand beyond their current state. The one certainty in our uncertain world is that time will continue to pass, so if you aren't convinced you are living to your full potential or getting the most out of life, act now to change that!

---

1. Mejia, Zameena. "Harvard's longest study of adult life reveals how you can be happier and more successful." CNBC MAKE IT. October 31, 2017
https://www.cnbc.com/2017/10/31/this-harvard-study-reveals-how-you-can-be-happier-and-more-successful.html

About Laureen

Laureen Gabrielle is a Healthcare Consultant and Health and Wellness Coach.

Whether Laureen is consulting with an organization, or coaching one-on-one, her approach accelerates her client's ability to perform at higher levels to successfully achieve goals. Laureen's expertise is in health care management, and personal health and wellness. For over two decades, she held various leadership positions in the health care industry focusing on the delivery of quality health care and operational performance.

Laureen graduated cum laude with a bachelor's degree in Health Care Administration from Quinnipiac University in Hamden, Connecticut. She went on to obtain a master's degree with high honors also in Health Care Administration from Quinnipiac University. Laureen did her residency at the University of Connecticut Health Center which involved creating a performance improvement curriculum for their clinical staff.

Laureen has a LEAN Healthcare Certification from the University of Michigan College of Engineering, and a Certification in Training and Instructional Design from Friesen, Kaye and Associates. Recognizing the neuroscience and psychology of achievement, Laureen became certified as a Neuro Linguistic Programming (NLP) Practitioner. In addition, Laureen is a PSYCH-K® Facilitator. Both NLP and PSYCH-K® practices enable a person to move beyond stress and resistance to achieve goals.

Laureen's volunteer interests include lobbying for patient rights in Washington, DC on behalf of the National Patient Advocate Foundation, as well as working with disadvantaged children with Big Brothers Big Sisters, and Kids in Distress in Florida. Laureen is a member of the South Florida Healthcare Executive Forum, the National Association of Experts, Writers and Speakers, and Women's Healthcare Executive Network.

Laureen was born and raised in Connecticut. While she considers herself to be a New England girl at heart, she enjoys the year-round warm weather in Florida where she currently lives. On weekends, you can find Laureen enjoying her downtime with her active and precocious daughter Julia, or watching the waves roll in at the beach.

You can connect with Laureen at:

- www.laureengabrielle.com

CHAPTER 29

THE 6 C's FOR A SUCCESSFUL RELATIONSHIP
ENDURING THE "HUFFING AND PUFFING"

BY CHARMAINE BETTY-SINGLETON (aka CBS)

"You Won't Blow Me Down." [1]
~ CBS

Have you ever thought about the children's story concerning the big bad wolf and the three little pigs as it relates to relationships? The pigs were intimated by the wolf because the wolf had a reputation for going after and destroying anything he wanted. Because of the wolf's reputation, when the pigs saw him coming, they ran away from him hoping to be safe. The first pig ran to his house built out of straw; the wolf ran after him, got to the house, huffed and puffed, blew the house down and ate the pig. After seeing what happened to the first pig, the second pig ran to his house built out of sticks; the wolf ran after him, got to the house, huffed and puffed, blew the house down and ate the second pig. The third pig, seeing what happened to his friends, ran to his house built out of bricks; the wolf ran after him, got to the house, huffed and puffed, puffed and huffed and blew with all his might, but was unable to blow down the house and the third pig was saved.

Hearing that story as I child, I remembered being scared and thinking the wolf would never get me. But upon reflection, I can honestly say that while I heard the story, I did not truly understand it, therefore, I did not learn from it and apply it to my life. If your relationship is built on a solid foundation and it is properly maintained, it will withstand all the "huffing and puffing" – which may be long distance, transformation, merger, death of business deal, partner or child, illness, competition, and/or ethical or moral dilemmas, to name a few.

Several of my relationships crumbled in front of my eyes and I was determined to understand the why, so I could learn from my mistakes and help others have successful, long lasting relationships both in business and in their personal lives. After much reflection and soul searching, I discovered the very simple, but profound answer: build it and then "WORK" at it, consistency is the key. I found that no matter the relationship, be it friendship, business, work, school, marriage or ministry, all these relationships require dedication, determination and appreciation of the "little things". It may not be important to you, but it's important to him, her or the organization. Now, let's outsmart the wolf/the problems of life and build our house/relationship to endure the "huffing and puffing".

The most important part of any relationship is building the foundation. My foundation for any relationship begins with my relationship with God. The bible says, *"But seek ye first the kingdom of God, and his righteousness; and all these things shall be added unto you."* [2] I realize that by putting God first, submitting to someone bigger than myself, I am then able to submit to other relationships. As I give of myself to others, the more I receive in return. I seek Him, God, to add good things to my relationships, like joy, peace and love.

Once the foundation is established, then the following six essential bricks are used to erect the house/relationship:

1. Communication. You read about a business opportunity in the newspaper that grabs your attention or observe a person across the room that takes your breath away, what do you do? You communicate to obtain more information, to get their attention and determine if this is something you want to pursue. You keep the communication going to determine it this is the right "fit" for either your personal or business relationship, or maybe even a combination of both. True communication and obtaining feedback helps one make an honest

assessment of whether they should take the time and effort to learn about this opportunity or person.[iii] If the answer is yes, you continue to communicate and move onto the next brick.

2. Courting. Courting is spending "quality" time with the item or person and learning about the good and bad. During this, the courting phase, you are showing and simultaneously obtaining all the necessary and ancillary information to determine and analyze the risks associated with this endeavor. One should look for and uncover the flaws, not to magnify them but to be aware of them, then make an educated decision whether to continue to communicate and move onto the next brick.[4]

3. Cleaving. Cleaving is the establishment of trust and sticking close to the object or person of your desire. Because you have taken time to observe, research and analyze, you have determined that this item is worthy of your attention, flaws and all, and it is a risk that you are willing to take, whether temporarily or permanently. The object or thing may come with "baggage" and one must determine how to respond, when others bad-mouth, question or dislike one's decision. Sticking close to the object or person when you are being scrutinized or judged is cleaving. Oftentimes, how one responds is a precursor to handling future challenges "huffing and puffing".[5] Surviving this phase requires more communication as one moves on and lays another brick.

4. Covering. Covering is just another word for prayer and "prayer works". The most important and powerful part of any relationship is knowing when to speak and when to pray. The bible says, *"Death and life are in the power of the tongue: and they that love it shall eat the fruit thereof."* [6] If one loves life they will say things to empower, edify and encourage others. However, if one loves death, they will say things that will belittle, embarrass and hurt another. When someone frustrates or hurts you it is easy to respond with hurting words. Rather than responding in anger, this is the opportune time when one must walk away and pray.

Once damaging words are spoken, it is impossible to take them back. It is better to take a moment to get one's emotions under control and then go back to the supervisor, friend, teammate, or spouse and speak to them from a standpoint of speaking "life" and strengthening the relationship, even during a difficult time. One doesn't always have to be right or have the last word. And if one must have the last word, then pray and talk to God about it. One's prayers can speak things into existence and ask for wisdom, help, direction, understanding and patience as the couple or team works through the problems together. Also, the prayers ask for protection from outside forces, requesting that nothing or no one will be able to sever the relationship. Prayer is a special type of communication that keeps things together. The relationship that prays together, stays together.[7] Let's move on and lay another brick.

5. Comfort. Comfort is another word for motivation and praise. In every relationship, people want to know that they are important and valuable to the team. One of my favorite sayings is: "it is the little things that count" – the Thank You's, the I Love You's, the Good Mornings, 'You mean the world to me,' 'We couldn't have accomplished this without you,' the bonuses, you deserve it, the achievement medal and 'Take some time off.' Comfort is also moral support: telling another (and sincerely meaning it) your happiness is my happiness, your pain is my pain, we are in this together, you are not alone. Finally, comfort doesn't necessarily mean that one can fix it. Rather, he/she will sit there with you saying nothing, holding your hand, handing you tissues, or maybe eating ice cream or sitting with you, until you are willing to talk, get up, or just doing nothing. It is really about the other person, the team, not about you.[8] Let's move on and lay the last and most important brick.

6. Continuous. Continuous is the brick that keeps everything together and does not allow the consistent "huffing and puffing" to penetrate over time and erode the relationships. Continuous means constant, never ending, without interruption. One must constantly communicate (verbally and nonverbally), court, cleave, cover and comfort every day, every hour and sometimes every minute. Simply put, 24/7/365. Ensuring that action, not just mere words, is demonstrated to your partners (whether in business, personal or on a team), showing how important this relationship is to you, how much you value them, and how you will do all you can within your power not to take the relationship for granted.[9] Your actions signifies to your partners, the world and the wolves, that you will do whatever

it takes within your powers to protect, bring honor and cherish your relationship, to keep it thriving and alive. To weather, endure and overcome the "huffing and puffing".

I wish to turn your attention back to the three pigs. As I stated earlier, the third pig who built his house with bricks was able to live. My honest desire for you is not only to live, but to be successful. Once you establish the right foundation and communicate, court, cleave, cover, and comfort continuously in all your relationships, you shall be successful and leave an impact on the people in your home, on your job, on your community and maybe even the world, and people will call you blessed. And because of your actions you will have established a foundation/legacy that will be remembered for generations to come.

Today is a new day and I wish you all the best. Here's to your future, here's to your success, here's to your legacy!

WITH GOD, NOTHING IS IMPOSSIBLE!

Reference Notes:
1. No weapon that is formed against thee shall prosper...." Isaiah 54v17 (KJV)
2. Matthew 6 v 33
3. James 1 v19, Proverbs 15 v1, Psalm 141 v3
4. 1 Timothy 4 v 12, Jeremiah 29 v11, 2 Timothy 2 v 22
5. Genesis 2 v 24, Proverbs 18 v 22, Genesis 2 v18
6. Proverbs 18v21
7. Psalm 91, Luke 6 v 12, Romans 8 v 26
8. 1 Thessalonians 4 v 18, Proverbs 3v 5-6, Isaiah 41 v 10, Psalm 139 v 14
9. 1 Corinthians 15 v 58, Galatians 6 v 9Hebrews 13 v 8

About Charmaine

Charmaine E. Betty-Singleton (aka CBS), author, advocate, veteran, entrepreneur, attorney, and motivational speaker extraordinaire, is the CEO/Owner of PTK Enterprises LLC, a business focused on supporting other business owners, community activism, and empowering individuals to greatness.

Charmaine is also the owner of Victorious Vibes radio station housed on SIBN. She is an avid lover of God and all people. She attributes her success first to God, and then to her parents and mentors—one of which is the late Dr. Myles Munroe. Charmaine strongly believes that with God ALL things are possible, and wishes to "die empty," successfully fulfilling ALL that God has called her to do.

Charmaine is a native of Kingston, Jamaica and refers to Queens, New York as home.

You may connect with Charmaine at:

- www.ptkenterprises.com
- www.facebook.com/CharmaineBettySingleton
- www.twitter.com/ptkenterprisesllc@ptkenterprises
- www.instagram.com/ptkenterprisesllc
- Email: ptkenterprisesllc@gmail.com

CHAPTER 30

CONFLICT RESOLUTION – THE SUPER HERO POWER WITHIN YOU

BY CAROL BARKES, CPM

Peace is not the absence of conflict; it is the ability to handle conflict by peaceful means.
~ Ronald Reagan

Conflict. Have you ever stopped to consider how you feel about this word? I'm willing to bet you haven't given it much thought.

Conflict is a topic we all encounter repeatedly throughout life and yet one most of us try not to think anything about. In fact, most of us prefer to avoid the topic altogether. Our brain pays a lot of attention to this topic even though we may have no conscious idea. Typically, our brains recoil, shut down, fight and seek ways to minimize the damage caused by potential conflict. Regardless of the unconscious approach on which it decides, our brain seeks to approach conflict in a manner which uses the least amount of cognitive resources. In essence, it is our caveman way of survival of the fittest; minimize risk with the least use of energy and help our genes survive for another generation. This is the purpose of our limbic system and a couple of little guys within that system called amygdalae.

Typically this means considering conflict an enemy; something to be avoided at all costs. While avoidance may sound like a relief, it simply does not work. Why? Because conflict is everywhere. We struggle within our own psyche with natural thoughts of, "Are we enough?" We struggle with our most intimate relationships and our workplaces and society are full of conflict. In fact, in 2008, CPP Inc. (publishers of the Myers-Briggs Assessment and the Thomas-Kilmann Conflict Mode Instrument) initiated a study on workplace conflict and uncovered the astonishing fact that U.S. employees spent 2.8 hours per week dealing with conflict. Translated into economic dollars, this represents approximately $359 billion in paid hours (based on average hourly earnings of $17.95) or the equivalent of 385 million working days lost to conflict. In short, ineffective conflict resolution skills come with a high cost, whether emotionally or financially.

So how do we take this daunting topic and turn it into something not so threatening to our brain? Surprisingly, it can be as simple as reframing how we view conflict. For instance, what if we stopped viewing conflict as a threat and recognized it as a natural route to progress and innovation? If you have ever been in sales, you know a simple "No" can be the end of the deal. However, a "No" with a reason is really a door opener; it is the start of a conversation. Likewise, so is conflict. A conflict gives us a way to make a new reality, a way to better understand each other and ultimately a better route to that which we all seek – peace and happiness.

Trust me. I can hear your brain as it resists. The risk versus reward can be hard to define. The retreat from the topic can seem easier than the conversation. But remember, that is our lazy, caveman brain telling us to conserve resources for another day - for the day the woolly mammoth attacks. Did you catch that? For the day the woolly mammoth attacks. In case you are not a news follower, woolly mammoths are EXTINCT. Not only can you afford to utilize some of those resources, you can utilize them in a manner which minimizes your resource outlay well into the future. This is something your brain will LOVE!!! It just needs your help to understand and fight its unconscious drive.

As a conflict resolution expert, hardly a day goes by when I am not tackling some version of conflict. Many tell me this seems like a terrible line of work. I find it exhilarating. I say this because I whole-heartedly believe conflict is a portal. We resist change and conflict because we cannot see what lies beyond. Yet, if we only give it a chance, that which lies beyond a well- resolved conflict is almost always a future brighter than we had imagined in the middle of the storm.

Consider the story of "John" and "Julie". They had been married for ten years and had three children. Over the course of time, their communication had broken down, passion had died, the realities of life had taken main stage and they decided divorce was their only option. When we met, they were on edge, emotional, angry and hurt. While this is completely normal for these types of mediations, and conflict in general, what was not normal was the way in which they spoke. For instance, while they seemed resigned to the reality of their divorce, nothing about their words indicated they really wanted a divorce but rather relief from their fighting. I couldn't help but see there still seemed to be a lot of love and solidarity. Consequently, I asked one simple question, "Are you sure?" I wondered if they really needed a divorce or rather a different way to approach conflict.

After a long discussion and a significant amount of soul searching, John and Julie realized they had gotten stuck in the desire to relieve the tension cause by years of conflict but were actually seeking an answer (divorce) which really did not provide the solution they both wanted. They loved each other, wanted to stay married and just wanted to stop fighting. Instead of ending the marriage, we shifted focus to developing conflict resolution techniques. Three years later, they are still married, their family is thriving and they report being happier than they ever remember.

Stories such as John and Julie overcoming conflict occur regularly in my world. These stories are not always about relationships. Sometimes they are about workplace conflict, sexual harassment, neighborhood disputes, family feuds, business transactions, customer service, the principle of the matter, etc. You name it, people fight about – people just like you. In fact, I am betting you can already relate to some of these categories. So what if conflict were not such a threat? What if we could change our automatic response to conflict and instead embrace all the possible gifts which accompany conflict?

So how do we leverage this conflict resolution superhero power and develop these methods? It is easier than you think. In fact, it is profound in its simplicity but it does take some serious attention and practice to master the process and change bad habits. In the end, however, your newly discovered superhero power will be well worth the effort.

Broken down, there are five key steps to efficiently develop this superhero power:

1. Listen like Sherlock Holmes.

Most people do not listen with the intent to understand;
they listen with the intent to reply.
~ Stephen R. Covey

As Stephen Covey observed, most of us are terrible listeners. We listen with an agenda, filter out that which does not align with our beliefs and use the listening process primarily as a time to formulate our next statement or response. Unfortunately, by doing so, we miss the opportunity to understand. So, too, do we miss the opportunity to discover possible resolutions.

Instead, seek to listen like a detective. In other words, listen with the real, authentic desire to learn and understand. Ask questions. Pay attention to non-verbal cues and respond primarily with what you have heard. Clarify meaning, do not assume and resist putting words into the other person's mouth. And finally, consider the value of silence. Sometimes simply creating the opportunity for silence allows another to really share thoughts which can move conflict forward.

2. Speak to be heard.

Be sincere; be brief; be seated.
~ Franklin D. Roosevelt

If only our brains could remember to speak briefly and sincerely when dealing with conflict. In reaction to stress we often speak faster, use more words and a higher pitch than normal. You can also probably remember times during conflict when you were spoken "at" and not "to". This phenomenon, while common, rarely generates meaningful resolution. In fact, this can make it more difficult for others to hear the important points we wish to convey. To have more meaningful conversations, speak slower, use fewer words and speak more softly. These tools allow others to hear us better and feel as though we are more present and engaged. Slow down, be brief and be heard.

3. Look for ways to collaborate instead of compete.

If you want to make peace with your enemy, you have to
work with your enemy. Then he becomes your partner.
~ Nelson Mandela

John Nash, the Princeton mathematician, won a Noble Prize partly for his work on this issue. In case his name is not familiar to you, he was characterized by actor Russell Crowe in the movie, A Beautiful Mind. Nash mathematically proved the 1755 hypothesis of Swiss philosopher Jean-Jacques Rousseau. Rousseau posited that individually four hunters could each only catch one rabbit while together they could collectively bring down a deer. Unfortunately, we tend to metaphorically "hunt rabbits" alone. When we look for ways to collaborate, we remove the "I win at your expense" mentality. Collaborative solutions are known to be more universally satisfying and generally stronger than those which only take into consideration the needs of one party.

4. Pay attention to interests rather than positions.

For a wise solution, reconcile interests not positions.
~ Roger Fisher and William Ury

One of the biggest mistakes people make when addressing conflict is they tend to focus on positions rather than interests. Simply put, positions are one's demands while interests are what a party really needs. Seek to understand one's needs and look to move beyond demands. For instance, many times in court, parties demand specific amounts of money for the perceived wrongdoings of another. Oftentimes, mediations over these matters initially surround the dollar amount demanded. However, we often find resolutions more naturally fall into place when we discover what people actually need—such as an apology, acknowledgment of frustrations, the correction of wrong doings, etc. There is magic in stopping long enough to discover, and acknowledge, each party's needs.

5. Look at things differently and consider you may be wrong.

*Holmes and Watson are on a camping trip. In the
middle of the night Holmes wakes up and gives
Dr. Watson a nudge. "Watson" he says, "Look
up in the sky and tell me what you see."*

"I see millions of stars, Holmes," says Watson.

"And what do you conclude from that, Watson?"

Watson thinks for a moment.

*"Well," he says, "astronomically, it tells me that there
are millions of galaxies and potentially billions
of planets. Astrologically, I observe that Saturn is
in Leo. Horologically, I deduce that the time is
approximately a quarter past three. Meteorologically,
I suspect that we will have a beautiful day tomorrow.
Theologically, I see that God is all-powerful, and we
are small and insignificant. Uh, what does it
tell you, Holmes?"*

"Watson, you idiot! Someone has stolen our tent!"
~ Thomas Cathcart

Many times we get locked into our position and become unable to
see any other reality. Just like Watson, we may be correct in our
observations yet we may also be missing the bigger point. From a
neuroscience perspective, this can be a result of our unconscious
brain utilizing neuropathways. Neuropathways help our brain
process information more quickly but in doing so, our brain naturally
filters out that which is not in alignment with what we believe. Step
back and take time to consider there may be more than one way to
view a situation and, in fact, you may very well be incorrect in what
you are thinking. There is tremendous honor and value in being able
to say you were wrong.

By combining these skills and continuing to learn more about conflict
resolution, you can fine tune your new abilities into an incredibly cool
superhero power. This power will provide you with the ability to see

through positions that really have nothing to do with what people really need, **hear things that are not even verbalized**, speak in ways that **generate real change** and **strengthen relationships like steel**.

But remember, at the end of the day, this superhero power has been waiting within you to be utilized all along, now you just need to need to put on the cape.

About Carol

It can be hard to imagine someone would choose to surround themselves daily with conflict, yet that is exactly what Carol Barkes does. Not only does she work with conflict, she enthusiastically embraces it. Those who work with Carol immediately find her approachable, kind and spirited style both engaging and effective. As a result, she has become a sought-after conflict resolution leader who dynamically guides people through conflict in a more efficient and empowered manner.

Carol's ability to transform difficult situations and positively change lives is her passion. This passion drives her goal of helping clients, whether organizations or individuals, prevent conflict before it begins and embrace conflict as a portal to positive change and progress when it cannot be avoided. But her goal doesn't stop here; she also intends to reshape how the world approaches conflict. Her motto: *RETHINK CONFLICT*, embodies her purpose.

A lofty purpose such as changing the world is not new to Carol. As an American Academy of Achievement Golden Scroll Award recipient, Carol received the award with the promise of achieving success like the famous personalities present at the award ceremony. This was no small promise as attendees included wine mogul Robert Modavi, the prince of Bavaria, Henry Heimlich, President Ford, Walter Peyton, Elizabeth Taylor, astronaut Chuck Yeager, several Nobel peace prize recipients and many others.

Throughout life, Carol's promise has driven her as she pursued a diverse variety of careers in search of the most meaningful way to make her contribution. For instance, she managed financial institutions, was a firefighter/engineer in the San Francisco Bay Area, directed a therapeutic riding center, was a hospice caregiver and became an entrepreneur who created a manufacturing company, lifestyle store and wine bistro.

While all very rewarding in their own way, these careers did not completely lend themselves to the higher purpose she knew was within her...until now. Her latest chapter arose from a difficult period in life which shook every aspect of Carol's world. In search of insight derived from the experience, she discovered neuroscience. In neuroscience, she found answers; answers that helped her and ultimately helps those she serves. Carol has observed how life-changing it can be to understand how our brains process information. Consequently, she crafted a spirited and scientifically-based approach to conflict resolution that is refreshing and informative, while also being straight-forward and enjoyable. Her presentations are engaging and powerful additions to anyone's toolbox.

Professionally, Carol is a Certified Professional Mediator, peak performance specialist, public speaker and educator focused on neuroscience and conflict resolution. She runs a private practice/consulting business while also serving as the Mediation Services Coordinator for Idaho's largest District Court and teaching at Boise State University.

Carol holds an AA in Fire Science, a BBA in Global Leadership & Influence, an MBA in Negotiation & Conflict Management and is pursuing a PhD in Peak Performance Psychology.

You can connect with Carol at:

- Carol@carolbarkes.com
- www.facebook.com/CarolBarkes
- www.carolbarkes.com

CHAPTER 31

FLYING HIGH

BY GINA BROWN

As the days emerged with the glow of the golden sun, so did her vibrant personality and vision for the future.

Attending college to learn the noble career of teaching kids who have physical and cognitive disabilities and elementary children, filled her days. She attended a Community College so her dual degree would be affordable, for she was paying for it from her waitress tips. She lived with her loving parents. Making connections with people her age and Vietnam War veterans twice her years, while consuming french fries with cheese in the cafeteria was where she learned about sacrifice. The real-life exploitation of agent orange, some grim War details, but usually too difficult to talk about, and the unappreciative fanfare upon her new friends' return, made this college student feel honored to know them and insignificant simultaneously. She grew an affinity for older men for their wisdom, perspective, and calmness but had fun experimenting with crazy and amusing folks her age at the party scenes and trips to beaches.

Smiling, studying, boundless energy, and experiencing the night life illegally were as constant as the visible illuminated moon.

One day, while wasting time trickle by like a drought-ridden creek, she noticed a good friend's older brother enter the house where they were hanging out. He caught her eye and immediately she was drawn to him and his businesslike demeanor, but in a humble sort of way. She noticed the respect he was given by his youngest brother, their friends, and herself. They talked for a while and she felt an instant magnetism.

He would visit her at the restaurant where she worked, wait for her to finish her shift, and take her out on the town late nights. The successful business owner and fun-spirited college student, friend of his youngest brother, were stimulated and merging. They enjoyed dinners, going out with friends, skiing (which she hadn't been able to afford), and many other thrilling things.

The feeling of love, exhilaration, and adventure was stronger than an unforeseen storm. She wanted to always be around him and experience the racing in her heart, this man's protection, and stability from his established career, and excitement.

Shortly after their whirlwind relationship began, he asked her to marry him. With love ravaging through her veins, she said yes! Love, excitement......what else could a young girl want? The idea of having children together, arousing nights, merging loving and fun families together, thrilling vacations, and financial security were intoxicating to say the least.

The bird that glides across the sky is what she felt like... weightless, soaring, and on top of the world!

EXCITEMENT

Wedding planning began.

Good times with her friends began to dwindle as she spent more time with her fiancée and his friends. Her wings that were spread so proudly and effortlessly began to get weighed down by acquaintances' warnings about his track record of breaking girls' hearts, accusations of cheating, and inability to locate him on several occasions.

The glow she once had which permeated through her smile and personality became sallow and lacked energy. The attraction began to feel one sided. On a few occasions prior to the wedding, she sadly but somewhat confidently addressed him about the turbulent times and lack of love she felt by him. Each time resulted in him making her feel like she was creating things that didn't exist and a plea to not call it off. She would leave feeling a little better but not whole.

After collecting several dresses from a friend's bridesmaids because of the threat of her wedding dresses not being in on time, almost calling it off three times, and a deflated self-worth, the big day came!

The ceremony was held at the biggest and most beautiful cathedral in the city by lying and claiming a different residency. It was grand. She cried tears of fear of not being loved instead of tears of joy. Her love for him was powerful yet confusing; unyielding yet unmatched. Her sister's first child's baptism, which she was the Godmother, was the morning after the wedding and she felt depleted and didn't make it. The guilt of that haunted her for many years.

After the honeymoon, which she had very little recollection of, included days of her commuting to finish her college education while he worked on the first floor where they resided. She felt like an intruder at times. He had lived there for many years before and it didn't feel like a welcoming home. It was noticed by many who cared for her that she wasn't the same happy and spirited person.

Overhearing her husband on the phone seeming like a verbal fight with a girl was explained that it was his brother's girlfriend and he wasn't fighting with her. She doubted her ability to accurately assess a situation. She was called jealous as a response.

The wife became suspicious often but couldn't have a conversation that seemed to lead to anything positive. She found recently developed pictures which showed another girl who she suspected him of having an affair with because she was at his office several times per week. He adamantly denied it which seemed to be the only consistent trait of their new marriage.

Days were filled with exhaustion, wandering mind, and resentment and nights were pervaded with fighting, waiting to hear the garage door open in the middle of the night, and loneliness for her. The once vibrant and energetic soul was depleted, confused, and low.

They went to a marriage counselor a few times and then she continued on her own. She explained, "I yawn all day, have intense jaw pain-TMJ, don't feel well, and hollow."

He advised her to hire a private investigator so that she had proof (black and white) of the infidelity because anything between your ears you can change, manipulate, and essentially do anything you want with it. This was causing the extreme exhaustion. You can't change something tangible. He also explained there are pathological liars, which oftentimes these people believe their own lies.

She kept the infidelity, loneliness, and sorrow to herself. She hired a private investigator who sought to provide the tangible picture on a Saturday night. He reported that he couldn't keep up with him even after several attempts. The money bought her more ambiguity of his actions. Questioning whether having a child together would bring them closer was as constant as the day was long for her.

One day her good friend, his youngest brother, called and asked if he could use the ski condominium. Her husband told her he would be at a seminar all day, so she called there to page him for his permission. They informed her the seminar was cancelled and it had been for several months. She waited until he returned eight hours later and asked how it was. He lied once again until she revealed her knowledge. He said he just needed to get away.

AIMLESSLY WANDERING

She took one change of clothes and drove aimlessly for 10 hours, with no direction. The atmosphere was dark and dismal which matched her mood perfectly. She went from a hotel to a friend's house and eventually resurfaced.

A divorce was an idea that embarrassed her after her parents spent so much money on the wedding, short duration, and dismal truth of rejection. She was raised with the belief system that you stick it out in good times and bad. It had only been a little less than a year but felt like years of punishment.

Things were looking up…he didn't try to talk her out of getting a divorce, but secretly she was hoping for it—always hoping he would reciprocate the love.

She proceeded with getting an attorney and appeared to be strong, but still loved him and felt compelled to cut ties to their friends. Because when talking to them, she wanted to know what he was doing, whether he was dating someone, and felt like she couldn't be a good friend. She knew it was going to be another loss which would cause even more sadness.

During the next year or two, she found too many reasons to call him and ask questions about the divorce, car, etc. This was attributed more to her not being able to come to grips with being rejected than it did with having the answers to the questions.

She began dating many, many frogs, but compared each to the feelings she had for her ex-husband. If the new guy was too nice, he wasn't exciting enough. One man had a mother who cheated on her husband and as soon as she got this news, she severed the relationship. Trust was not there for anyone.

FRIGATE – SOARING & HOVERING

A few years later, a smiling, full of life, and handsome man was met in a bar. They enjoyed a very connected conversation. There was a magnetism. Somewhat intoxicated, she spoke about her relationship that went south. She left to use the restroom and anxiously came back, and he was gone. She thought he left because he wasn't interested.

When he returned he saw she wasn't there. He searched a few "hot spots" around the area to find her but with no luck. She couldn't get him off her mind. He explained her to people – asked if they knew her or had her phone number. He was on a persistent course to fine her. One year later, he called her and asked her out on a date. They shared common interests, passion to do fun things and for each other. They fell in love. They spent many exciting days and nights together. She felt love, comfort, and excitement.

A fork in the road was seen by her a couple of years later. Was marriage in the future or not? After a few wonderful years together, she broke it off with him because she wasn't sure whether or not it was true love.

Her sister gave her an article in hopes of it helping her in the quest. It was called Love vs. Lust. She read it and discovered instantaneously she never loved her husband and knew what true love was for the very first time ever, but already let him go. She had a belief system of what love looked and felt like. She literally got on her knees and begged the true love back into her life. He accepted with some hesitancy because his ego had taken a hit.

They have now been growing in deeper love for 25 years, have 4 children together, encourage each other to reach their dreams, support one another, and are excited for the future together.

WE LEARN MORE FROM OUR FAILURES THAN WE DO FROM OUR SUCCESSES

Learning from a challenge, disappointment, and mistake will make you all the wiser. Knowledge is not your ultimate power but use it to then act on what you truly desire.

Trust your gut. If something doesn't feel right, it isn't!

Thoughts, beliefs, and visualization are powerful! They can propel you to live a life full of joy and fulfillment or negativity and drudgery.

- If you have a goal, write it down, break it into smaller attainable steps, and start taking action steps toward achieving it.

- If you have a challenge, write it down, break it into smaller steps, and start taking action to solve it.

Had you not experienced one failed relationship, you probably wouldn't have a successful one. Don't let it define you, but use everything learned to your advantage.

When dating take the time to discover whether you are experiencing love or lust. Love is always kind and looking for ways to show the other partner its true self. Lust is always trying to hide its true nature by deceiving and manipulating.

You don't know what you don't know. Reach out to a coach, therapist, or trusted friends for support. You could be led to a vision you haven't been able to see. People connect more through challenges than triumphs. Connectivity and helping others fulfills people.

About Gina

Gina Brown is a Speaker, Educator, Success Coach, and Culture Transformation Specialist. She grew up and resides in Pittsburgh, PA with her husband, four sons, and a Golden Retriever. She has more than 20 years as an educator and has trained with some of the best coaches in the world, Jack Canfield and Tony Robbins.

Gina is a Strategic Interventionist through training with Tony Robbins, Chloe Madanes, and Mark and Magali Peysha. She leads individuals, relationships, and organizations to understand themselves better, and directs them toward positive and sustainable change through strategic planning of skillful interventions – in steps or stages. She helps people create the life they always wanted! Using human needs psychology, she assists people to understand why they do what they do (how they meet their six basic needs) and facilitates the change that is sustainable. She has helped people overcome anxiety, fears, depression, guilt, auto immune diseases and a lot more! Unleashing the power within people is her specialty, and she has helped many manifest the life of their dreams. Clients have gone from couch-ridden, confused and unhappy to happy, healthy and thriving. Some of these people entered the workforce after being unemployed for a long time while others found more meaning in their work. Clients report improved relationships with their spouses, family members, friends and colleagues after Gina's unique coaching.

Gina became a Canfield Methodology Trainer by studying with Jack Canfield. As a certified Canfield Methodology Success Coach, she helps people and organizations reach their personal and professional goals. She experimentally teaches the Principles of Success, so people understand how they work, and she facilitates individual and group transformation. People who have worked with Gina report significantly higher incomes, getting clear on what they want out of life, and living with more purpose, joy, and fulfillment.

As a Culture Transformation Tools Specialist, Gina works collaboratively with leadership and teams to build a values-driven culture. She assesses the values of people, current culture, and desired culture in an organization and leads them to a higher performance environment with highly engaged people. If you were showing up living your values in your work place, wouldn't you be more engaged and productive? The companies and organizations who invest in this work outperform the S & P 500 significantly.

You can connect with Gina at:

- info@nowsuccesscoach.com
- www.nowsuccesscoach.com

CHAPTER 32

CAN I WALK MY TALK?

BY ROSIE UNITE

*Then be prepared... To be... **Amazed**.*
~ Rosie Unite, "Can I Heal and Connect with The Unified Field?"
(from *The Big Question* with Larry King)

I am amazed. Every day. More often than I'd like to admit, however, I'm also not.

It's hard to stay conscious (alert to my thoughts and their direct effect on my body) – and to hold myself absolutely accountable for my life. But I keep doing the work, and I've learned new ways to live in awe.

After a lifetime of *chasing* success – in the last 12 months, I've *lived* it by giving myself a break and celebrating successes small and large every day.

So, what does success mean for me now?

I. *MANIFESTING* MY PERSONAL AND PROFESSIONAL FUTURE

Life's like a movie. Write your own ending. Keep believing. Keep pretending.
~ Kermit the Frog, *Sesame Street*® and *The Muppet Show*®

In *The Big Question* (TBQ), I shared my Five Paths to Possibilities™ **D** - **R** - **E** - **A** - **M**. The **M** stands for <u>M</u>anifest Your Future.

283

It's not a "one-and-done-I-want-everything-now!" concept. I must manifest my future every day. That doesn't mean things drop from the sky – although sometimes they do! I believe it means staying open to everything that might support me, taking spirited action, and then letting go of the *How* and *When*.

No matter how crazy or daunting a new opportunity may seem, I explore it, saying, "Yes, and what more?!" I now also know that asking for help is not a weakness, but rather an act of generosity – which allows others to use their talents to help me thrive (Cheryl Richardson, *The Art of Extreme Self-Care*). I've since had spectacular breakthroughs: personal and professional, practical and mystical, fundamental and radical.

The most important relationship I have is with *me*. It's the launchpad upon which I manifest other relationships in my *personal* future – which then catapults my *professional* future. I continuously ping my electromagnetic signature – clear thoughts and soul-filled emotions – into the Unified Field of Energy, *knowing* that all will happen in a way just right for me.

What a ride it's been!

II. <u>MANIFESTING MY *PERSONAL* FUTURE</u>

When you read, don't just consider what the author thinks,
consider what you think.
~ John Keating (Robin Williams), *Dead Poets Society*

Every day, I manifest breakthroughs for healthy, vibrant relationships with myself, the past, and with the Unified Field. The more I love myself, the more I can love – people, things, experiences, life. It's really a capacity issue. If I have US$46 million, I can invest, donate, or buy things worth US$46 million. But if my bank account is negative... In essence, I can't give what I don't have! As I flourish in this new state of being, I love more deeply those closest to me and learn to love things I formerly didn't.

<u>ME, MYSELF AND I</u>

If **D - R - E - A - M** is my daily nourishment – then staying conscious of my thoughts, emotions, and actions is veritable tiramisu! But getting a hold of that delicious dessert isn't easy.

Why? My external environment constantly bombards me with triggers, each one feeling like an Olympic challenge. I have to assemble a top-tier team of neurons in my head to return my heart and mind to coherence (orderly, harmonious synchronization) and my body to homeostasis (equilibrium) whenever I'm triggered.

My daily Olympic challenges and new responses?

1. Seeing an athletic man sitting in a subway seat for mobility-challenged passengers:

   New response: *Sorry to interrupt your video game, sir, but would you consider giving your seat to this elderly woman?*
   [Old response: Fury.]

2. Trying to untangle six twisted electrical cords:

   New response: *Breathe... isn't this the best puzzle ever?!*
   [Old response: Irritation.]

3. In a rush, just missing the elevator in a 15-floor building:

   New response: *Perfect... time to center and ground myself.*
   [Old response: Anxiety.]

4. Being ignored by an unfriendly neighbor:

   New response: *To that part in you, Mr. Neighbor, that's closed, unloved, and unhappy – this smile is for you.*
   [Old response: Hate.]

5. Criticizing myself:

   New response: *Dear one, is this how you treat Divine Energy within you?*
   [Old response: Justification.]

To win such mental-emotional sports, I must be mega-alert to say to myself: "Is this it? You're choosing to go unconscious (into survival emotions and reptilian brain), ditch everything you've worked on, give away your power, and forget who you *really are* and what you can *do?* Seriously?!"

That always snaps me back, and I remember what I share with others: "One thought. One second. One breath. *Your* power." Gold medal!

THE PAST

I've learned to forgive, knowing that people who've chosen to be mean are internally blocked from loving themselves. How could they give something they don't have?

Forgiving is one of the greatest gifts I've given *me*. I've liberated energy and gained wisdom – recalling painful memories without the emotional charge. This doesn't mean I forget how people act. I'm not a pushover.

As I **D - R - E - A - M**, I've had to make excruciating decisions to **D**isconnect and **D**etoxify from some people. I still love and care for them, but given that I choose *100% goodness through all five senses* for myself – I make no exceptions.

THE UNIFIED FIELD

I'm not religious. And although I don't believe in coincidences, I also don't search for hidden meaning in everything. I *know* everything is energy. Solid matter is simply energy vibrating at the slowest frequencies, thus perceptible by the human eye. I know I'm powerful energy (as we *all* are), and I experience abundance everywhere. The "old" me was asleep to this concept. Thank goodness I woke up.

The stream of synchronicities I ride is fast and fresh. I've had so many lightbulb moments that I should stop being surprised! Regardless, in every instance, I still chuckle, and with a big grin on my face, and my hand on my heart, I say, "Thanks, again!"

Recently, I've had two profound mystical experiences that have imbued me with absolute energetic connection with the Unified Field. One happened in a week-long meditation retreat in Spain. It was ineffable. Days later, people told me they could still feel my energetic field in *their* bodies.

The other keeps happening! I saw the same meaningful four numbers (military time) on digital clocks everywhere – in the short 60 seconds they appeared on any day. It happened so frequently that I laughed in gratitude each time. But just when I got used to seeing them, I no longer did. Weeks later, I "randomly" noticed a different set of four numbers – deeply symbolic – on clocks everywhere. You can guess what happened next. Once I was no longer surprised to see *those* numbers, they didn't "appear." What did? The first set – in a weeks-long fun fury! The Field has a wicked sense of humor!

MY *PERSONAL* BREAKTHROUGHS

- Getting out of my own way.
- Knowing everything is a gift, even the tough stuff.
- It doesn't matter if I fall off my path, as long as I jump back on.

How quickly have these breakthroughs catapulted my *professional* future?

III. MANIFESTING MY *PROFESSIONAL* FUTURE

Do one thing every day that scares you.
~ Eleanor Roosevelt

Launch and grow new technology companies on behalf of large corporations globally? No problem. Start my own venture – born from a deeply personal story (my *TBQ* chapter), where science kisses spirituality, for the world to know? Exciting, but also scary.

Backstory: For several years, I wasn't employed, mostly by choice. I'd had a phenomenal career and sought something spectacular and meaningful. So, I rejected opportunities at two adored tech companies. And I was rejected by others for being "all over the map" and having *too much* enthusiasm (no joke).

This prolonged gap slammed this Type-A overachiever. I believed I *was* what I *did* for a living. But now I know who I *really am* and what I can really *do* (as we *all* can) – manifest my intentions through my powerful thoughts, emotions, and energy.

Result? The most prolific 12 months of my life!

Everything was new. My right brain was rocking, creating, and developing my own IP. I received not only what I sent out to The Field but also gifts that I never expected or even knew existed!

MARCH
After leading two Success Principles™ workshops in London, I was surprised by the testimonials. People said: "I'd love to work with her." and "If she believes what you're capable of, then you believe it yourself!" Others found me "open, honest, authentic, and fascinating." I was surprised and humbled.

JULY
At an entrepreneurial retreat in San Diego, I felt "behind" and overwhelmed. When asked for a Venn diagram of new things I wanted to do, I drew three interconnecting circles: keynote speeches, books, and private clients – with a smiley face in the middle. A colleague wrote atop the circles: "Happy Birthday!" (in the spirit of the words).

Although I'd never professionally done any of the three, I had an exciting feeling that all had already happened – in my future!

At a different kind of retreat in Italy, I asked if I could beta-test my scrappy keynote for a group of Europeans and Americans. Again, the feedback floored me: "I was gripped by it… this inspires me," "Made me feel so optimistic… exactly what the world needs now," and "Opened my heart and mind to new possibilities." Again, I was humbled.

AUGUST
I had no professional writing experience. So, at an advanced meditation retreat, I continuously filled the energetic field within me and all around me with groovy intentions of writing my personal story in a book.

A few weeks later, I was selected to write a chapter in Larry King's *TBQ* book, in which I did just that!

SEPTEMBER
In awe, I met and watched the legendary Larry at a private filming in Hollywood. I'd said "Yes!" to be one of the Executive Producers of the groundbreaking TV Special *The Voice of a Generation: An Evening with Larry King.* Another first!

DECEMBER
I had my first TV media interview on *Success Today* and gave my first formal keynote at *Success Live* at Universal Studios in Orlando! Again, the response was go-go-go!

FEBRUARY
Kids are my greatest teachers and partners in (fun!) crime. So, not-so-randomly at a trade show, I met an altruistic, young author who's written and illustrated a beautiful series of children's books to help kids befriend their myriad, and often crippling, emotions. Within minutes, we *knew* we'd collaborate.

For the record, the show's organizers don't know me (yet!) – but I *will* be a guest speaker at their UK and US events next year. Just saying.

MARCH
Phenomenal.

This "non-author" wrote a second time with *another* legend – this book! Thrilled, I also contributed my life-affirming message in the lovely children's book *Leo Learns About Life*. I then said "Yes!" to a fourth book, *Professional Performance 360 Special Edition: Success Second Edition* – co-authoring with Sir Richard Branson.

I also attended the premiere of Larry's TV Special – hosted by the EMMY® Award winning Director and film team. To boot, I was selected to deliver a keynote at the Global Entrepreneurship Initiative at the United Nations in New York.

When it rains, it generously pours!

Almost forgot… I also launched my new company, ImaginateLife™.

MY *PROFESSIONAL* BREAKTHROUGHS

- Realigning Rosie.
- Flying on my *Why!*
- Fearlessly saying, "Yes!"

Your future can also happen that fast. In ways wild and wonderful. Through gorgeous people, resources, and opportunities that come at the perfect time for you to receive. How do you know if you're successful?

7 SIGNS
YOU'VE MANIFESTED *YOUR* BREAKTHROUGHS
TO
S - U - C - C - E - S - S ™

You are...

1: SYNC-ING

To your *Why*. To your Purpose. Proverbial doors keep opening.

Why? Because you're fully *you*.

2: UNLIMITED

In how you feel every day, in every facet of your life, knowing you *can* and *will*.

Why? See S above.

3: CREATING

More than ever. New thoughts, ideas, visuals, melodies, wonders, solutions, experiences, and adventures.

Why? You neither self-criticize nor care about other's judgments. You trust the unknown – allowing pent-up creative power that you've *always* had surge through you.

4: COLLABORATING

Because you see opportunity everywhere (even with competitors) – enhancing your vision, mission, products, services, and reach.

Why? You're driven to make meaningful, valuable, sustainable, scalable, and memorable impact on the people, organizations, and communities that matter to you.

5: ENERGETIC

Indefatigably so. Like my little niece after inhaling a bowl of custard!

Why? You're operating at a higher vibration, higher frequency. You know that one second in survival mode (e.g. worry, hate, doubt, fear, guilt) is one second of *wasted energy*. You have a gazillion other ways to use it.

6: SMILING

Inside and out. And you don't care if strangers think you're nuts!

Why? You're happy – not because you've achieved some metric – but because you just are. It's your state of being. Even if life throws you curveballs, you raise your energy as soon as possible – for yourself and others. Smiling does that in a flash.

7: SOARING and SAILING

You're soaring in the sky and sailing the high seas.

Why? Because you're…

> ➢ Wide-open to possibilities.
> ➢ On-point.
> ➢ Alive!
> ➢ *Amazed.*

In my morning rhythm and ritual, I always ask for surprises – for breakthroughs. Despite many blips on my internal radar (still human!), I soar and sail every day.

Do you believe you can too? I do.

BON VOYAGE!

About Rosie

Rosie Unite is the Founder and CEO of ImaginateLife™, a for-profit global social impact venture (www.imaginatelife.com).

She's passionate about the power at the nexus of neuroscience, epigenetics, quantum physics, and spirituality to heal bodies, elevate minds, and transform lives. Known as *The Possibilities Whisperer*™, Rosie shares her extraordinary experience to help others stretch beyond their perceived selves and connect with life's abundance.

ImaginateLife™ offers the knowledge, skills, and awareness that inspires and empowers others to discover their innate power, live fully, and seed a greater consciousness. Services include keynote speeches, workshops, special events, and advisory services.

Rosie's deeply grateful for the visionaries on her amazing journey.

Dr. Joe Dispenza is a renowned neuroscientist, educator, and *NY Times* best-selling author. To-date, Rosie has completed nine of his workshops globally – the majority Advanced and Advanced-Follow-Ups.

She's honoured to have participated in his extensive research on meditation effects on brain and body. Rosie has been QEEG (quantitative electroencephalography) brain mapped by U.S. and German neuroscientists; heart coherence measured by HeartMath Institute; individual energy field tested by GDV technology; and group-measured for energy in workshop environments by GDV Sputnik sensors.

She continues to support breakthroughs in *neuroplasticity* – the brain's ability to change via new neural connections – and *epigenetics* – the study of heritable changes in gene expression not involving changes to underlying DNA.

Rosie has enjoyed co-authoring this book with the innovative and generous Jack Canfield. She has also worked directly with Jack as a Certified Trainer in *The Success Principles*™ (one of his numerous *NY Times* best-selling books) and *Canfield Methodology*™. She is grateful for his legacy and forever inspired by his endearing guidance to share her story with the world.

Rosie also appreciates the inimitable Larry King. She was not only a co-author of his book *The Big Question* but also one of the Executive Producers of the groundbreaking TV Special *The Voice of a Generation: An Evening with Larry King*. Captivated by people's lives, Rosie watched the legendary *Larry King Live* on CNN for years. She found his unique, humorous way of engaging with guests across the spectrum –

some admired, others not – always edifying and entertaining.

Previously, in her 30-year global career, Rosie was a leader and executive in the *Fortune 500* corporate, start-up, and social impact sectors. A Wharton MBA, she helped launch and grow new companies and emerging mobile, telecommunications and digital technologies. She began building businesses in the Peace Corps – helping community-based microenterprises.

Rosie's worked with well-known organizations, including: Sprint, GTE (Verizon), DoubleClick (Google), Johnson & Johnson, France Telecom, Deutsche Telekom, Intelig Brazil (TIM Italy), World Bank, Inter-American Development Bank, Women's World Banking, Foreign Affairs, Academy for Educational Development, and Habitat for Humanity.

A globe-trotting, life-long student, Rosie is a Sivananda Hatha Yoga Certified Instructor and has completed Vipassana 10-Day Meditation and Levels 1-2-3 of EFT Universe's Certification Program (i.e. Tapping). Fulfilling a childhood dream, she's traveled in 65 countries and lived in eight: USA, Brazil, Netherlands, Hong Kong, Spain, Bulgaria, Dominican Republic, and the UK.

CHAPTER 33

LOVE AND LET GO

BY CLAUDEL E. KUEK

THE KEY TO LIVING IN PEACE

It was not always this way for me. I was the first-born in a strict family where obedience, discipline and constant drive toward excellence were the core of our daily lives. I grew up under close scrutiny and a relentless pressure to dive, nose in to every deep end, and swim to achieve every goal. Indeed, this visual image of being pushed without warning to swim without aid across the pool at my first swim lesson remains seared in my memory.

From as far back as I can remember, all I wanted was to break free from my parents' strong hold and any form of authority surrounding me, and to be free to live a life by my own terms.

My parents are wonderful and loving, albeit strict and controlling. Yet, they had a way about them which rubbed off on me and my siblings as we were a close knit family. They were highly strung and often emotionally volatile. I picked these up from an early age, and deemed that it was quite alright to be temperamental and transparent about one's emotions. I was impatient with anything that stood in the way of my progress, and learned that the way to deal with setbacks was to show rage.

God bless my parents who are today separated by choice and living happier lives for it. I would not change them for anything in the world. However, because of their profound influence during my formative years, I have had to constantly work on my limiting beliefs, my persistent need to charge into projects at break-neck speed, my inability to trust and to relax.

Who I am Today

As I am writing this, I am a very different person from who I used to be. It has been a long, winding walk to get to this place where I have always wanted to be: calm, balanced, happy and relaxed.

In the early years after stepping out from the shadow of my parents, and to realize my passion for learning and for dance, I put myself through college overseas, leaving home against my parents' wishes. I had been an accomplished ballerina as a child, and continued dancing there to capture hearts and fulfil my need to excel. At the same time, I worked with great fortitude and stamina to accomplish as much as I could in the shortest time possible, anxious about my limited study funds running out. It seemed like a constant race to reach my destination, and I was immensely pleased to graduate magna cum laude.

Today I have evolved to become the person I am proud to be: happily married, deeply connected to the most inspiring persons in my life - my children, founder and director of award-winning Pilates studios in Singapore - PowerMoves, leading in the community as a success coach for aspiring youths, and at peace with the choices I have made and the contributions I am able to make.

How do I know life?

We know with great certainty that life really is a journey to be savored and cherished. The many moments, both good and bad, all come and go in a flash. The frivolity of time that we think we have plenty of fades into scarcity before we realize. Inconveniences that make our blood pressure go up too often fall away into one last heartbeat. I should have understood right from the start that we really ought to be abstracting the most out of the every breath we take, every dream we contemplate, and every thought we formulate.

I am now more mindful about the race of life, and not to be forced into a pace that will leave me panting and breathless, the way it was for me growing up. Now that I am in my mid-50s, what I know to be most precious is to have more of time to share with the people I love and to make a real difference in my corner of the world. I want more of life. I want more of everything that is important to having more of life.

Why it has to be Love

Love is what it is. Inasmuch as you understand the meaning of love, it is accurate to say that the most compelling reason for our existence is to love. When we give ourselves up to loving everything before us, we will more clearly understand its meaning and that of life. To stretch time out, live a little longer, and live a little better - we just all need to do a lot more loving.

> *Owe no one anything, except to love each other,*
> *for the one who loves another has fulfilled the law.*
> ~ Romans 13:8

- Love the home that you live in, love the food that nourishes your body.
- Love the reason you awake every morning, love the day for turning into night.
- Love your parents for they tried, love your children for they only want to make you proud.
- Love your neighbor for sharing in your space less lonely, love your colleague for making your race more worthy.
- Love the traffic for its buzz, love the weather for its mystery.
- Love the government for its structure, love the economy for its challenge.
- Love what you do as a reflection of independence, love who you married as a gift from your Creator.
- Love who you are as a triumph of your spirit, love who you can be as you work towards your goals.

When we surround ourselves with the emotion of love, we are wrapped in an abundance of gratitude which in turn helps to center us toward an inner peace and calm. This attribute will bring forth a life more forgiving, more beautiful and more in touch with your higher purpose.

The secret to achieving any level of quietude and peace lies in the art of letting go.

Let Go of the Past

There is beauty and wisdom in all things past - your accomplishments, your triumphs, all your wow-was-that-really-me moments. There may also lie, in your past, regrets, pain of events gone wrong, and all the I-should-have-known-better moments. Would life not be as colorful without these layers of good and bad that represent a life well lived? Everything happens for a reason and it helps make us who we are. Be thankful for all the opportunities, for better or for worse, as we had the time and we had our chances. But yesterday is gone. There is nothing more we need to do about yesterday for we cannot bring it back.

Our purpose for today is to be our best self and we can only do this when we let go completely of the past. Focus on the now, do something special for yourself and for those around you, keep abreast with your renewal and continual growth. Release the attachment to all things past. For today is your time and your gift to yourself. Do not let anybody else own it but you.

Let Go of the Future

The future is beyond our control as it is yet unborn. How so very unexciting it would be if we all knew exactly what the future holds. Without an uncertain future, we might not need to strive further or stretch ourselves ever again. The beauty about the future is its element of surprise and the opportunity to do it differently. The lessons of hindsight take us forward and help us create a future that seems less unfamiliar. However, whatever happens in the future cannot be predicted nor guaranteed. Lying awake worrying about the unknown, playing out the fears and imagining the worst possible scenarios is not keeping the future in the future. The best way to embrace the future is to leave it there in the future as you live in and experience the present.

Today is our gift and it will last for only 24 hours; don't use it spending any time in the past or in the future. Be open to the wonder and magic of every surprise that the future holds for you. Stay strong and steadfast about making today your best possible creation and keep those future calls in the future where they belong.

Let Go of what You Cannot Control

It seems so very obvious – why would we ever obsess over something we have little or no control over? Whether it be dwelling over the outcome of an event or the response of a loved one, it is rationally futile even before we begin exploring the options. But indeed we will always be tempted to try. The trying is what will cause us to feel a loss of control and an increase of overwhelm, over an outcome that we never had control over anyway. We cannot control everything that takes place, but we can control how we look at it and how we choose to respond to it. We can control what action steps we will take in the direction of an outcome we so desire. We can become more mindful of what is really in our present and focus on whatever it is we do have the power over.

In learning to let go of everything we have no control over, we must remain grounded in the thoughts we hold of the present moment. Stay aware of the positive in the situation, keep breathing into the moment, focus on your strengths and let go of all else.

Love and Let Go

All the art of living lies in a fine mingling of letting go and holding on.
~ Henry Havelock Ellis

In all my time reaching for the stars, what I was truly searching for was my freedom. The freedom to love as I please, to love everything that pleased me, and the freedom to be able to let go of all things holding me back from being the best version of myself. At the point when I could let go and just be thankful for who it is I am really meant to be, I found peace. Letting go is pre-requisite of healing, of achieving, and of being free.

I count myself lucky to be standing here at mid-life understanding that I can finally stop trying to figure everything out. All we need in our hearts is love and even more love. Love yourself, love the others, love the process, love this wonderful life that belongs to you. Be grateful for another new day to be alive. It is not about being perfect in every moment; it is about having fun, staying cheerful and being real. Enjoy every moment with your loved ones; cherish every hug, accept every compliment, and seize every opportunity to make someone else smile.

In learning to love freely and let go unabashedly, therein you will find peace.

<u>To just Be</u>

Believe in yourself. Believe in your purpose. Believe that the universe is unfolding as it should and that your role is to go with the flow and find your rhythm in the now. In holding on too tightly to the past or the future, or the inconsequential thoughts, this could in fact be holding you back from the big-picture purpose and vision of who you are meant to be.

Be flexible while staying true; allow the pathways to unfold as it will, opening you up to courage and surprise, spontaneity and opportunities. Flex and flow with the current of your life. Be grateful for everything. Be strongly focused on the every moment of now. Remind yourself that this very moment in time is the only one you know you have for sure. Let love be your guide. Remember to breathe.

Learn to love and let go, and just be you. Therein you will find beauty in every moment and one day soon, a complete peace of mind.

It was the mantra of 'live and let live' that held us toward the greater understanding of how this world belonged to us all equally, and with the hope that we could all find peace and happiness in. For me, it has evolved to 'love and let go' – *this is my key to living in peace.*

About Claudel

Claudel E. Kuek believes that "our greatest wealth is our health". On the strength of that conviction, she founded PowerMoves Pilates-in-the-Park with its first studio in the healing serenity and soothing ambience of the city central park in 2006. Over the next 12 years, PowerMoves went on to start up other branches across the country, each housed within a distinctive lifestyle destination surrounded by fine gourmet restaurants, art shops, specialist medical clinics, and nature.

An accomplished ballerina formerly with the UK Royal Academy of Dance and a professionally-certified Pilates trainer, Claudel's founding philosophy was a heartfelt desire to endow and empower individuals with "a rhythm and confidence that transcends mere exercise and becomes a way of life." Not unlike ballet, the visible benefits of Pilates are manifested as a combination of energy and elegance that can be perceived even in the way a person moves. Her passion led to PowerMoves becoming a renowned fitness and wellness brand in the country. Her multi-award-winning studios have gained numerous accolades, such as "Most Beautiful Studios in the World" by *Balanced Body Inc.*, "Best Pilates Classes" by *SHAPE* magazine, "Best of Singapore" by *Tatler* magazine; and scoring first place over multiple years consecutively for Most Outstanding Service Quality in the sports and recreation arenas.

Claudel holds a Bachelor of Science, *magna cum laude*, degree in International Business and Marketing from Hawaii Pacific University. From 2007 to 2010, she also held the position of President of the military officers' wives club – responsible for the welfare and social interactions of the wives of military personnel. She has an avid interest in Interior Design and is lauded for her work in features with *Harper's Bazaar, Tatler* and *Prestige*.

At 53 today with two grown-up children, Claudel is a role model for working women and mothers everywhere. She is a Jack Canfield trainer (creator of the *Chicken Soup for the Soul* series), and is developing a Success Coaching enterprise to help aspiring youths and women discover a new capacity and confidence that is founded from fitness and wellness of the mind, body and soul.

CHAPTER 34

MASTERING THE ART OF EDUMARKETING

BY GINGER BELL

LEVERAGING YOUR EXPERTISE FOR MARKETING SUCCESS

An investment in knowledge pays the best interest.
~ Benjamin Franklin

Whether you are a Financial Planner, Chiropractor, Real Estate Agent, Dentist or Mortgage Professional, you have an expertise and you have information to share. Google processes over 40,000 search queries every second. Consumers today do not want to be sold, they want to be educated and they are looking for information. In fact, 73% of purchase decisions begin with research conducted on either Google or Amazon. So, the question is, what are you doing to position yourself as the expert in your field? What are you doing to Edumarket your business?

WHAT IS EDUMARKETING?

Let's start by breaking down the word Edumarketing, as it may be a term you are not familiar with.

Edumarketing combines two words: "Education" + "Marketing" = "Edumarketing"

Edumarketing means to use education to market yourself while educating your potential clients, clients and business partners about yourself, your expertise and your business.

It is really a very simple concept. Edumarketing is combining education with a marketing plan to deliver Edumarketing.

Edumarketing, or education-based marketing is the sharing of knowledge with the purpose of building trust. It is a strategy that establishes credibility and positions you and your company as the expert in your field.

Edumarketing is more than just hiring a ghost writer to write a blog article for your website to help improve your SEO. Edumarketing is incorporating a variety of channels to deliver your expertise and educate in your marketplace.

The best Edumarketing plan includes using a variety of distribution channels including:

- Blogs on your website and partner websites
- Micro-blogs such as LinkedIn, Twitter and Facebook
- Online videos
- Live workshops
- Webinars
- Online education
- Radio shows
- Magazine and newspaper articles
- Whitepapers
- E-books
- Print books

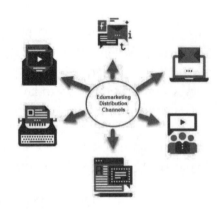

If used correctly, Edumarketing will provide long lasting referral customers who will look to you, and only you as the resource.

THE POWER OF BEING THE EXPERT

Marketing is telling the world you're a rock star.
Content Marketing is showing the world you are one.
~ Robert Rose

The growth of information available online today has made consumers more educated and informed about their options than ever before. Prospects are spending more time doing independent research and getting information from their peers and other third-party sources. At the same time, professional networks, trade publications and associations have become a valued resource for prospects to look to for recommendations and insight. Establishing yourself as the expert and utilizing education-based marketing is one of the most valuable additions you can add to your business.

EDUMARKETING CHANNELS

I've learned that people will forget what you said, people will forget what you did, but people will never forget how you made them feel.
~ Maya Angelou

There are a variety of channels you can use for educating. When creating your Edumarketing plan it is important to remember to include your potential and existing customers as well as your aligned partners in your strategy as they can be a valuable referral resource for your business. To create a truly successful Edumarketing plan you should include the following channels.

BLOGS, WHITEPAPERS, ARTICLES AND BOOKS

A common method used in marketing today is content marketing. Content marketing includes blog articles, white papers, industry publication articles, e-books and studies. Content marketing does not have to be complicated or long. In fact, shorter articles are more effective. Today's best content marketing strategies involves shifting from trying to find the perfect way to explain an idea or process to instead think of each step along the journey and slowing publishing articles to take the reader through the process. Simply put; instead of having them drink from the firehouse, provide them with the water that they need at that moment.

ONLINE VIDEOS

YouTube has revolutionized how people 'learn'. Videos are one of the most effective vehicles for storytelling, educating and connecting with people. According to Statista, people spend over 1,000 minutes per month watching online videos. YouTube has become one of the leading search engines on the web. Including video in your Edumarketing plan is an absolute must and YouTube is not the only channel to include video's in. You should include videos on social media, email marketing and most importantly your online e-learning portal which we will detail later.

PRESENTATIONS AND WORKSHOPS

One of the most effective methods of positioning yourself as the expert includes speaking at the front of the room. Local chambers often host education for their members. Associations are another great venue for speaking about your expertise. You should not just look at Associations in your field either, think about potential related fields that could benefit from your expertise and become a valuable referral partner. If you are not comfortable with speaking, then put together a panel of experts. A Real Estate Agent could speak on the advantages of home-ownership for First-time Home Buyers by compiling a panel that includes a Mortgage Professional, Home Inspector and Insurance Agent. The panel would provide information in their field of expertise and it would take the pressure off one person speaking the entire time.

Being the "expert" at the front of the room is one of the most powerful methods of Edumarketing. Be sure to "socialize" your speaking so that others see that you 'ARE' the expert. You can do this by having someone take photos of your event with you at the front of the room. You can post the photos on social media, your website and newsletters.

VIRTUAL AND ONLINE COURSES

You don't need to have a complicated software or product to bring value to your customers by including online education in your Edumarketing plan. While customer training may be a necessity in some areas, for most it is a valuable way to use your expertise to attract new customers as well as build 'Goodwill' with your existing customers. It can also provide an increase in your SEO. It isn't necessary to create extensive "how to" guides to have a powerful education plan. If you are an Insurance Agent, you could create a course on "How to Vacation Ready Your Home". It could include an info-graphic or a checklist that they can download.

Remember, people are looking for information online so having an online university of courses that people can take for free is a valuable method to increase your database. There are a variety of technology products you can use to host your online education including live webinars, recorded webinars, e-learning courses, white papers, checklists, videos and how to guides.

PODCASTS AND RADIO SHOWS

Podcasts have become a powerful marketing tool. A podcast is a set of digital audio files that are available on the internet for downloading. Podcasts have become the new talk radio on mobile devices. Including Podcasts in your Edumarketing plan can help you reach new audiences. Podcasts allow you to develop a relationship with a listening audience. Podcasts are easy to create and highly engaging. It is also a great way to develop public speaking confidence. Radio shows and community cable shows are still a viable method for building a new market share.

Look to local stations and find out what their audience has for questions. You could do a segment on "Overcoming a Stiff Neck" if you are a Chiropractor or "Inexpensive Decorating Tips" if you are an Interior Designer. Education can be entertaining if done correctly and a valuable means to market your expertise.

CREATING YOUR EDUMARKETING PLAN

You have the power to achieve greatness and create anything and everything you want in life, but you have to take action.
~ Jack Canfield

The quickest way to get started with your Edumarketing plan is to complete these steps:

Step One: Identify Your Expertise

The first step is to identify your expertise. If you are a Financial Planner, your expertise is helping people invest, save and increase their wealth, if you are a Mortgage Professional, your expertise is helping people qualify for financing a home of their dreams. Your broad definition of your expertise is great for the local Chamber 30-second elevator pitch, but to successfully build an Edumarketing plan, you need to know a bit more. To drill down on your expertise, answer the following questions:

1. What problems do you solve?
2. What questions do you answer?
3. What specialized solutions do you offer?

(Be sure to write down all your answers. These are all possible articles, videos and courses.)

Step Two: Determine Your Topics

Next, take your answers from Step One and write down each as a topic on a sheet of paper. Don't expand on them yet, simply write each answer down. Save this sheet as your topic list. You will find that you can constantly add to this list over time. No matter the question, if you have an answer, you have a topic. When determining your topics, you want to consider who you want to read, view or learn from the topic and what action do you want them to take.

Step Three: Develop Your Content

Before you determine your delivery method, you need to develop your content. Start with the following:

1. Take a topic
2. Write out the answer or information to the topic
3. Determine your delivery method(s)
4. Develop your deliverables

You may use the topic and information in a blog post or create a quick info video to place onto YouTube. You may create a check list to use to capture leads on your website or an online course for your eLearning site. You may create a PowerPoint slide deck to use in a webinar or you may use the topic as a discussion in your podcast. You can develop several different deliverables for each topic. The most important thing to remember is to take your topic and write your content, then develop your deliverables. Yes, this process does take a bit of upfront work, but once you have done it you will be thankful because you will end up with a strong list of topics that will support you in your marketing and business goals and position you as the expert in your field.

Create a content hub to organize your content for your various distribution channels like blog posts, videos, social media, presentations, eLearning, eBooks, etc. If your topic is long, then you may want to create one cohesive paper and/or presentation. Although the content you create may be divided into multiple deliverables, creating one single presentation or whitepaper gives you more control and will help you:

- Divide your broader topics into smaller topics
- Develop multiple content for various distributions channels
- Build FAQ's

Step Four: Identify Your Distribution Channels

Distribution is how you get your content out to your audience so that you can engage them and eventually turn them into customers or educate them, so they will continue to buy or refer business to you. Your distribution channels may be determined by your geographic location or industry but should not be determined by your development expertise. It is easy to outsource to experienced professionals. For example, you may use a ghost writer to write your content and a videographer to create your video's. If you are looking to develop a complete Edumarketing plan that includes online learning, you will want to hire a professional who has a complete understanding for developing educational marketing programs. You don't have to start out utilizing all distribution channels. You can begin by adding blog content to your website and then move on to creating videos and then an eLearning channel.

These days, people want to learn before they buy,
be educated instead of pitched.
~ Brian Clark

Whatever Edumarketing strategy you determine is best for you, the most important steps are to identify your expertise, share your knowledge and expand your business. It will make a difference in your bottom line!

About Ginger

Ginger Bell helps her clients use education to market and brand themselves as experts. A previous Dale Carnegie Training Consultant, Ginger learned early in her career to use education as a means of marketing, and today helps companies build their business by leveraging their expertise.

Ginger is a Multi-Best-Selling Author, Education Specialist and Marketing Expert who works with companies, experts, and entrepreneurs. She utilizes the power of education, new technologies, media, and personality-driven marketing to attract new clients and position her clients as experts in their field.

Ginger helps companies and entrepreneurs create educational marketing campaigns and strategies to increase their customer base and grow their business. Her clients hire her to develop training, communication and sales programs, design online education programs and create education, marketing and branding strategies.

Her client list includes Re/Max, Nike, Motto Mortgage, Finance of America, FirstFunding, Tovuti, Fidelity National Title, Mentor Graphics, Merrill Lynch, Arch MI, Windermere and countless entrepreneurs and small-business owners across the US.

Ginger is experienced in training management, presentations, webinars, learning management, instructional systems development, project management and online training development.

A sought-after national speaker and published author to audiences nationwide, Ginger has been named as one of the 50 Most Connected Professionals and Elite Women of Lending. Ginger has also been awarded the "Professional Woman of the Year" award by the National Association of Professional Women for her commitment to training and education.

You can connect with Ginger at:

- ginger@go2training.com
- www.GingerBell.net
- www.Go2training.com
- www.linkedin.com/in/gingerbell/

CHAPTER 35

FIVE MINDSETS FOR SUCCESSFUL FITNESS

BY FRANCIS PAPINEAU

The first wealth is health.
~ Ralph Waldo Emerson

Good health is the basis for anything you wish to accomplish. But sometimes your couch looks so inviting, and once you sit on it, you're glued to it. The couch potato mindset takes you away from the actions needed to be in good health.

Have you ever heard of the expression '...having a millionaire mindset'? That refers to deciding to be a millionaire and doing the activities necessary to become one.

Why not do the same for your health? Decide to be healthy and do the activities that will get your there. Are you out of shape? Are you a busy mom who takes care of everyone else in the family? Think that you are too busy to exercise? This chapter is for you.

MINDSET #1: SET A REALISTIC ROADMAP

May your troubles in the New Year be as short-lived as your resolutions.
~ E.C. McKenzy

It's January 2nd. You've partied. You've eaten 'til you can't bend down.

You've had too many cocktails. But that's ok because you are 'gung ho' about joining a gym tomorrow.

- In January, you are an Ace, you attend the gym 6 days per week without fail.

- February comes along, you do ok too, going 4-5 times per week.

- March. St. Patty's day: Time to celebrate once again. "It's been a long winter." you think, "I deserve a break" and there go your good intentions.

One of the reasons for this phenomenon is the lack of progression when adding exercises to your schedule. Couch potatoes go from doing nothing at all, to training 5 or 6 days a week, and then quit. The key is to make this change smooth and gradual. Drastic doesn't stick! Instead, *be realistic*, set aside two 30-minute blocks of time per week to exercise. Then do it! Be proud of yourself for being consistent. After a month, add another exercise day. Once you are able to exercise three times per week for another month without fail, then add a fourth workout day in your week. So, if you started your regimen in January, instead of quitting by St. Patrick's Day, you would be exercising four times per week and sticking with it. Celebrate with a green drink, a green salad and make people green with envy.

MINDSET #2: TAKE ACTION

Movement is a medicine for creating change in a person's physical, emotional, and mental states.
~ Carol Welch

Taking action is the first step to making a change.

What do you do when you get home totally exhausted after a tough day at work?

- Sit in front of the TV?
- Workout?
- Sit in front of the TV and eat junk food?
- Go for a walk?
- Sit in front of the TV, eat junk food and sleep on the couch, because by then you are too tired to walk to your bed?

You're like a bear before hibernation! You lie around on the couch, gathering more and more food, moving less and less. The more you lie around, the less energy you have to enjoy life.

Getting off the couch makes you think like a horse. You start to gallop and then run. The more you run, the more you want to run and capture that feeling of freedom and health. A few months of this makes your brain more alert and, over time, might bring along the lean and powerful demeanor of the horse.

In other words, no more monkeying around! Start moving! Choose an activity that is meaningful to you and make it part of your days:

- walk with your dog or a friend at a moderate pace
- walk around your work place at lunch time with a coworker
- use the elliptical while reading a book
- use the treadmill while watching your favorite show
- ride your bike
- dance, turn the music up and move

> *In the wise words of King Julien, "I like to move it, move it..."*
> ~ (Sacha Baron Cohen, *Madagascar*)

You don't have time to exercise? Create time! Watch one hour less of TV 4 times per week or wake up one hour earlier. Here is an eye opener: let's say you wake up an hour earlier four times a week, which is:

> 1 hour x 4 times/week = 4 hours per week
> 4 hours x 52 weeks= 208 hours/year

Now divide 208 hours/year by 40 hours (a full work week) = 5.2 weeks.

Amazingly, by waking up an hour earlier four times per week, you just created over five 40-hour work weeks in a one-year span to workout. The early bird gets the fitness benefits!

And, say you wake up an hour earlier and workout at home, saving yourself the drive to the gym, traffic and possibly having to wait to use the equipment, now you have extra time on your hands. This is a wonderful way to start the day and be ahead of schedule.

After exercising, your mind is clear and ready to be challenged. This is a great time to schedule your most difficult task of the day, or work on that project that you put on the back burner.

MINDSET #3: PRIORITIZE YOURSELF AND COMMIT

The key is not to prioritize what's on your schedule,
but to schedule your priorities.
~ Stephen Covey

Make exercise part of your schedule, make it an appointment with yourself. Would you cancel an appointment with a client over and over again? No? Then treat yourself with the same respect, schedule it and show up! *Don't think about it, just do it.*

As adults, we have such busy schedules. We are always thinking about what's coming next, what we have to get done today, tomorrow, next week plus what we did not have time to do yesterday.

When you are stressed or have too much on your schedule, the first thing you forgo is workout time, right? It should be the other way around. Exercising provides great stress relief and gives you renewed energy.

Jill has never been a morning person, but to get her exercises done she made herself become one. There are days when Jill gets home at a decent time. She puts dinner together, washes dishes, helps the kids with their homework and bed time routine, then goes through mail and emails and is in bed by 9:00 p.m.

The next morning, her alarm clock rings at 5:30 a.m. and she gets up to workout.

There are days when Jill gets home later and gets to bed at 10 p.m.

The next morning, her alarm clock rings at 5.30 a.m. and she gets up to workout.

Some days, Jill has meetings at night and gets to bed at 11:00 pm.

The next morning, her alarm clock rings at 5.30 a.m. and she has a hard time getting up to exercise. The bed is so comfy. But Jill reminds herself how well she feels after exercising and how proud of herself she is once she is done. This thinking is more powerful than a snooze button to get her up.

Jill has _committed_ the first 30 to 45 minutes of her scheduled workout days to exercise. _This is not negotiable_. Vince Lombardi said it well: "Most people fail, not because of lack of desire, but, because of lack of commitment."

Find out what works for you and make it fun!

You can rename your workout time, "play time" – if that helps. Just like kids, you might end up wanting more play time. Have fun along the way.

MINDSET #4: BE THANKFUL

The more you express gratitude for what you have, the more
you will have to express gratitude for.
~ Zig Ziglar

How many times have you heard someone say:

  o I used to work out every day.
  o I used to be able to do 50 push-ups.
  o I used to be in great shape.
  o I used to walk five miles every day.
  o I used to have more energy.
  o I used to fit in those pants.

You get the picture. It's time to say, "I am able to" and move forward. Take action, get moving, focus your energy on what you can do. Be thankful for what you have at this point in time. Being thankful is the first step in being ready to receive more. Here are three (3) ways to be grateful, stay focused and move towards your goals:

1. Start the day by writing three things you are grateful for.
   As an example: you are thankful for your family, your health and your friends.

2. At the end of the day write down <u>three</u> "victories".
   For example: you've made that important phone call; you didn't eat that piece of cake; you worked out.

3. At night write down <u>three</u> actions that you want to accomplish the next day to move towards your goals.
   Examples: take a 30-minute walk at lunch time; write the first ten pages of your dream book; send a thank you card.

Then you'll realize that your actions become victories and your victories will create more actions, giving you more and more to be grateful for. This is a nice circle to be in.

MINDSET #5: VISUALIZE

I believe that visualization is one of the most powerful
means of achieving goals.
~ Harvey Mackay

See yourself as being fit. What does it feels like to you to be healthy:

- Do you have more energy?
- Do you breathe better?
- Do you have more self-confidence?
- Do you fit in those "skinny pants"?

Have a clear picture in your mind and make it happen. Visualization is a surprisingly effective way to get results. Olympians and professional athletes use visualization to see themselves performing their sport and succeeding at it. My friend Jack saw a poster once of a man, probably in his seventies from looking at his face, but with killer abs and toned muscles doing biceps curls. That poster inspired him. He thought if a guy in his seventies can look like that, why couldn't he?

Every time Jack saw that poster, he believed more and more that he could get a body like that once he focused on eating well, setting time aside for, and being consistent with workout sessions. Within a few months he went from waist size 38 to size 34.

Jack was thankful for the outstanding progress that he had made since he first saw the poster. He is now more active, more engaged in life and says, "I used to say I used to, now I say I can."

Why was Jack successful?

1. He set a realistic time frame. – (Set a Realistic Roadmap)
2. He stayed away from the couch. – (Take Action)
3. Jack decided he could do more to improve his health and stuck to it. – (Prioritize Yourself and Commit)
4. He was thankful for his progress every step of the way. – (Be Thankful)
5. Jack had a clear picture of what "healthy" felt like to him. – (Visualize)

To be successful, the change has to come from within. Go deep enough to find your ultimate reason to make a change. If the reason has meaning to you, you will stick to the program. Jack's friend unsuccessfully attempted to quit smoking several times in his life. Then came the grandkids who did not want to be around a cigarette-stinking grandpa. Guess what? Playing with his grandkids had enough meaning for him to stop smoking. He can almost keep up with the grandkids now.

CONCLUSION

Only changes in mindsets can extend the frontiers of the possible.
~ Winston Churchill

Picture a beautiful wild horse in the pasture with limitless energy and a total sense of freedom. Your mind is like that wild horse, it goes 100 miles per hour and wanders around. To channel your power and keep your mind focused on achieving your goals, use the five mindsets for successful fitness as your guide:

- Set a Realistic Roadmap
- Take Action
- Prioritize Yourself and Commit
- Be Thankful
- Visualize

Use these mindsets time and time again to keep you moving and engaged.

Happy fitness!

About Francis

Francis Papineau has been changing his clients' lives for the past three decades by sharing his knowledge of health and wellness, and by implementing exercise programs focused on stretching, core strengthening and proper lifting techniques.

After receiving his Degree in Occupational Therapy from the University of Montreal, he moved to sunny Florida and oversaw work conditioning and work hardening programs to prepare patients for their return to work following various injuries, surgeries and health issues.

Francis has also been a consultant for a Certified Nurse Assistant program teaching proper body mechanics and posture and transfer techniques when handling patients using core muscles to prevent back injuries. Francis was featured in a newspaper article highlighting a client's progress and success in getting back to his passion of playing his favorite musical instrument. In addition, he has given numerous talks in the community on physical health issues and therapeutic treatment options.

Francis is the author of the upcoming book *The Couch Potato's Guide to Fitness* in which he sets you up with a simple and complete exercise program to get you on your way to better fitness. He is writing this book because, over all of his years in health care, he has come across countless people who wanted to get fit but did not have the knowledge nor the time to find an adequate exercise program, therefore did nothing instead. *THE COUCH POTATO'S GUIDE TO FITNESS* is there to help millions of people across the globe improve their fitness level in a simple, effective and meaningful way. Be on the lookout!

If you have enjoyed reading this chapter, you may Follow him on Facebook/The Couch Potato's Guide to Fitness.

Francis is always excited to share his expertise and enjoys speaking at different events to address the five mindsets for fitness success. To invite Francis to speak at one of your events please contact him by email at:

- CouchPotatoBook@gmail.com